FREE IN THE WORLD

AMERICAN SLAVERY AND CONSTITUTIONAL FAILURE

Mark E. Brandon

PRINCETON UNIVERSITY PRESS PRINCETON, NEW JERSEY

Published by Princeton University Press, 41 William Street,
Princeton, New Jersey 08540
In the United Kingdom: Princeton University Press,
Chichester, West Sussex

Library of Congress Cataloging-in-Publication Data

Brandon, Mark E.
Free in the world : American slavery and constitutional failure /
Mark E. Brandon.
p. cm.
Includes bibliographical references and index.
ISBN 0-691-01581-3 (cloth : alk. paper)
1. Constitutional history—United States. 2. Constitutional law—
United States—Philosophy. I. Title.
KF4541.B684 1998
342.73'029—dc21 97-25835 CIP

This book has been composed in Sabon Typeface

Princeton University Press books are printed
on acid-free paper and meet the guidelines
for permanence and durability of the Committee
on Production Guidelines for Book Longevity
of the Council on Library Resources

http://pup.princeton.edu

Printed in the United States of America

1 3 5 7 9 10 8 6 4 2

For Kathryn and Rachel

Contents

Preface

IN RECENT YEARS nations have adopted written constitutions in numbers unprecedented in the history of the world. By one count, 183 countries are now using (or at least can point to) written constitutions for making and maintaining various forms of politics.[1] In fact the adoption and use of written constitutions have come to define many of the basic problems of constitutionalism. Several reasons account for these trends, but one probably arises from the perception that the world's oldest active constitution—the Constitution of the United States—has been a profound success.

But to what extent can we reasonably expect written constitutions to establish or constrain politics successfully? I begin here to answer that question by peering beneath the surface of the prototypal story of success: the constitutional experience of the United States. Specifically I examine the breakdown of constitutional order in the United States in the nineteenth century, paying special attention to slavery as an institution and an element of constitutional discourse. The basic aim of this study is to take up questions concerning constitutional failure. In the process I shall also have a few things to say about constitutional theory and the American constitutional experience.

One of the basic lessons I draw from my analysis is this: In order to succeed as a constitutional enterprise, a polity must be willing to risk failure. Much of the book explores some of the reasons for and implications of that claim.

Chapter 1 introduces some of the themes of the study. Among other matters, it deals with the relationship between constitutional theory and history. Concerning the former, the chapter describes a form of constitutional theory—or constitutionalism—that, from the perspective of traditional constitutional scholarship, is controversial. For one thing, the "new" constitutionalism I describe takes the "writtenness" of constitutions as central to the constitutional enterprise. For another, the new version is normatively thinner than many traditional accounts of constitutionalism. Notwithstanding these deviations—some scholars might call them perversions—I hope the reformulation is fruitful and believe it

[1] Gisbert H. Flanz, ed., *Constitutions of the Countries of the World*, Release 96-5 (August 1996). This figure probably overestimates the precise number as it includes Israel, New Zealand, and the United Kingdom, which most people concede do not employ written constitutions. But if it is an exaggeration, it is only slightly wide of the mark.

is consistent with widespread contemporary conceptions of the character of the constitutional enterprise.

Chapter 1 also presents a typology of constitutional failure. It argues that constitutional failure is multidimensional, that there are several types of constitutional failure. It describes those types and concludes with an account of the original failure of the Constitution of the United States: the failure to supply the means by which slaves and even free blacks might construct their political identities by reference to the Constitution. The general account of history in chapter 1 is not controversial; nor are the particular historical accounts in the rest of the book especially novel. But I draw some lessons from the history that cut against the contemporary grain.

Chapters 2 through 5 focus on sources of division and cohesion in the constitutional polity. They show how the successful operation of institutions and norms in constitutional politics can generate not only attachment but also division. They also show how those divisions can lead to constitutional failure of one sort or another and can sometimes even undermine the capacity of a particular constitutional regime to sustain itself.

Chapter 2 shows how the logic of constitutional authority incites the production of foundational narratives or myths and how they can contribute to constitutional division. Myth serves two basic functions in this context. First, it helps render the constitutional regime coherent and therefore comprehensible and useful. Second, it helps justify the very existence of the regime that lays claim to a new constitution. But chapter 2 shows how the exigencies and ambiguities of a constitutional founding can engender more than one myth. In the case of the United States there were at least two, each suggesting its own account of constitutional authority, values, and institutions. The chapter shows how those myths competed with and sometimes reinforced each other, not only for general primacy but also in supplying a solution to the problem of slavery.

Chapter 3 is the first of two chapters illustrating how the allocation of interpretive authority can foster constitutional division. It attends to the authority and activity of nonjudicial actors—especially Congress—in interpreting the Constitution. It suggests that the very function of Congress and the character of congressional action in a constitutional polity make the constitutional dimensions of that function and action inescapable. In short, Congress, when it acts, is unavoidably "interpreting" the Constitution. The functions and composition of Congress as an institution render it an interpreter with distinctive characteristics, one of which is its institutional tendency toward pragmatic accommodation and compromise. Notwithstanding this tendency, when Congress solves problems in a way that appears to be institutionally successful, it can precipitate or exploit divisions in the polity. Such divisions occurred repeatedly with respect to Congress's attempts to deal with slavery.

Chapter 4 continues the discussion of allocations of interpretive authority and their implications for political division. It addresses the authority of courts, especially the Supreme Court, and suggests that the Court has its own distinctive way of approaching constitutional problems and the Constitution. As with Congress, the Court's approach grows largely out of its institutional makeup and function but is also colored by the character of the judiciary's public commitment to "rule of law." If Congress has an institutional inclination toward accommodation and compromise, the Court tends toward principle, at least as its most publicly visible mode of justification. Acting in this way, the Court responded to issues relating to slavery in ways that were comparatively coherent but deeply divisive. If they were also immoral by our present lights, they were nonetheless constitutional. But ultimately they threatened the survival of the order.

Chapter 5 reflects on an example of what we might think of as false division. The debates between Abraham Lincoln and Stephen A. Douglas supply the context for the discussion. The chapter shows how two astute politicians could exploit competing foundational myths in order to generate the appearance of disagreement over slavery. I argue, however, that the appearance was illusory and that apparently irreconcilable myths led to virtually identical policies with respect to slavery. Hence what appeared to be multiple constitutional meanings were in fact not very different at all. But if the division between the two men was illusory, it nonetheless successfully divided the polity, though not along lines that Lincoln or Douglas intended.

Chapters 6 and 7 deepen the theoretical connection between division and failure. Chapter 6 claims that the political breakdown leading up to the American Civil War was constitutional in character. It was constitutional not simply because its consequence in the short run was an alteration of the constitutional order but also because it involved disputes over what the Constitution was and what it meant. But if the ultimate failure of the order was constitutional in this sense, then constitutional discourse must be autonomous from other ways of talking about the world. Chapter 6 goes on to show how American constitutional discourse was partially autonomous from—at the same time that it was connected to—other forms of discourse. The chapter also argues that disputes of the type that precipitated political breakdown are a natural function of constitutional interpretation and that interpretation is central to the constitutional enterprise. Thus working constitutions—at least those that are interpretable—unavoidably possess both integrative and disintegrative properties. But the fact that disputes over interpretation might cause the breakdown of a particular constitutional order does not necessarily signify a "failure" from the standpoint of constitutionalism.

Chapter 7 presents a constitutional theory of secession, arguing that the secession of the southern states in 1860 and 1861 was constitutional in at least three respects. First, it potentially represented an attempt to deconstitute and reconstitute "a people" through reflection and choice instead of through accident and force. Second, its aims were to secure constitutional forms and limitations, including ostensible constitutional rights, that many Southerners believed were threatened under the existing order. Third, and in some ways most important, its method was consistent with a prevalent foundational myth of the existing order.

Chapter 8 briefly takes up questions about the significance of the Civil War in the context of the Radical Republican program of Reconstruction, which represented a potentially new beginning for the order. The chapter also considers, however, some reasons in constitutional theory that the Radicals' program failed to achieve most of its apparent purposes. Thus it reflects again on what it takes to authorize a constitutional regime.

The epilogue supplies an impressionistic sketch of the current condition of the American constitutional polity. Specifically the chapter speaks to the legacy of slavery, as well as to sources of present constitutional division and their possible relation to constitutional failure.

This study does not aim to supply a normative defense of constitutionalism, whether new or traditional. The purpose, rather, is to understand constitutionalism by coming to terms with the operating logic of the constitutional enterprise. That logic includes certain principles that purport to constrain or direct the enterprise and thus to shape the forms of political life it might engender. I make no attempt here to argue that the enterprise is (or is not) desirable, though I can imagine such a project in the future.

The questions I raise here and the approaches I take may well be susceptible to comparative analysis. In a sense the study is already comparative in that it analyzes institutions, norms, and economic forms by region within an entity. But in suggesting comparability, I intend not *intra*national but *inter*national comparison. I do not claim to have performed or described a methodology for conducting such further research. I provide instead what Clifford Geertz would call a "thick description" of the conceptual and material "webs of significance" that animated the political cultures of the United States.[2] But this case study may suggest basic ideas and categories of analysis—a reconception of constitutionalism and a typology for constitutional failure, for example—that can supply a space within which systematic comparisons are possible.

The precise character of such studies would vary according to the questions asked. Studies concerning the extent to which written constitutions can constrain politics, as well as the ways they would do so, might look quite different from studies directed toward other types of questions, such as the logics of constitutional authority, the forms of constitutional justification, and the unconscious and self-conscious dissolution of constitutional regimes. Whatever the questions, however, once we have redefined constitutionalism, the potential number of cases expands dramatically, across both time and place.

If we were to look for cases involving substantial constitutional failures (in the sense of either institutional breakdown or the failure of constitutional texts) we would likely find many, including the national unifications of Europe in the nineteenth century, the demise of Weimar Germany, the challenges of European Union, the current constitutional politics of Eastern and Central Europe, the disintegration of the Soviet Union, and the fates of the numerous constitutional experiments of Latin America. If we were to look for cases in which social division might produce constitutional failures of various sorts, we could point to the difficulties of racial, ethnic, and tribal divisions in the Americas, the Middle East, Africa, and South Asia. We might also examine the claims to autonomy by indigenous peoples virtually worldwide. If we were to inquire about the particular problems and possibilities connected with secession, we could look toward movements of secession or self-determination in Canada, India, Pakistan, Sri Lanka, Burma, Chad, Ethiopia, Nigeria, the Sudan, Uganda, Zaire, Zambia, the Philippines, Iraq, the former Yugoslavia, the former Czechoslovakia, the former Soviet Union, Russia, Italy, and the Basque regions of Spain and France.[3] Even within the United States, some people talk seriously about the division of California and the secession of Staten Island from the rest of New

[2] Clifford Geertz, *The Interpretation of Cultures* (1973), at 3–30. For a rich and suggestive account of the comparative potential of such an approach, see William Ewald, "Comparative Jurisprudence (I): What Was It Like to Try a Rat?" 143 *U. Pa. L. Rev.* 1889 (1995).

[3] For a useful catalogue of movements for autonomy, self-determination, or secession, see Morton H. Halperin et al., *Self-Determination in the New World Order* (1992). See also Donald L. Horowitz, *Ethnic Groups in Conflict* (1985); Larry Diamond and Marc F. Plattner, eds., *Nationalism, Ethnic Conflict, and Democracy* (1994).

York City.[4] Further, members of Hawaii's native population are now formally talking with the state's other residents about assuming sovereign authority over part of the territory presently governed by the state of Hawaii.

In urging the utility of comparative analysis, I offer no firm judgment about whether investigations may or should proceed through the building and testing of hypotheses[5] or through other, perhaps less positivist means.[6] But what we may discover is that even regimes that appear to be similar—in their structure or normative commitments or modes for establishing and maintaining political authority, for example—are actually quite diverse, with respect at least to constitutional failures and perhaps to other characteristics as well. I do not think this is a conclusion scholars should bemoan, as though we might never know the scientific truth about politics. Instead, as Reinhard Bendix has argued, it may simply be that diversity is constitutive of human experience and we cannot adequately comprehend that condition without "understanding . . . the contexts in which more detailed causal inferences can be drawn," if in fact they can be drawn.[7]

I offer a final word about the controversy to which I commit myself in this book. Earlier I indicated that some of what I say here flies in the face of current conventional wisdom about constitutionalism and the Constitution. The extent to which this is so came home to me recently. I had presented my theory of secession at a conference at Boalt Hall School of Law when one of my discussants, an historian, became visibly agitated, responding to my paper with a passionate defense of Lincoln. Later he would tell me that my attempt to justify secession was "repugnant" and an implicit assault on the civil rights movement. He was not the only one at the conference troubled by my argument. A prominent law professor cornered me after my presentation and—hands waving, voice rising to a shout—railed against my theory of secession, claiming,

[4] These potential secessions would probably have a constitutional status distinct from the others just mentioned.

[5] See, for example, Arend Lijpart, "Comparative Politics and the Comparative Method," 65 *Am. Pol. Sci. Rev.* 682 (1971); Giovanni Sartori, "Comparing and Miscomparing," 3 *J. Theoretical Pol.* 243 (1991).

[6] See Theda Skocpol and Margaret Somers, "The Uses of Comparative History in Macrosocial Inquiry," 22 *Comp. Stud. Soc. & Hist.* 174 (1980).

[7] Reinhard Bendix, "The Mandate to Rule: An Introduction," 55 *Social Forces* 247 (1976); Bendix, *Kings or People: Power and the Mandate to Rule* (1978), at 5, 15.

among other things, that I was illicitly favoring Jefferson Davis over Abraham Lincoln.

Unable to salve these scholars' tender feelings then, I fear this book may do no better. But to avoid misunderstanding, I wish to clarify two points at the outset. First, I intend neither to assail the civil rights movement nor to defend racism or slavery. On the contrary, I am gratified that some of the most sympathetic readings of this study have come from African-American scholars. Second, although I disagree with Lincoln's constitutional positions against secession, that does not mean I want to disparage his legacy unfairly or resurrect the old Confederacy. I want to do neither.

But I believe we get nowhere as constitutional scholars or as citizens of this country by sanitizing constitutional theory or the American constitutional experience. Thus my effort here is to contribute to a conversation about what we — in the United States and elsewhere — might realistically expect from written constitutions and from constitutional union. What we might expect is both less and more than some of us might imagine.

Acknowledgments

In writing this book I have enjoyed the intellectual companionship, enlightenment, and criticism of a number of teachers, friends, and colleagues, though some will surely deny complicity in this project.

Among my teachers I have especially valued my relationship with Walter Murphy, for whom the word *retired* has meant simply that he has moved his office to a sunnier location. He embodies the best of academe: an engaging mind, generous spirit, breadth of knowledge, and, not least, a humility that is increasingly rare in the academic world. At Princeton he provided a space in which students and scholars with diverse agendas—some at odds with his own—could find their own voices. Walter has repeatedly read drafts of the manuscript and frequently saved me from error. (Doubtless he wishes he had saved me from more.)

I am grateful to other teachers as well. One, who later became a colleague, is Kim Scheppele. She combines a creative and empathetic intellect with limitless energy of tornadic intensity. It has been my good fortune to benefit in countless ways from her association, friendship, criticism, and advice over the years. Will Harris is a gifted scholar and teacher. Happily I have known him in both capacities. He has an extraordinary ability to conceive the problems and possibilities of constitutionalism with comprehensiveness and subtlety. His account of constitutional theory has significantly influenced my own. I am grateful, too, to Robert George for asking hard questions, some of which I still have no good answers for.

Special thanks are also due two friends, Judy Failer and Wayne Moore, who have consistently bestowed their unselfish wisdom on this project. If they have sometimes generously read the project in ways that were more insightful than it was, they have nonetheless helped me make it stronger.

At the University of Michigan I am grateful to Pradeep Chhibber, Ann Lin, and Elizabeth Wingrove for reading part of the manuscript and to Hanes Walton for reading the whole thing. I am also indebted to the graduate students here who have helped make the study of law and politics stimulating, challenging, and rewarding.

Across the country I have enjoyed conversations with and comments from teachers, colleagues, friends, and acquaintances too numerous to name. Some, however, deserve specific mention: Sotirios Barber, Michael Les Benedict, Keith Brandon, John Brigham, Dan Deudney, John

DiIulio, George Downs, Don Drakeman, Steve Engelmann, Louis Fisher, Lawrence Friedman, John Goldberg, George Grassmuck, Michael Hanchard, Luke Harris, Jennifer Hochschild, Ralph Hummel, Ellen Kennedy, Mark Killenbeck, John Kingdon, Donald Kommers, Sanford Levinson, Don Maletz, Steve Mazie, Pratap Mehta, Anne Norton, Noah Pickus, Robert Post, Andrew Richards, Donald Robinson, Tony Sebok, and Jeff Tulis.

Princeton University Press has made the process of publication humane and sometimes even happy. Malcolm Litchfield has been especially helpful in getting the book to press. Rita Bernhard has read and edited the manuscript with care and sensitivity.

The following groups provided forums in which I publicly rehearsed ideas related to this project: the American Political Science Association, the Southern Political Science Association, the Southwestern Political Science Association, Princeton's Colloquium in Political Philosophy, the Princeton Conference on Public Law, the University of Michigan's Junior Faculty Seminar in Political Science, and Boalt Hall School of Law's Conference on Reserved Powers. A summer fellowship from the University of Oklahoma supported research for chapter 8.

Finally, I thank my undergraduate teachers—especially Murray Flynn, Justin Fuller, and Douglas Rodgers—for showing by example the ways in which an academic life can be an honorable one.

FREE IN THE WORLD

CHAPTER ONE

Constitutionalism, History, and Constitutional Failure

I

Americans are accustomed to thinking of their constitutional experience in comedic terms. It is a comedy, not in the sense of being humorous, but because it is a story with a series of happy endings.[1] The American constitutional experience, on this account, is a story of success.

There is much to this view, and the impulse to embrace it is both powerful and understandable. Many aspects of the American constitutional experience do justify both satisfaction and celebration. But even when aspects of the experience have been undeniably unhappy, Americans have frequently searched for accounts that turn water into wine or, more prosaically, try to make sense of what might otherwise be difficult to bear or comprehend. Consider, for example, the felicitous ways in which many Americans have come to terms with what most now recognize as the moral horror of slavery and its legacy, and with the horrific sacrifice of civil war.[2]

Such psychic resilience is in some ways commendable. But however understandable the inclination or impulse may be to render experience in comedic terms, embracing accounts of success too readily comes with costs attached. For if we can plausibly claim that learning occurs in the human species, it is more often a consequence of failure than of success. Hence, even if the presentation of American experience as comedy is largely accurate, dwelling on success may teach less than evaluating the significance of failure. And to the extent that a comedic account of American constitutional history is inaccurate, Americans lose the in-

[1] The notion of happy endings comes from Sanford Levinson, *Constitutional Faith* (1988).

[2] Among the most powerful and insightful of the happy accounts are the following: James M. McPherson, *Battle Cry of Freedom: The Civil War Era* (1988); McPherson, *Abraham Lincoln and the Second American Revolution* (1991); Garry Wills, *Lincoln at Gettysburg: The Words That Remade America* (1992); Bruce Ackerman, *We the People: Foundations* (1991); Christopher L. Eisgruber, "Justice Story, Slavery, and the Natural Law Foundations of American Constitutionalism," 55 *U. Chi. L. Rev.* 273 (1988); and Eisgruber, "Justice and the Text: Rethinking the Constitutional Relation Between Prudence and Principle," 43 *Duke L. J.* 1 (1993).

sights they might gain from a realistic appraisal of their constitutional history.

One reason for Americans' tendency to view their constitutional experience as comedy may be the common perception that the document that calls itself "the Constitution" is a kind of sacred text whose power depends on its ability to generate "religious" attachment.[3] These days, many people worship at the altar of American civil religion whose holy scripture is the Constitution. I propose, however, that we leave the church. I do so, not out of some nihilistic impulse to destroy any domain for the sacred, but out of respect for and attachment to many of the ideas and institutions that the Constitution represents. It is my hope that in reflecting candidly on those ideas and institutions, we might come to a deeper appreciation of the things of value in the constitutional enterprise and embrace them rationally instead of as articles of faith.

Alexander Hamilton suggested that "it seems to have been reserved to the people of this country . . . to decide the important question, whether societies . . . are really capable or not, of establishing good government from reflection and choice, or whether they are forever destined to depend, for their political constitutions, on accident and force."[4] Hamilton's suggestion evokes a sense more of scientific speculation than of religious affirmation. He viewed the Constitution, after all, as an "experiment," not a divinely inspired vision.[5] Moreover, the image of experimentation implies the possibility of failure, that the experiment might not succeed. As a consequence his assessment of the Constitution's principal challenge captures some of the central problems of constitutional theory and of any putatively constitutive text: Is it possible to self-consciously construct a society?[6] To what extent (if at all) can writ-

[3] On the Constitution as a foundation for American civil religion, see Sanford Levinson, "'The Constitution' in American Civil Religion" 1979 *Sup. Ct. Rev.* 123 (1979). See also Levinson's later expansion on those arguments in *Constitutional Faith* (1988), especially at 9–53.

[4] *The Federalist*, No. 1 (1787).

[5] Hamilton was not alone in conceiving the project of American political thought as scientific. See I. Bernard Cohen, *Science and the Founding Fathers: Science in the Political Thought of Thomas Jefferson, Benjamin Franklin, John Adams, and James Madison* (1995). But see Madison's comment: "It is impossible for any man of candor to reflect on . . . [the drafting of the Constitution], without partaking of . . . astonishment. It is impossible for the man of pious reflection not to perceive in it, a finger of that Almighty hand which has been so frequently and signally extended to our relief." *The Federalist*, No. 37 (1788). For another reverential account, see Catherine Drinker Bowen, *Miracle at Philadelphia: The Story of the Constitutional Convention, May to September 1787* (1966).

[6] Hamilton's dichotomy of reflection and choice on the one hand and accident and force on the other is too simple in some respects (as dichotomies tend to be). Even so, it is useful in identifying a spectrum of alternatives.

ten constitutions contribute to that self-conscious construction? Simply put, do constitutions matter, and if so, how much?[7]

Hamilton's speculation was pregnant with an affirmative answer. Americans have rarely lacked confidence in their capacity to forge a new world out of a political and physical wilderness. From the beginning they seem to have thought (or feared, in the case of the Antifederalists) that they could construct a politics out of the Constitution.[8] If the task were fearsome or difficult, however, the idea did not seem absurd that people might imagine a possible political world, write a blueprint for it in the form of a constitution, and then build a politics from the blueprint (melding imagination, text, and will). In fact the possibility that political forms and practices might arise out of language appeared to be confirmed by pre-Constitutional experience.[9]

Some Americans, now poised at the precipice of the twenty-first century, have made a full-grown dogma of Hamilton's pregnant affirmation. Even among the less worshipful or dogmatic, it has become something of an unreflective (sometimes begrudging) assumption. The Constitution, they hold, clearly does make a difference, has effectively authorized institutions of government for more than two hundred years, has made "us" who "we" are as a people and a nation, for better or worse.[10]

[7] Some of the questions that arise in connection with the constitutional enterprise resemble questions raised by literary critics. See, for example, Stanley Fish, *Is There a Text in This Class? The Authority of Interpretive Communities* (1980); Ronald Dworkin, "Law as Interpretation," 60 *Texas L. Rev.* 527 (1982); Sanford Levinson, "Law as Literature," 60 *Texas L. Rev.* 373 (1982); Stanley Fish, "Working on the Chain Gang: Interpretation in Law and Literature," 60 *Texas L. Rev.* 551 (1982); Owen Fiss, "Objectivity and Interpretation," 34 *Stanford L. Rev.* 739 (1982); Paul Brest, "Interpretation and Interest," 34 *Stanford L. Rev.* 739 (1982); Thomas Grey, "Do We Have an Unwritten Constitution?" 27 *Stanford L. Rev.* 703 (1975).

[8] That confidence did not commence with the constitutional founding. Tocqueville noted the sense of mission that motivated the English settlement of the continent, especially New England. Alexis de Tocqueville, *Democracy in America*, vol. 1, part 1, ch. 2 (Meyer, ed., 1969), at 42–47. For Tocqueville's account of the constitutional founding, see vol. 1, part 1, ch. 8, in id., at 112–170, in which he concludes with the following: "How wonderful is the position of the New World, where man has as yet no enemies but himself. To be happy and to be free, it is enough to will it to be so."

[9] For a detailed list of what Lutz calls "constitution-like documents" before the constitutional founding, see Donald S. Lutz, "From Covenant to Constitution in American Political Thought," in *Covenant, Polity, and Constitutionalism* (Elazar and Kincaid, eds., 1980), at 101, 129–133.

[10] Compare, e.g., the platitudinous pronouncements of Warren E. Burger, "We the People," 37 *Case W. Res. L. Rev.* 385 (1987); Burger, "Tell the Story of Freedom," 72 *ABA J.* 54 (May 1986); and Burger, "Lawyers and the Constitutional Convention," 34 *Fed. Bar News & J.* 106 (1987), with Bruce A. Ackerman, "The Storrs Lectures: Discovering the Constitution," 93 *Yale L. J.* 1013 (1984); Ackerman, *We the People: Foundations* (1991);

But what if we take seriously Thomas Hobbes's critique of the capacity of words to constrain politics? "The force of words . . . [is] too weak to hold men to the performance of their Covenants," he said.[11] "It is therefore in vain to grant Soveraignty by way of precedent Covenant. . . . Covenants, being but words, and breath, have no force to oblige, contain, constrain, or protect any man, but what it has from the publique Sword."[12] If Hobbes was right, then written constitutions are in big trouble. And our conventional assumptions about the capacity of our own Constitution to construct a political world may deserve reevaluation. I propose to undertake such a reevaluation.[13]

Taking its cue from Hobbes, this book is about constitutional failure. It speaks not only to Hobbes's "realist" challenge (that a constitution cannot govern apart from the power of the sword), but also to the subtler challenge of twentieth-century Hobbesians: that a constitution is largely incapable of making a world that is distinguishable from the imperatives of economics, morality, culture, or politics.[14] The suspicion that drives the book is this: In the events leading up to and following the bloody campaigns of 1861 to 1865, Americans mislearned basic lessons about constitutionalism and the character of their own Constitution. In so doing, they have often missed the ways in which their constitutional experience has been marked—not by happy endings, but by unhappy ones, frequently poignant, sometimes tragic.[15] They have missed the ways in which their Constitution has failed.

---

and the much less happy account of Staughton Lynd, *Class Conflict, Slavery, and the United States Constitution* (1967).

[11] Thomas Hobbes, *Leviathan* (Macpherson, ed., 1968), at 200.

[12] Id., at 231.

[13] The reevaluation has already commenced at the hands of a number of able scholars. See, among others, Walter F. Murphy, "The Art of Constitutional Interpretation: A Preliminary Showing," in *Essays on the Constitution of the United States* (Harmon, ed., 1978), at 130; Murphy, "Constitutional Interpretation: The Art of the Historian, Magician, or Statesman?" 87 *Yale L. J.* 1752 (1978); Murphy, "An Ordering of Constitutional Values," 53 *So. Cal. L. Rev.* 703 (1980); William F. Harris II, *The Interpretable Constitution* (1993); Sotirios A. Barber, *On What the Constitution Means* (1984); Sanford Levinson, *Constitutional Faith* (1988); Bruce A. Ackerman, *We the People: Foundations* (1991).

[14] Mark V. Tushnet comes close to this position in "Following the Rules Laid Down: A Critique of Interpretivism and Neutral Principles," 96 *Harv. L. Rev.* 781 (1983), at 824–827. Lawrence M. Friedman embraces it explicitly in *A History of American Law* (2d ed., 1985), at 12. See also Wythe Holt, "Now and Then: The Uncertain State of Nineteenth-Century American Legal History," 7 *Ind. L. Rev.* 615 (1974).

[15] That experience has sometimes been "tragic," not only in the sense that it has been unhappy but also in the classical sense of the word; that is, it has been tragic because it involves conflicts among values and ways of political life that are both fundamental and incapable of being resolved rationally. See Isaiah Berlin, *The Crooked Timber of Humanity: Chapters in the History of Ideas* (Hardy, ed., 1991), at 191–192.

The South has known the conflict of the 1860s as "The War Between the States"; the North as the "Civil War."[16] The names in and of themselves might be arbitrary but for the fact that they signified distinct notions of the character not only of the war but of the Union over which it was fought. And the character of the Union was at issue not only because it supplied justifications for both secession from and preservation of the Union but also because it simultaneously derived from and informed people's understandings of the Constitution—what kind of thing it was, what it meant, what it required or permitted or prohibited.

In exploring the Constitution's capacity to constrain politics, this book focuses on American slavery, for slavery shoves a sharp wedge into the general problem of constitutional failure. First, although I am not directly interested in slavery as a "cause" (or not) of the Civil War, slavery was an important part of a complex set of values, institutions, and ways of life that were at stake in the breakdown of the American constitutional order. That slavery was so intimately bound up in that breakdown makes it an excellent medium for tracing the ostensible failure of the Constitution. Second, the problem of slavery lay at the juncture of morality, economics, culture, politics, and the Constitution; therefore it can shed light on the relationships among all of them. In doing so, it can also shed light on what I shall call the "autonomy" of the Constitution.

Slavery was present in the polity in two forms. One was institutional: it embodied values, practices, and relationships that were part of the ways of life in the United States. The other was discursive: slavery was a subject of public discussion. In the beginning much of the discussion surrounding slavery was not what we might think of as "constitutional" in character. Over time, however, the character of the discussion changed, as parties on all sides were increasingly impelled—often against their inclinations—to think and speak of slavery as a constitutional subject. As an issue of public discussion, slavery raises a set of questions about the character of constitutional conversation: Is there a distinctively "constitutional" discourse? If there is, what are its contours and character? What distinguishes it from other ways of talking about the world? What is the role of interpretation in constitutional discourse? Are there limits to interpretation?

With respect to interpretation, the problem of limits implies two additional questions. First, to what extent are there constraints on the very

[16] Following conventional contemporary usage, I shall use "Civil War" to describe the conflict; however, "The War Between the States" has received sanction from surprising quarters in recent years. See, e.g., *Roe v. Wade*, 410 U.S. 113 (1973), at 140.

activity of interpretation? Does a constitution ever "run out" or is it infinitely elastic in its ability at any given time to generate authoritative meanings over a particular issue within a political society?[17] Second, and related to the first matter, are there moments in political society when constitutionally authoritative interpretation becomes impossible?

II

Questions about constitutional failure, autonomy, and discourse logically incite questions about the character of American constitutionalism and of constitutionalism generally. When commentators today speak of "constitutionalism," they are speaking typically of a form of politics roughly equivalent to liberalism.[18] But the historical roots of constitutionalism extend far beyond the rise of liberalism.

Constitutionalism arose in history primarily as an attempt to solve a persistent and pervasive problem in human experience: how to constrain and direct political power;[19] that is, it is fundamentally, if not exclusively, concerned with the problem of limits. In this respect, constitutionalism is unavoidably linked to the idea of rule of law. The problem of limits presents itself to Western thought (as we have inherited it) in the form of a dialogue between Socrates and Thrasymachus in Plato's *Republic*. There Thrasymachus claims that justice is nothing more than

[17] This problem is related, but not identical, to the issue of reasons running out in moral deliberation. See Robert P. George, *Making Men Moral: Civil Liberties and Public Morality* (1993), at 8–18.

[18] See, e.g., Edward S. Corwin, *Liberty Against Government* (1948), at 1–9; Gordon J. Schochet, "Introduction: Constitutionalism, Liberalism, and the Study of Politics," in *Constitutionalism: NOMOS XX* (Pennock and Chapman, eds., 1979). See also Murphy, "An Ordering of Constitutional Values," supra note 13. Murphy has since recanted in his "Staggering Toward the New Jerusalem of Constitutional Theory: A Response to Ralph F. Gaebler," 37 *Am. J. Jurisprudence* 337 (1992), but even his post-recantation constitutionalism bears a strong familial resemblance to liberalism. See Walter F. Murphy, James E. Fleming, and Sotirios A. Barber, eds., *American Constitutional Interpretation* (2d ed., 1995), at 45–53. Liberalism also seems the unavoidable upshot of James E. Fleming's constructivist constitutionalism. Fleming, "Constructing the Substantive Constitution," 72 *Texas L. Rev.* 211 (1993); Fleming, "We the Exceptional American People," 11 *Constitutional Commentary* 355 (1994). See also Rogers M. Smith, *Liberalism and American Constitutional Law* (1985); Stephen Macedo, *Liberal Virtues: Citizenship, Virtue, and Community in Liberal Constitutionalism* (1990).

[19] See, for example, Stephen L. Elkin, "Constitutionalism: Old and New," in *A New Constitutionalism: Designing Political Institutions for a Good Society* (Elkin and Soltan, eds., 1993), at 20, 21. In citing Elkin for this proposition, I do not intend to incorporate his usage of *old* and *new* constitutionalism. Although I employ those terms, my usage departs from Elkin's in several respects.

the rule of the strongest. In short, he suggests, there are no limits apart from whatever limits there may be to power itself.

Much of Western political thought from Plato to Nietzsche has represented an attempt to meet the challenge of Thrasymachus. (It is not clear that Socrates succeeds in doing so.) One reason for the persistence and normative power of constitutionalism is that it has represented an especially useful strategy for dealing with the problem of limiting political power. Its strategy is sometimes encapsulated in the notion "higher law," a law binding not only subjects and citizens but even the ruler (eventually, the state).

As Corwin pointed out, the notion of higher law has a long pedigree in the West, extending back through Rome at least as far as pre-Socratic Greece and, though Corwin barely mentions it, ancient Israel.[20] Whatever the form of higher law may have been in these primordial times, by the time of the hegemonic rise of Christianity in Europe, the higher law was unquestionably metaphysical. That orientation owed a great deal to Plato's transformation of philosophy and to Aristotle's subsequent systematic revision of Plato's metaphysics. Notwithstanding these pre-Christian roots, by the Middle Ages the higher law had taken on a distinctively Christian character.

The aim of this metaphysical higher law was to discover transcendental moral principles. In this connection "principles" connoted general rules, "moral" connoted bindingness, and "transcendental" connoted some source outside the ruler or state (indeed, in its most abstract forms, outside human beings altogether).

If the notion of higher law were to succeed in constraining political authority, however, it would have to answer a series of questions: First, where does higher law originate? (What is its source?) Second, what makes it binding? (What is its authority?) Third, how do we know what it tells us to do? (How do we discern or recognize the general rules at a level of abstraction that permits us to solve problems in the world?) Fourth, how is higher law to be enforced?

Even within the confines of Western thought, a comprehensive genealogy of answers to those questions would be exhausting. It is probably accurate, however, that the most durable theoretical framework for supplying answers in the West has been natural law, which has presented a number of faces to the world. Three of those faces are important for genealogical purposes: the natural law of Aristotelian teleology, the rationalist natural law of Medieval Christian theology, and the con-

[20] Edward S. Corwin, "The 'Higher Law' Background of American Constitutional Law," in *Corwin on the Constitution* (Loss, ed., 1981), at 79.

tractarian natural law that arose with greatest force in seventeenth-century England in the wake of the fracturing of Christian institutions.[21]

Without pursuing the genealogy in detail, I want merely to suggest here that each of these prominent versions of natural law failed in its own way to answer adequately all the four basic questions attaching to higher law. Chiefly they failed to supply satisfactory answers to the questions of knowability and enforceability.

These failures helped spawn an innovation in higher law that fundamentally altered the very character of constitutionalism. The first useful and enduring historical example of that innovation was the Constitution of the United States. Stated most boldly, the Constitution represented a point of departure, a quantum step that led constitutionalism out of the old metaphysical paradigm of natural law and into a new paradigm in which constitutionalism is concerned with a particular kind of *enterprise*. In the new constitutionalist enterprise, (1) people, or "a people," (2) self-consciously attempt (3) to conceive the design for a new political world, (4) to embody that design in some sort of text, and (5) to implement it in the world.[22] As John Marshall would later comprehend,[23] what was crucial to (though clearly not exhaustive of) this reconception was that the new constitutionalism had to do with the ways by which people try to make a politics using what we have come to think of as "constitutions."

By "constitutions" here, Marshall meant (and I intend) *written* constitutions. This usage creates a potential confusion, for in Aristotelian terminology, which many twentieth-century commentators have adopted, "constitution" refers roughly to the institutions and values of a political society, not to texts. I shall be departing from Aristotle's terminology here. Specifically I shall use "constitution" to mean the textual kind and

[21] Each of these three "schools" of thought has attentive contemporary adherents in the United States. For Aristotelian natural law, see Barber, supra note 13. For Thomistic natural law, see George, supra note 17, and John Finnis, *Natural Law and Natural Rights* (1980). For liberal, though perhaps noncontractarian accounts of natural law, see Ronald Dworkin, *Taking Rights Seriously* (1977, 1978); and Macedo, supra note 18. Including Dworkin as a natural lawyer is potentially problematic. Some genuine natural lawyers, for example, have criticized Dworkin for being a conventionalist or a moral relativist. For reasons I shall take up in chapter 2, I think the Dworkin we see in *Taking Rights Seriously* may well be pressing a version of natural law.

[22] With respect to "conceiving the design," the implicit role of imagination may seem simply naive. Still, the notion has an impressive pedigree. Early in this century, for example, Albert Einstein suggested to Heisenberg that "[w]hether you can observe a thing or not depends on the theory which you use. It is the theory which decides what can be observed." Quoted in Michael Polanyi, "Genius in Science," 38 *Encounter* 43 (1972), at 48. And see Nelson Goodman's claim that what one sees depends simply on "the way of the taking." Nelson Goodman, *Ways of Worldmaking* (1985), at 2.

[23] *Marbury v. Madison*, 5 U.S. (1 Cranch) 137 (1803), at 176–177.

shall refer to the two elements of the Aristotelian constitution as "institutions" (or "government" or "polity") and "values" (or "norms" or "ethos").

In making claims about the new constitutionalism, I do not intend to suggest that the framers of the Constitution had clearly in mind that their proposed solution to the problems of constraining and directing political power departed so from older notions of higher (natural) law as to step into a new paradigm. Nor do I suggest that institutional arrangements, social organization, or normative or ethical considerations are not material to the new constitutionalism. Nor do I claim that the domain of constitutionalism is now exhausted or captured by the notion of "interpretation."

The emphasis on writtenness does not eliminate institutions, society, or values from constitutionalism, but does transform their place and function. Thus the new constitutionalism has a discrete operating logic that leads to distinct conclusions about what it might mean to be a "constitutional" society. These conclusions, I believe, reflect our current conceptions of what a constitution and constitutional government are. And they may permit us to evaluate constitutional failure with greater analytical subtlety than was possible before.

III

This account of constitutionalism is controversial in at least two respects. First, one might criticize it for overlooking Israel, New Zealand, and Great Britain (countries that lack a written constitution) as "constitutionalist" societies. At bottom, this criticism represents a belief that the "new" constitutionalism simply is not "constitutionalism," which has an historical meaning that we are not at liberty to alter.[24] My brief response to this criticism is simply that history, not I, has altered the definition of constitutionalism. But even to the extent that I am an active agent in the redefinition, I believe it is a useful way of adapting and applying inherited concepts to a changing world. A corollary concern that might animate this first criticism is that the new constitutionalism excludes certain political societies—basically liberal with limited governments—that might claim to be constitutional and might even be attractive. This claim is accurate but misses the point. My primary aim here is not to identify desirable forms of politics but to understand how constitutional regimes work (and fail).

The second criticism, which might be more serious than the first,

[24] See Murphy, "Staggering Toward the New Jerusalem," supra note 18, at 346–347.

characterizes the new constitutionalism as a form of "constitutionism" that fails to acknowledge certain substantive norms, without which Nazism, Stalinism, and Maoism would belong to the genre of "constitutionalist" societies, as each had one or more texts that the regime claimed as its "constitution." In short, whatever the written constitution says, goes.

This criticism may assume that the abandonment of metaphysical sources for norms implies or logically requires the abandonment of norms altogether. Or perhaps the criticism is merely skeptical of the possibility of deriving extra-textual norms from a text-centered constitutionalism. I hope to be able to show that the new constitutionalism can and does presuppose certain norms without positing them as metaphysical props. Hence, although the new constitutionalism is normatively thin, it is not normatively empty. But "constitutionalist" regimes need not be liberal, may in fact be reprehensible by our lights. Hence, although I do not concede that the new constitutionalism includes the regimes of Hitler or Stalin or Mao, it does permit a multitude of sins.

I have suggested that certain norms of the new constitutionalism might be derived from viewing constitutional politics as a form of purposive enterprise. This perspective presupposes one purpose that connects the new constitutionalism with the old: Constitutionalism is concerned with the problem of limits. Put somewhat differently, one basic reason for having a written constitution in the first place is to constrain or direct—to limit—politics. Or, more cynically, one reason for having a written constitution is to foster the belief that it can or will constrain or direct politics. Again, we need not think of limits in liberal terms, but the purpose of limiting is fundamental to the constitutional enterprise.

Given the character of the enterprise I have described so far, this presupposition implies three further notions. First, the limits should be, in some form or fashion, *voluntary*. Second, constitutional limits are limits of *principle*. Third, if a constitution is genuinely to constitute, it requires the possibility that people can *attach* to it, though the attachment need not be worshipful or "religious."

Let us first take up the notion of voluntariness. This is not another way of saying "consent." It is instead to invoke Hamilton's idea that the aim of the written Constitution was to establish and maintain a politics through "reflection and choice," not through "accident and force." Even if we put aside what William F. Harris II calls "the elemental preposterousness" of the idea that words can make a polity, reflection and choice would seem to be quite weak in the world. Especially if we try to divorce choice from the power of the sword, it seems the height of hubris to suggest that people can make a political world simply by choosing or willing to do so. The limitations, those aspects of life that are largely beyond human control or prediction, are enormous.

Nevertheless, most people—at least in political societies we might call "modern"—do not see themselves as enslaved to fate. They believe (or act as if) they have meaningful freedom to shape and direct their lives. In the most constrained situations, people frequently imagine that the choices they make matter. Even slaves in America tried to carve out a world of their own in the face of extreme oppression.[25] What accounts for the perception that human beings are free to pursue chosen ends by chosen means? I do not know. Perhaps the perception is simply true, and so obviously so that we need not inquire any further. Perhaps it is little more than illusion, in which case we either judge that existence is absurd or conclude with Isaiah Berlin "that if freedom [is] an illusion it [is] one without which one could not live or think."[26] Or perhaps some strange paradox rescues freedom from determinacy in a manner akin to the way a supposed big bang created space and time from a state in which neither previously existed. Whatever the account, constitutionalists must assume that it is possible to make a "real" world through "reflection and choice."

Almost by definition, making a world from reflection and choice implies diminishing the role of what Hamilton called "accident." But does it make sense to try to distinguish a "constitutional" world from one that is established or maintained by force? For whether force refers to violence (using physical means to enforce one's will on or constrain the action of another) or to coercion (using the threat or possibility of violence or other sanctions to enforce one's will on or constrain the action of another), it may be essential to making a political world, especially at the level of a nation-state. Certainly if politics concerns authoritative allocations of coercive power to make and implement a wide range of decisions for a society, the connection between politics and force should not be surprising. At the very least, force is essential to policing the ideological as well as the geographical boundaries of such a world. Weber's notion—that politics essentially consists of "the monopoly of the legitimate use of physical force within a given territory"—reinforces the connection.[27] And force is fraught with additional political significance, if politics has also to do with the construction of social and personal identities.

[25] See Eugene D. Genovese, *Roll, Jordan, Roll: The World the Slaves Made* (1972, 1974).

[26] See Berlin, *Crooked Timber*, supra note 15, at 4.

[27] Max Weber, "Politics as a Vocation" (1919), in *From Max Weber: Essays in Sociology* (Gerth and Mills, eds., 1946), at 77, 78.

But if it is quixotic to think that one can (or should) purge politics of all traces of force, there might still be reasons for wanting to limit its influence. As a constitutional matter, the problem with force is threefold. First, again taking Hamilton as a point of departure, the stronger the role of force, the weaker the role of some forms of choice. Second, to use force to make a world is not necessarily to understand that world. The absence of understanding is problematic because Hamilton's "reflection" must presuppose or imply comprehensibility if it is to be meaningful. Third, and here we begin to see the second notion that follows from the presumption of limits, a world that is substantially a creature of force is essentially a standardless world, as force becomes its own justification. Standards are crucial because they make principle possible. Without principle, there is no distinguishing authority from power or a constitutional world from a world of accident or force.

In sustaining a constitutional world, interpretation takes on special significance. Indeed it is central to the life of a constitutional society. One aim of a constitution is to construct a new political world from the world of the text. If that new world is to be a "constitutional" one, it must reflect (and be reflected in) the text. Word and "political reality" must be compatible with each other on some level. In order to test that compatibility, we have to assume that one can interpret the text. Actually we have to assume that we can interpret both the text and the political world. The act of interpretation presupposes that interpretation can generate understanding or "meaning." Meaning in turn suggests some sort of order or "coherence." Although that term inevitably implies some notion of internal consistency or fit, it does not require anything resembling mathematical exactness.

Even without a strong requirement of precision, however, three general considerations threaten to undermine both the norm of coherence and the reciprocity of society and text. The first is simply the character—one is tempted to say the inherent ambiguity—of language itself. In *The Federalist*, No. 37, James Madison acknowledged the difficulties inherent in the medium, though he affirmed its utility.

The second consideration is the complexity of society. Even supposedly simple societies have a subtlety and complexity that challenge consistency. The difficulties are all the greater in a society that "contain[s] multitudes," diverse tensions, even contradictions. If Walt Whitman's dismissal of the problem of contradiction—"Do I contradict myself? / Very well then I contradict myself"[28]—is facile or glib, it is also instructive. For tensions and contradictions may be essential to sustaining knowledge, perhaps to creating and sustaining life itself. Thus the

[28] Walt Whitman, "Song of Myself" (1855), at Section 51.

creation of new worlds may be possible only at the level of paradox, and sustaining a world may depend on playing out, while not entirely extinguishing, the tensions arising from the creative paradox. But a constitutional society cannot, without undermining the constitutional enterprise, abandon some form of fidelity to coherence and consistency with text.

The third consideration is "blending." In trying to understand a text, interpreters import assumptions, theories, and biases from outside the text, as they do in their attempts to understand the political world or themselves. The outside and inside are constantly blending into each other.[29]

Blending occurs in at least three ways. First, "coherence" has to do substantially with *appearance* or *perception*. Consequently, given the belief of the post-Einsteinian world that unmediated perception is an impossibility, any hard distinction between inside and outside is at least partly illusory. But the distinction cannot be entirely an illusion if constitutionalism is to succeed as an enterprise, unless imagination can manufacture by trick a "real" or possible world from one that does not exist.

Second, the meaning of a text is not immanent in its words but is culturally grounded; that is, the source of meaning is not exclusively in the words themselves but in the culture that confronts them. This account of meaning has at least two implications.

One implication is that "plain words," as an interpretive mode, rests on a fallacy. Consider one of the simplest of the Constitution's provisions: that a person is ineligible to serve as president "who shall not have attained to the age of thirty-five years." To interpret that provision, we must import understandings (usually culturally shared) that are partially autonomous from the words themselves. Presumably we would understand, among other things, both what counts as a year (a single revolution of the Earth around the sun) and when years are assigned for the purposes of a person's age (such that "year one" is not assigned at birth or conception or viability). Neither of those notions is evident

[29] An alternative way of thinking about the problem of blending is to imagine that constitutional coherence operates along two axes, one horizontal and the other vertical. The horizontal axis represents the "internal" coherence of the text. Its principal mode of expression is theoretical. The vertical axis represents consistency with political society's ethos, its values, habits, and self-understandings. Its principal expression is experiential. Constitutional meaning operates in proximity to the intersection of these two axes. For a fuller description of these ideas, see Mark E. Brandon, "The 'Original' Thirteenth Amendment and the Limits to Formal Constitutional Change," in *Responding to Imperfection: The Theory and Practice of Constitutional Amendment* (Levinson, ed., 1995), at 229 et seq.

from the words themselves but instead derives from social conventions and expectations that attach to the language.[30] Of course this last observation poses a challenge to the success of any text whose purposes include making a society on which it depends for its very meaning.

The other implication of the account of meaning I have proposed is that it is clearly distinguishable from a naturalist or "moral realist" account of meaning. As Michael Moore has described it, moral realism holds that the source of meaning is not cultural understanding but the scientifically (and morally) true characteristics of the events, persons, things, or ideas for which the words stand. Here is an example: What, Moore asks, is the meaning of "death"? A society or group might hold that a person is dead who is unconscious and whose respiratory and coronary functions have ceased. But would it be right? Moore insists it would not be, under certain circumstances.[31]

For example, he says, what about a person who has "drowned," who is unconscious and whose heart and breathing have stopped? Is the person "dead"? Moore says that if the person is revivable using "certain procedures," any group that claimed the person was dead would be wrong. It would be wrong not because it misapplies the culture's conventions but because it misunderstands the natural scientific truth about when a person is dead. According to Moore, death is a subclass of events that are "natural kinds of things" that possess "true natures." The aim of interpretation, he says, is to comprehend the truth about their natures. The nature of things is not merely a scientific matter, however, but a moral one as well. Hence, he says, words like *justice* and *responsibility* have true meanings that reflect or are determined by moral reality.[32]

I reject Moore's view, at least for the purposes of this study and perhaps for deeper reasons as well. Chapters 2 and 6 will take up the relationship between morality and constitutional interpretation in greater detail, so I shall limit myself here to a brief response. People—even those who are similarly situated—often disagree fundamentally with one another about matters of morality. It is my impression that frequently at the most basic levels of disagreement, neither reason nor

[30] See Mark V. Tushnet's discussion of this very provision in Tushnet, "A Note on the Revival of Textualism in Constitutional Theory," 58 *So. Cal. L. Rev.* 683 (1985), at 686–687. But see John Hart Ely, *Democracy and Distrust: A Theory of Judicial Review* (1980), at 13, who argues that the reference in the provision is "clear." I do not claim the contrary, but if, in Ely's words, "the language is so clear that a conscious reference to purpose seems unnecessary," it is so because of the cultural grounding of meaning.

[31] Michael S. Moore, "A Natural Law Theory of Interpretation," 58 *So. Cal. L. Rev.* 277 (1985), at 293 et seq.

[32] Id., at 291–301.

scientific inquiry can adjudicate the differences. Hence there is no authoritative natural or transcendental means for validating one position or another. But even if there were such means, and I shall make this point again in chapter 6, they would *appear* as cultural—or "conventional"—artifacts.

Take, for example, another type of argument about the "nature" of death: Is there "life" after "death"? This question may be answered in many ways, but I shall restrict myself to two. One popular school of thought holds that people do survive death, at least in a spiritual sense, and live on in heaven, hell, or purgatory. Another school holds that people do not survive death in either a material or spiritual sense, but may live on, if at all, only in the memories of those who survive them. What is the answer to the question? I do not know, though I have met people in both camps who insist that they do. I suspect their confidence is misplaced, at least as an epistemological matter; that is, even if in fact they happen to be right, they cannot know that they are. I assume, then, that we in this world cannot know the truth about such matters and know that we know. This is not necessarily to suggest that the question is not important. It is merely to claim that the ultimate rightness or wrongness of the answer is not at the heart of its importance, at least for my purposes.

What is important is that the two sides begin from fundamentally different premises. Each side takes its premises to be true. From its premises, each side builds and employs its own relatively coherent worldview that not only answers certain questions (like whether there is life after death) but logically excludes the view of the opposing side. The difference between the two worlds is not negotiable, much less resolvable, by means that both sides can coherently embrace. As I view them, then, these are contests of meaning, not transcendental truth.

I suspect that these considerations concerning the cultural ground for meaning apply not only to the peculiar issue of life after death but also to many of the most basic questions of political morality, identity, and interest. This suspicion leads to the third way in which blending occurs between what is inside and outside the constitutional text. Once the authority of the text is established or assumed, people are often impelled to see themselves as embodying the text. They can convince themselves that their identities, self-perceptions, or interests coincide with their constitution. The constitution to which they have attached themselves can thus become the filter through which they interpret their political lives. Or perhaps in the most extreme situations, the constitution is not merely a lens after all, but a mirror, reflecting instead of filtering.

All these observations about blending impede not only the construction of meanings from texts but also the construction of a politics congruent with the text. And they are even a challenge to the idea of coherence itself. Nevertheless coherence is central to constitutionalism. First, it is inextricably tied to the notion of comprehensibility, which is essential to the constitutional enterprise. Second, coherence is linked to the notion of standards, and hence to principle, in systematizing normative values or establishing boundaries within which a politics of institutionally constrained will takes place. A polity willing to forgo coherence must also be willing to forgo standards and thus stands ready to undercut the very authority of constitutional government. For such a willingness subverts the idea of limits in government. It undermines institutional accountability. It breeds cynicism, even despair. In short, although government can exist and society will not crumble without standards, that government and society will cease to be *constitutional* in the sense I use the word. They will cease to be constrained in any meaningful way by constitutive text(s).

IV

These notions concerning constitutions and the character of constitutionalism might seem to imply fairly distinct assumptions about constitutional failure. For example, one view that might follow from them is that to be a constitutional society is to hold the world(s) together, to maintain a form of order. Hence, when a constitution ceases to hold its normative or institutional political world together, it has "failed." Certainly, on most versions of such a view, the American constitutional order had failed by 1861. But constitutional failure is potentially more complex than this notion implies.

In fact we can imagine a typology in which constitutional failure is multidimensional; that is, it exists in four distinct but related domains or, alternatively, at four levels of abstraction. The types of constitutional failure that reside in those domains are failures of *constitutionalism*, of *a constitution*, of *constitutional order*, and of *constitutional discourse*. As we shall see, constitutional failure sometimes operates in ironical or counterintuitive ways precisely because it may reside in those different domains. Thus a constitutional *failure* at one level may actually suggest a constitutional *success* at another.

First, there is a failure of *constitutionalism*, or a failure to employ basic principles of constitutionalism within a regime or in moving into or out of such a regime. In ascertaining these principles, one need not resort to transcendental or natural principles of political morality. Instead we can turn to inferences that follow from viewing constitutionalism as an enterprise in a particular mode of establishing, directing, and limiting political power.

I have suggested that a basic vehicle of that enterprise is a written constitution. The very character and purpose of the enterprise presuppose the existence of standards that define and direct the enterprise, that make it sensible and perhaps useful. To depart from them is to abandon the enterprise, the experiment, and to render it, in fundamental fashion, a failure. Although they are not transcendental or universal principles for guiding human behavior, they are "objective" — they supply a fairly firm ground for evaluation and criticism — because they are constitutive of the enterprise at hand. They are part of what it means to be engaged in that enterprise.

Thus, drawing on Hamilton, a constitution possesses the possibility for failure not simply because it is a human creation and therefore fallible according to whatever transcendental standards there may be, but because it is an experiment and therefore fallible according to the standards or principles implied by the character of the enterprise itself. In other words, it is fallible according to the standards that inhere in the enterprise of attempting to establish, direct, and constrain political power by written constitution. Of course a constitution may also be fallible in the pragmatic sense that the system it establishes is simply unworkable, but I am interested here in speaking to standards.

We may deduce some such standards from the principles and presuppositions that we saw in the preceding section. Some of the standards that follow from those principles and presuppositions are these: Any regime that purports to aim for government by reflection and choice depends for its success on its ability to act on the human mind. Specifically (and here we see the third notion that follows from the basic presupposition of limits), it must act on the mind in a way that permits those who would be subjects or citizens of the regime — or of the constitution that the regime holds up as authority for its own existence — to attach themselves to the regime using a modicum of free will. That attachment is, in part, a psychological phenomenon which in turn generates certain expectations among potential constitutional subjects.

Those expectations are a double-edged sword from the regime's standpoint, for while they form part of the glue that holds any constitutional society together, they also imply certain obligations that the regime is bound to recognize. The specific content of those obligations may take many forms and be present in varying intensities, depending on the character and experience of the people doing the attaching and on the precise form and origin of the regime itself.

But certain general expectations or standards may pertain to any constitutional regime. First, to the extent that a regime's constitution arises from or includes some process (as the Constitution of the United States did), the regime should follow its own procedures. Second, procedures for establishing the regime (or for ratifying its constitution) should represent the fundamental principles and presuppositions of constitutionalism; that is, they themselves should represent, among other things, a degree of reflection and choice. Third, "normal" procedures for operating the regime—normal constitutional process—should also represent reflection and choice, though perhaps in ways different from those of constitutive procedures. Fourth, policies pursued by the regime should be "rational" in the sense that their validity should be subject to testing by reference to public, constitutional norms and standards. Finally, the regime is estopped from challenging the constitutional legitimacy of other regimes that claim authority by the same modes of creation that it claims for its own existence and authority. Thus it is possible to imagine conditions under which the creation of a new regime by secession from the old is permissible not only according to the specific logic of authority of a particular regime but also under principles of constitutionalism.

A failure of constitutionalism is not the only possible form of constitutional failure. The second form is a failure of *a constitution*, which involves discarding, abandoning, or ignoring a particular constitution. This form of failure may involve a contemporaneous reconstitution by a new constitution, as was the case for the Confederate States of America after the rescissions of the Constitution of the United States of America, but need not do so.

A constitution may fail for reasons compatible, or incompatible, with the principles of constitutionalism. It may fail because a society wants to make different substantive choices from those in the former constitution or because it wants to devise new institutions or procedures for enacting choices or because it is motivated by other, less noble impulses. But if the failure is a self-conscious discarding or abandonment, and especially if it involves a contemporaneous reconstitution, the failure almost by definition must be compatible in some form with principles of constitutionalism. It must be so because it involves the exercise of some form of choice; however, according to principles of constitutionalism, the original choosing of a constitution must presuppose the possibility of choosing to reject that constitution, either in the beginning or later.

Third, there is a failure of *constitutional order*, which is signified by the breakdown of a political regime established or authorized by a constitution. Often the failure of the order is unreflective and unself-conscious, perhaps gradual, even almost imperceptible. For that reason, it need not implicate a failure of constitutionalism. Moreover, it may well leave the existing constitution in place and therefore need not occur in conjunction with a failure of that constitution.

In fact the failure of a constitutional order may well grow out of or be caused by *adherence* to a constitution. Sotirios A. Barber notes an argument widely used to justify deviating from conceded constitutional rights in times of threat to national security. Such times, the argument goes, justify the polity's departing from the text: The Constitution is not a suicide pact.[33] Barber recognizes both the power and pitfalls of such an argument. One can easily imagine circumstances in which a society is faced with a choice between its survival as a political order and the survival of its constitution. Abraham Lincoln chose the former at the expense of the latter, and backed his choice with guns.[34] Hugo Black, on the other hand, may well have embraced, at least in one case, a theory that reversed Lincoln's values and thus revised what might count as the survival of the order.[35]

Fourth is a failure of *constitutional discourse*, which occurs when a constitutional order is unable to speak coherently or, more seriously, to sustain itself through constitutional interpretation or through discourse pertaining to its constitution.

In the United States the most vivid and serious account of this form of failure occurred in the decades preceding the Civil War. During that period an interpretive schism between Northern and Southern states—over the character and allocation of political authority, mainly in the context of disputes over the extension of slavery into the territories—deepened and widened to such an extent that the two regions adopted distinctive interpretive paradigms that could not accommodate each other. In a sense each side was faithful to the Constitution in its own way. Hence the mere presence of competing interpretive paradigms did not signify a failure of the Constitution. But the conflict between the two did precipitate the breakdown of the constitutional order, when the South eventually abandoned the order and seceded from the Union in a manner that may have been consistent with principles of constitutionalism.

One can perceive discursive failures, however, that do not precipitate a breakdown of the order. For example, the deep divisions in our own time over the constitutional status of abortion reflect a kind of discursive breakdown in which neither side can speak meaningfully to the

[33] See Barber, supra note 13, at 108–113.

[34] Lincoln sometimes denied there was a contradiction between the two choices. At other times he claimed that he was not obliged to adhere to particular provisions of the Constitution when doing so put at risk what he considered to be the fundamental purpose of a constitution: to create a union in perpetuity. See Lincoln, "Message to Congress in Special Session," in *The Collected Works of Abraham Lincoln* (Basler, ed., 1953), vol. 6, at 421, 430.

[35] *Barenblatt v. United States*, 360 U.S. 109 (1959), Black, dissenting, at 134.

other. In some respects, such divisions may well indicate the success of the Constitution, as each side sees or expresses itself as being faithful to the Constitution's values. Thus the battle is over not only the *meaning* of the Constitution but the Constitution itself. And because the battle is incapable of being resolved happily for all sides, the stakes are sufficiently high that social disruption can and does occur; the lines of division, however, are sufficiently complex and cross-cutting that they do not threaten the failure of the order itself. But if they were to precipitate such a failure, it would not necessarily signify a failure of constitutionalism. Constitutionalism does not ensure harmony, unity, or happy endings.

As Gayatri Spivak has suggested, it may be that the Constitution is not teleological (or substantively purposive) after all but is instead paralogical and morphogenetic.[36] To see a constitution as part of a "process" in this way, however, is to revise our expectations about what might amount to a "constitutional failure" (or success). For the story of constitutional significance is at least partly a history of constitutional change; but it is a history in which dispute and division play a constitutive role.

V

What follows, then, is not simply an analytic study of constitutional failure or the character of constitutionalism. It is also an interpretation of American history. "Out of our conceptions of the past, we make a future."[37] Whether history—the discourse we use for constructing or reflecting our conceptions of the past—can succeed in making a future depends neither on its ability to predict the future nor simply on its ability to give a causal account of how we got where we are. For the importance of history does not lie entirely in its revelation of the forces that determine our existence.

History is important for constitutionalism because it participates in the self-conscious construction of political society.[38] Through it we give ourselves narrative accounts of who we are here and now. It is a means

[36] Gayatri Chakravorty Spivak, "Constitutions and Culture Studies," 2 *Yale J. of Law & the Humanities* 133, 135 (1990). *Paralogical* refers to fallacies in reasoning or logic. *Morphogenetic* has to do with the evolution of and structural changes in organic forms.

[37] I have seen the quotation attributed to Thomas Hobbes, *Behemoth, or the Long Parliament* (1668); however, having searched *Behemoth* for the quotation, I have been unable to confirm it. Perhaps it is sufficient to suggest that if Hobbes was not its author, he should have been.

[38] I do not claim that people can self-consciously construct every aspect of their (collective or individual) lives. However, I am interested here in exploring the extent and ways that they can.

by which we both choose our own ancestry and construct our own political identities.[39] To borrow from Nelson Goodman, it is one way of making our political world(s).[40] Thus history is not simply a discourse through which we attempt to reconstruct the past, even given the truism that we invariably read the past through the lens of the present, that our understanding of the past is shaped by our standing in the present. Just as often, perhaps more often, history is a way of constructing the *present*, of reading the present through the artifacts, myths, and received accounts of the past. By giving ourselves an "historical" understanding of our present condition, we generate a means by which we might "make a future." It can inform our understanding of a constitution at the same time that the identities it generates are potentially distinct from the identities that emerge from reflection on the text.

With respect to the Constitution of the United States, the relationship between history and text is not that suggested by the jurisprudential phenomenon of intentionalism. The oft-repeated justification for intentionalism is to promote certainty, legitimacy, and limits in constitutional interpretation. It aims to achieve those objectives by embracing the intentions of the Constitution's historical framers as the sole appropriate standard for determining its meaning. Simply, authorial intention is equivalent to meaning.[41]

At least one constitutional theorist has suggested that intentionalism is categorically incompatible with constitutionalism.[42] I am disinclined to read intentionalism out of constitutionalism a priori. Nonetheless there are three sets of central objections to intentionalism, objections that limit its utility in the constitutional enterprise. The first is the epistemological objection. It aims at the difficulty of reading people's minds, especially people who have been dead a century or more. We simply cannot know with certainty today what they thought about anything then. We can make guesses on the basis of received accounts of what they said and did. But the accounts themselves are often "flawed" in that they are sometimes contradictory, often partial, and usually only the most ephemeral approximation of what "really" happened. We can construct plausible stories about what people said and did. Even so,

[39] On history as a way of choosing one's ancestry, see Robert Cover, "Foreword: *Nomos* and Narrative," 97 *Harv. L. Rev.* 4, 18 (1983). On the relation between history and the construction of political identity, see Anne Norton, *Alternative Americas: A Reading of Antebellum Political Culture* (1986).

[40] See Goodman, supra note 22.

[41] See, e.g., Gary L. McDowell, *The Constitution and Contemporary Constitutional Theory* (1985); Robert H. Bork, *The Tempting of America: The Political Seduction of the Law* (1990); and Antonin Scalia, "Originalism: The Lesser Evil," 57 *U. Cin. L. Rev.* 849 (1989).

[42] See Harris, supra note 13, at 159.

such stories but dimly manifest the mental operations that motivated them. If people in former times were even remotely like people seem to be now, they did and said things from a variety of motivations, intentions, and impulses, many of which were hidden even to themselves. Sometimes they might have been strategically deceptive about their reasons for action. Sometimes their justifications were merely pretexts that not just imperfectly, but falsely, portrayed what they took their actual reasons to be. Politicians of all eras have been masters of such games.

Those difficulties have led some scholars—still sympathetic to the notion that meaning should be grounded firmly in the time and place of original authorship—to modify intentionalism in order to save it from the epistemological critique. Under the modification, authoritative meanings would be those that comport with our best account of the *pronouncements* of the framers of the original Constitution or its amendments. The assumption would be that those pronouncements are a rough but workable approximation of the intentions of the author(s). As modified, intentionalism avoids the need to understand actual mental processes but cannot cure the problems of the (in)accuracy of the historical record and of the potentially pretextual uses of language. Still other problems persist in intentionalism.

One difficulty, and the second general objection to intentionalism, is an ontological problem that folds back into the epistemological objection. It asks: Who counts as a framer of the Constitution or of any particular constitutional provision? Is a framer only one who drafted the provision? Does "framer" also include anyone who participated (or sat) in the constitutional convention? Does it also include a person in Congress—which authorized the convention, but not its product—or a person in a state legislature or ratifying convention who voted for the provision(s)? What voice of a framer is an appropriately authorial (or authoritative) voice? (For example, when John Marshall wrote opinions as Chief Justice of the United States, was he still speaking as a framer, as he himself claimed? Or was his later, judicial voice a different, though not necessarily less authoritative, voice?) How do we resolve the dilemma of multiple purposes presented by the fact of multiple authors? Do we include dissenters as framers?[43] If so, how do we incorporate the opinions of dissenters on questions of meaning? Dare we take seriously the myth, which originates in the Preamble itself, that the people are the ultimate authors of the Constitution?[44] And what do we make of Jeffer-

[43] On this point, see Justice Clarence Thomas's dissenting opinion in *U.S. Term Limits v. Thornton*, 115 Sup. Ct. 1842 (1995), which invoked antifederalist arguments on behalf of the authority of a state to limit the terms of members of Congress from the state. See also Justice Felix Frankfurter's dissent in *Trop v. Dulles*, 356 U.S. 86 (1958).

[44] For a nuanced discussion of the complex ways "the people" can be configured, see Wayne D. Moore, *Constitutional Rights and Powers of the People* (1996).

son Powell's paradoxical conclusion that the historical record of the convention in Philadelphia indicates that it was the framers' intention that their intention not be followed in constitutional interpretation?[45]

In an effort to finesse such questions and difficulties, one might modify intentionalism still further. For example, we might try to construct interpretations that might have comported with the ethos or spirit of the ages during which the Constitution and its amendments were proposed and ratified. We might call this modification "originalism," whose aim is not intentions per se but *understandings*.[46] Essentially we would be looking for interpretations that would have been plausible or acceptable to the people, or perhaps more narrowly to potential interpreters, at the time of the framing. This version solves one problem—identifying the framers—but it raises another similar problem: Who counts as an authoritative original interpreter? And it suffers from an epistemological difficulty similar to that of intentionalism. It requires some understanding of the original interpreter's mind-set, which may be more challenging than invading the mind-set of the framer. In a looser form, however, originalism might avoid that difficulty by permitting us to resort to extrinsic historical evidence of ethos or belief. But if we weaken originalism in this manner, we should remember that extrinsic evidence has but limited relation to intentions or understandings (of framers or anyone else). And the deeper problem remains that the choices we would make would be fraught with the same treacherous ambiguities that intentionalism or originalism is designed to obviate.

We face similar difficulties with respect to the third objection to intentionalism and originalism. It is strategic. It asks: At what level of generality do we read a framer's intentions or purposes? In other words, precisely what must a framer have intended or assumed? Take, for example, the oft-discussed problem of the reach of the Fourth Amendment's prohibition against unreasonable searches and seizures. Does electronic eavesdropping implicate the Fourth Amendment?[47] If the framer must have thought of *a particular practice* in order for it to be covered by the Fourth Amendment, then surely the Amendment does not constrain electronic eavesdropping in any way. Of course this approach gradually disempowers the original Constitution in the face of

[45] See H. Jefferson Powell, "The Original Understanding of Original Intent," 98 *Harv. L. Rev.* 885 (1985).

[46] This appears to be the strategy adopted by Scalia, supra note 41.

[47] The Supreme Court squarely addressed the question in *Olmstead v. United States*, 277 U.S. 438 (1928), holding that "[t]he Fourth Amendment is to be construed in light of what was deemed to be an unreasonable search and seizure when it was adopted." [Quoting *Carroll v. United States*, 267 U.S. 132 (1925).] But see *Katz v. United States*, 389 U.S. 347 (1967), where the Court held that electronic eavesdropping was covered by the Fourth Amendment.

technological change, so perhaps it cannot be what intentionalism or originalism requires. Perhaps the Amendment covers forms of invasion *similar in type* to those particular forms the framers imagined. Or perhaps we can avoid this two-step analysis and invoke directly the *general types* of activity the framers had in mind and then reason from those types to modern practices that might be covered. Or might we simply invoke highly *abstract principles*—such as privacy of the home or a general interest in privacy of person or place—to determine what the framers intended?[48]

The point is not that one cannot supply tentative answers or solutions to the questions or problems that arise from any of the versions of intentionalism or originalism. It is that those answers and solutions, and what we make of the pronouncements we take to be authoritative, embody the very difficulties of interpretation, including unavoidable impositions of the present on the past, that intentionalists and most originalists insist we evade. Hence the point is not simply that intentionalism or originalism is a kind of illusion or trick, as many such enterprises are, but that it cannot work in the way its proponents say it can or must to provide certainty in constitutional interpretation. Antonin Scalia concedes as much, claiming that originalism nonetheless has fewer and less serious flaws than "nonoriginalism"; however, it is not clear what one should make of such a defense when the fundamental reason for originalism cannot be sustained on originalism's terms.[49]

Despite these and other criticisms, various accounts of some framers' "intentions" have always had rhetorical power in American constitutional culture. That power is understandable given the almost mystical importance of foundings and "fathers" in the lore about the nation and the Constitution. Indeed some notion of foundings may be crucial to understanding how constitutional regimes come to be legitimated. But to acknowledge the importance of foundings is not to justify making sovereigns or demigods of their perpetrators.

To be sure, the authorial act is a constitutive act of great importance and can even have an interpretive character. Making a constitution is a quasi-interpretive act. For example, we may assume that even founders have political agendas and personal fears that find their way into (the founders' understandings of) the text.[50] And they, like any mortals, are probably tempted to peek behind the veil (which is certainly not Rawls's "veil of ignorance"),[51] to make the world only too well, to anticipate in

[48] Part of Ronald Dworkin's argument is intentionalist in this last sense. See Dworkin, supra note 21, at 131, 132–137.

[49] See Scalia, supra note 41, at 862–865; see also Tushnet, supra note 14, at 793.

[50] Their agendas and fears may not be ours, however.

[51] For a discussion of the veil of ignorance as an imaginary device for making moral judgments, see John Rawls, *A Theory of Justice* (1971), at 136–142.

detail a picture of the constitutional world to be. All this presupposes some sort of "pre-textual" interpretation.[52] Indeed one might wonder what it would be like to write or ratify a constitution—even with great faith in the wisdom and capacity of succeeding generations to interpret and apply it as they will—without engaging in such anticipatory interpretation.

Both authors and readers interpret, then, and in some respects their interpretive perspectives may be virtually identical, as, for example, when the constitution maker imagines himself a constitutional "subject" or citizen. But their perspectives are also likely to be different in important ways. For one thing, even if the authors of constitutions do not "retire into the sky,"[53] they do eventually die. What makes that fact significant is the character of interpretation. Just as it is too simple to say that the author chooses the words (*constructs* the text) without interpretation, it is also too simple to say that a reader interprets them (*construes* the text) without choice. Just as construction implies construal, construal functions as a kind of construction. To interpret a text is to re-create it, if only briefly. Thus, in the sense (and to the extent) that space and time drive a kind of wedge between words and their authors' intentions, language might defensibly be considered "free in the world," as Heidegger suggested.[54] This freedom seems especially, but not exclusively, the condition of written, as opposed to spoken, language. The materiality of texts—hence their potential for greater longevity and dissemination—diminishes the authority of intention as a source of or standard for measuring meaning.

But language is assuredly not *free* in any radical sense of the word. Words, the constituent elements of language, are not like free-floating electrons, randomly colliding with or attaching to other particles. Nor, to draw on a metaphor more familiar to political philosophers, are they like "loose canons" on the deck of a storm-tossed ship. For if a text becomes freed from the intentions of its authors, it becomes in turn the property of its users, its interpreters, who give it life, who re-create it, by constructing meanings from it. A constitutional text, then, far from being free in the world, is unavoidably circumstantially grounded in particular times, places, and peoples. In showing how that is so con-

[52] "Pre-textual" (anticipatory) interpretation is not necessarily equivalent to "pretextual" (strategic, self-interested, or specious) interpretation, as the former may well be sincere, other-regarding, or principled.

[53] James Bradley Thayer, "The Origin and Scope of the American Doctrine of Constitutional Law," 7 *Harv. L. Rev.* 129 (1893). Of course many of the American constitutional founders did not retire (into the sky or elsewhere) but became active players in constitutional politics and often ardent opponents of one another as readers of the Constitution.

[54] The phrase is a paraphrase of Heidegger's observation. See Robert R. Magliola, *Phenomenology and Literature* (1977), at 81.

cerning the American Constitution, history can also show us something of who we are.

VI

Who "we" are is sometimes problematic, and therein lies the original failure of the Constitution: it failed to constitute slaves. That is not to say that the Constitution failed to *account for* slaves, nor even that it failed to *bind* them in some (literal) sense of the word. But it did not bind them *in a constitutional sense.* Put somewhat differently, although slaves were certainly not *free in* the constitutional world, they were in a theoretical sense *free from* that world. This failure was deliberate and largely self-conscious. It was perpetrated both through language and by silence.

Slavery was present in the Constitution in only four places. Article I, Section 2, counted slaves ("all other Persons") as three-fifths of persons for purposes of allocating representation in Congress among the states; Article I, Section 9, denied Congress authority to interfere with the slave trade ("the Migration or Importation of such Persons") before 1808; and Article IV, Section 2, provided for the return of fugitive slaves ("Person(s) held to Service of Labour"). Less directly, but just as importantly, Article V entrenched Article I, Section 9, by prohibiting for twenty years any amendment to the Constitution concerning the importation of slaves. Of course, in saying that slavery was present in the Constitution, one must take the word *present* somewhat loosely, as none of the four provisions actually used the terms *slaves* or *slavery.* But even if we take the provisions to refer to slavery, the text contained precious little to indicate what its constitutional status or future might be. In the face of a stingy text, perhaps the framers' intentions could supply clues as to the constitutive significance of slavery.

As it happens, however, intentionalist solutions to problems of textual uncertainty are themselves uncertain, as they become ensnared in the ontological question of who counts as a framer, the epistemological question of what counts as evidence of intention, and the strategic question concerning the proper level of abstraction at which to pitch intentions. Evidence suggests that many people at the time of the founding—before Whitney invented the cotton gin in 1793—believed that slavery would eventually die a natural death.[55] Walter Berns argues that many

[55] See James Madison, "Letter to Robert Walsh" (November 27, 1819), in *The Writings of James Madison* (Hunt, ed., 1910), vol. 9, at 1–6. See also David M. Potter, *The Impending Crisis, 1848–1861* (1976), at 38. This was Abraham Lincoln's position in his "Ad-

in the founding generation understood the commerce clause as authorizing Congress to prohibit the *domestic* slave trade.[56] And Herbert Storing goes so far as to claim that the founders not only were not proslavery but thought that slavery should be abolished, though not that blacks should be citizens.[57]

The picture David Potter paints is more complex and less happy. He notes that slavery did not pose a serious moral problem in the Colonies until the Revolution. In the wake of the movement for independence, many people, both Northerners and Southerners, condemned slavery and embraced the notion that it would eventually die. Some, intent on rooting out the institution, supported voluntary manumission, though apparently not abolition. But Potter notes that views of the immorality of slavery were not remotely universal. In fact "there is considerable reason to doubt that the antislavery philosophy . . . ever extended very far beyond the intellectuals in the South or very deep into the lower South even among the intellectuals."[58]

William Wiecek is still less sanguine about the framers' position on the place of slavery in the political order. He argues that slavery was inextricably tied to American practices and traditions at the time of the constitutional founding and was part and parcel of the founders' views of their world and of human progress. "[S]lavery," he says, "was wholly compatible with the American constitutional order; indeed, was an essential element of it. America then was a racist, slaveholding society, and its constitutional order conformed to that fundamental characteristic."[59] In the Constitutional Convention, Charles Cotesworth Pinckney of South Carolina gave voice to sentiments that others may have harbored but did not express: "If slavery be wrong, it is justified by the example of all the world. . . . In all ages one half of mankind have been slaves."[60] Perhaps the most we can say about the framers is that their positions on slavery were manifold, ambiguous, and deeply ambivalent.[61]

---

dress at Cooper Institute, New York City" (February 27, 1860), in *Collected Works*, supra note 34, vol. 3, at 522 et seq.

[56] Walter Berns, "The Constitution and the Migration of Slaves," 78 *Yale L. J.* 198 (1968).

[57] Herbert J. Storing, "Slavery and the Moral Foundations of the American Republic," in *Slavery and Its Consequences: The Constitution, Equality, and Race* (Goldwin and Kaufman, eds., 1988), at 45 et seq.

[58] See Potter, supra note 55, at 38–39.

[59] William Wiecek, "'The Blessings of Liberty': Slavery in the American Constitutional Order," in *Slavery and Its Consequences*, supra note 57, at 23 et seq.

[60] Quoted in James Madison, *Notes of Debates in the Federal Convention of 1787 Reported by James Madison* (Koch, ed., 1987), at 505.

[61] This is essentially Wiecek's position. Wiecek argues that notwithstanding the multi-

The bottom line is that notwithstanding its import as a moral and economic issue or the dire warnings of some that slavery would be the new nation's undoing,[62] there was little agreement on slavery's significance or its future. In fact a strange constitutive silence reigned in the country on many of the most fundamental questions pertaining to slavery.

Perhaps the silence was not so strange. For sometimes even those fundamental values around which a society organizes itself or through which people in political society construct their identities are not expressed in written constitutions. In fact constitutions often tell people what they need not (or may not) talk about just as they direct what they need to (or may) discuss. The reasons might be twofold. First, the matter may not actually need to be put in writing. If a value or practice be independently fundamental, if widely and/or deeply "ingrained" as part of a society's political existence, whether consciously or unconsciously, its expression might seem superfluous. It is constitutive regardless of whether it is embodied in a text. Second, some matters (because there is no consensus over them or because trying to achieve consensus would be too burdensome or potentially divisive) are left unresolved, and if spoken to at all, are addressed only partially. This second notion might mean that the matters are left to be resolved at a constitutional level at some later date. Or it might mean that they are left to be addressed through "normal" political processes of institutional and social compromise, rather than nailed down as constitutional values. Or it might mean that they are left simply as "private" matters, removed from public debate and treated as if they did not implicate public values.[63] Some-

---

plicity of framers and intentions, the delegations from South Carolina and Georgia "extorted acquiescence in their single-minded proslavery program from all the other framers." Wiecek, supra note 59, at 24. Compare Don Fehrenbacher's claim that the ambivalences of the text itself reflected the multiplicity of intentions with respect to slavery. According to Fehrenbacher, however, the interpretive practices of governmental institutions eventually transformed those ambivalences into a unidimensional proslavery gloss on the Constitution. Don E. Fehrenbacher, "Slavery, the Framers, and the Living Constitution," in *Slavery and Its Consequences*, supra note 57, at 1 et seq.

[62] See, e.g., Thomas Jefferson, "Letter to St. George Tucker" (August 28, 1797), quoted in William W. Freehling, "The Founding Fathers and Slavery," 77 *Am. Hist. Rev.* 81 (1972). Even earlier, James Madison warned that insurrection and faction would follow from the continuation of slavery. See Madison, *Notes*, supra note 60, at 224–225; Madison, *The Federalist*, No. 43 (1788).

[63] The seed for the second notion comes from Michael Foley, *The Silence of Constitutions: An Essay in Constitutional Interpretation* (1989), at xi–xiii. Foley's notion of silence or "abeyance" suggests a revision of Lynd's thesis that the Constitution was explicitly a pact between Northern capital and Southern plantation agriculture, for under Foley's scheme the Constitution was less a "truce[ ] between two . . . defined positions" than "a set of implicit agreements to . . . keep[ ] fundamental questions of political authority in a state of irresolution."

thing of both notions lay behind the constitutional silence on many questions pertaining to slavery.

But whatever the mode by which slavery was authorized, the presence of slavery in the Constitution and the constitutional order amounted to a failure from the standpoint of certain principles of constitutionalism. I suggested above that, from the standpoint of constitutionalism, constitutional success depends partly on adherence to Hamilton's principle of reflection and choice. I claimed that reflection and choice imply that the success of a constitutional regime depends on its ability to act on the minds of potential citizens or subjects in such a way as to generate some form of attachment through the exercise of their free will.[64]

In a modern state it would probably be too much to expect that free choice always be concretely or literally present. Sometimes it is present only mythically, and often people recognize it to be quite limited in scope. Usually, however, choice is present by approximation through representation. The representation of choice might appear in one or both of two temporal locations. One is at the creation of the order. To the extent that the founding frames subsequent expressions of will, the expression or representation of will at the founding is genuinely constitutive. The other location arises after the creation of the order. It occurs through participation or through other modes of representation in the life of the polity.

For example, children were not literally "present" in the institutions that participated in the constitutional founding of the United States; however, it might be plausible to think of them as "virtually" represented in at least two ways. First, since all founders of the new polity were children once, the perspectives of (male) children—though perhaps not their voices and probably not their choices—were virtually represented, though very loosely, in the experiences of those men who originally constituted the order.[65] Second, those children who reached adulthood could literally be represented in "normal" (post-ratification) political institutions on reaching the age of "majority."

The same could not be said of slaves.[66] Slaves were prohibited from asserting any meaningful political choice, not only at the time of the founding but until slavery was abolished in 1865. As long as one was a

[64] William F. Harris II suggests connections between constitutional text and mind in three domains. First, a constitution is a *projection* of human mind. Second, a constitution must be *intelligible* to the human mind. Third, it must be capable of being *imprinted* onto or *enacted* by the mind. See Harris, supra note 13, at 41–43, 84–113.

[65] This account of virtual representation draws on John Hart Ely's *Democracy and Distrust*, supra note 30, at 81–87, 160.

[66] Nor, for that matter, could it be said of women, to the extent that women's experiences, perspectives, and choices were not congruent with men's.

slave, one was constitutionally choiceless and voiceless. And inasmuch as the choices that might have been attributable to slaves were not present in the experiences of those whose choices were represented in the polity, even a virtual representation for slaves was not possible. Because of that disability, slaves had no way to attach themselves structurally to the Constitution as constitutional subjects. In no way could slaves construct a political identity by reference to the Constitution. Consequently they had little incentive even to speak of themselves in constitutional terms.

In fact this disincentive extended beyond slaves to free blacks as well. In the seventy years following the constitutional founding, black participation in the formal constitution of the Republic was so rare as to render blacks virtually invisible, as most public forms of participation were foreclosed to most blacks, slave or free, North and South.[67]

For these reasons alone, it should not be surprising that black voices were largely absent from the domain of constitutional discourse in the antebellum period. But two additional considerations reinforced the structural silencing of black voices. First, notwithstanding its protodemocratic institutions and the populist rhetoric surrounding its ratification, the Constitution of the United States was clearly a document of strongly elitist origins. In fact it would not be an exaggeration to argue that it was the very political *property* of elites in the country at the time of the founding (and in many respects afterward).[68] Staughton Lynd has argued persuasively that the Constitution was basically a pact between the two dominant economic (and social) forces of the age, Northern capital (at the time heavily commercial, but eventually also industrial) and Southern agriculture (eventually plantation agriculture).[69] Their compromise found sanction in the Constitution's (1) fortification of dominant economic forms through the commitment of a strengthened national government to protect them, (2) highly restrictive notions

[67] See Donald Robinson, *Slavery in the Structure of American Politics: 1765–1820* (1979), at 7. This is not, of course, to argue that blacks did not participate in the formation or constitutional history of the country. It is simply to recognize that they were rarely included in debates over the construction and maintenance of the fundamental structure of the political system. The most palpable public forms of "participation" among slaves were slave revolts, which were profoundly political (but arguably extraconstitutional) devices for challenging the order.

[68] See, for example, Jennifer Nedelsky's illuminating discussion in "American Constitutionalism and the Paradox of Private Property," in *Constitutionalism and Democracy* (Elster and Slagstad, eds., 1988), at 241, 244 et seq.

[69] Lynd, supra note 10, at 11, 16–17. That the Constitution might have served such a function does not, of course, exhaust its significance, even in 1789. But the fact that many of the founding elites also found their way to governmental positions meant that they also controlled constitutional interpretation to a large degree, which in turn helped fortify both their positions as elites and the elitist character of the Constitution.

of citizenship, personhood, and equality, and (3) significant constraints on the forces of popular democracy.

The second consideration, growing out of the first, is that most of those people who owned the Constitution simply did not care about how blacks—whether enslaved or "free"—perceived their connection to the order. But more was involved than simply the elites' unwillingness to listen. They also took active steps to deny to slaves and free blacks the means for acquiring an intelligible constitutional voice. Among those steps were the imposition on slaves of an exceptionally restrictive regime and the widespread denial of substantial educational opportunities to free blacks. Both steps produced a rate of illiteracy that was not only staggering in size but colossal in consequence.[70]

The Constitution's failure to constitute slaves and the polity's unwillingness fully to constitute blacks as constitutional subjects doubtlessly engendered a psychology of alienation (and worse) among those not constituted. Such alienation is a predictable consequence of the presence of a constitution to which the mind is disinclined to attach or from which certain minds are prohibited from attaching. But whatever its roots, the psychology of alienation reinforced the reluctance of blacks either to legitimate the Constitution by attempting to speak through its categories and institutions or to pronounce their political identities by reference to that constitution.[71] Thus, even when the constitutional history herein talks directly about slavery, it does so largely through the voices of others.[72] Those voices, however, were not univocal.

[70] Reliable data on the prevalence of illiteracy among slaves and free blacks are difficult to come by. Nevertheless it seems fair to infer from what we know of the regimes imposed on the two groups that the rate of illiteracy was very high. See, e.g., Sterling Stuckey, *Slave Culture: Nationalist Theory and the Foundations of Black America* (1987), at 53, 137, on legal prohibitions against teaching slaves to read. See also Genovese, supra note 25, at 41, 186; Kenneth M. Stampp, *The Peculiar Institution: Slavery in the Ante-Bellum South* (1956), at 208. Although legal prohibitions could not prevent literacy entirely, they could restrict it substantially. For one example of judicial enforcement of prohibitions, see "Trial of Mrs. Douglass," in *Documents of American History*, vol. 1 (Commager and Cantor, eds., 1988), at 327. Foner estimates that 90 percent of all adult blacks living in the antebellum South were illiterate. Eric Foner, *Reconstruction: America's Unfinished Revolution, 1863–1877* (1988), at 96.

[71] Of course many of the expressions of black voices were not likely to have survived because they occurred in narrative forms not likely to have been recorded, because of the neglect of the preservers of the dominant constitutional culture(s), or for other reasons. Still, where records exist, it is not surprising to see how infrequently slaves spoke of themselves in relation to the Constitution. See George P. Rawick, ed., *The American Slave: A Composite Autobiography*, vols. 1–19 (1941, 1972), and Supplement, series 1, vols. 1–12 (1977).

[72] But see Norton, supra note 39, especially at 1–16.

CHAPTER TWO

Foundings, Myths, and Constitutional Division

I

Far from univocal, constitutional voices in the country were fundamentally divided. That fact suggests another failure of the new Constitution: its inability to generate a definitive solution to certain constitutive problems. Alternatively, however, the Constitution did *succeed* in producing *multiple* solutions, though some were irretrievably incompatible with one another and thus produced problems of their own.

That the Constitution was capable of accommodating equal and opposing solutions to problems of the polity would come as no surprise to many. Certainly it would not have surprised Robert Cover, whose influential "*Nomos* and Narrative" describes with perceptive subtlety the capacity of human beings to generate a multiplicity of accounts of the "normative world" they inhabit.[1] The construction of that normative world—that *nomos*—employs several basic elements: rules, certainly, but also institutions, experience, and the rituals and practices that join them. Alongside those elements, indeed sometimes constitutive of them, is narrative, which takes two principal forms. The first, interpretive narrative, gives people not only the means to interpret and hence to make sense of their world but also the knowledge of "how to *live* in it." The second and more basic form, constitutive narrative, is often mythic in character, though it need not be strictly so. Constitutive narrative establishes, orders, and justifies boundaries for the world. Narrative, then, both *interprets* the world and *constitutes* it. It establishes paradigms within which certain forms of action are not simply meaningful but possible.[2]

Cover describes as "jurisgenerative" the manner in which narrative participates in creating a world and making it inhabitable. Put another way, narrative makes multiplicities of meaning possible. In fact, the generation of multiplicities of meaning—which recalls to mind Whitman's "multitudes"—may well be unavoidable. First, as was suggested in chapter 1, the very act of interpretation calls into life a being, much of

[1] Robert Cover, "Foreword: *Nomos* and Narrative," 97 *Harv. L. Rev.* 4 (1983).

[2] Id., at 4–9.

whose form and content could not have been predicted.[3] The unpredictability that arises from interpretation is a condition that permits—even if it does not guarantee—the emergence of alternative *nomoi*. Second, the structure of the American state, the operation of governmental institutions, and the potentially competing motivations among institutional actors at almost all levels of government virtually ensure a diversity of *nomoi* among institutions. Third, interpretive diversity in the constitutional polity extends beyond institutions of government into political society. As noted in chapter 1, the capacity of a constitution to constitute a *polity*, as opposed to establishing mere government, depends on the success of the constitution in acting on the minds of those who would be citizens. Hence, even if an authoritative interpretive center exists among institutions of government, the interpretive authority and autonomy of the *members*—the citizens and residents—of the polity can pull powerfully and sometimes contradictorily on institutional actors. Those members may even have the power to transform the field on which institutional interpretation occurs, though one would imagine that such transformations are exceedingly rare.

There is, however, a "jurispathic" quality to the creation of constitutive meanings. *Jurispathololog*y, in Cover's words, is a "process that destroys legal meaning in the interest of social control." Its most vivid demonstrations are often actions of state but, as Cover notes, it also has a social basis.[4] In fact, almost every jurisgenerative act will, in some sense, also be jurispathic, for to imagine a world is to render others invisible or impossible. If there is a binding power in myth and meaning, there is a blinding power as well. To *see* the world is simultaneously to uncover or reveal and to disguise or conceal.

Again, this dynamic of the creation and suppression of meanings would not surprise most people. But an element of constitutional theory sits in awkward tension with it. That element is "coherence," which, as I suggested in chapter 1, is fundamental to the idea of constitutionalism. If it is fundamental, its form is nonetheless a bone of contention.

In the United States the most familiar version of coherence with respect to law and the Constitution is sometimes called "formalism." According to one version of formalism, law consists of rules and principles that have two distinctive characteristics. First, they exist even if they are not positively articulated in human law or recognized by human institutions; that is, they exist independent from what human beings might say, do, or want. In this sense they are metaphysical. Second, they are

[3] See the similar claim and language by Justice Holmes in *Missouri v. Holland*, 252 U.S. 416 (1920), at 433.

[4] Cover, supra note 1, at 11–19, 40–44.

discoverable. The principal tool for discovery is human reason, which can function as an instrument of discovery because the very structure and relationship of rules and principles are rational. They form a "seamless web," a finely knit, coherent, logical whole. And they are true.

Oliver Wendell Holmes derided formalism, both because of its metaphysical character and because it expected too much of human rationality. Law, he said, is not "a brooding omnipresence in the sky."[5] Nevertheless Holmes himself could wax mystically that, in reflecting on law, one could "connect [one's] subject with the universe and catch an echo of the infinite, . . . a hint of the universal law."[6] In Holmes one might attribute this latter sentiment to a romanticism that, for psychological or intellectual reasons, may have been an irresistible counterpoise to his otherwise acidic cynicism. Or perhaps his historical location—that he lived too early to witness Legal Realism's purification of law—made it impossible for him to discern clearly the far-reaching implications of his critique of formalism.

Whatever the case may have been for Holmes, constitutional theorists today, far from shaking the vestiges of formalism, have heartily embraced it. Sotirios A. Barber claims, for example, "that the Constitution has a meaning independent of what anyone in particular might want it to mean" and that its meaning is grounded in a metaphysical moral reality.[7] And although Ronald Dworkin distances himself from the formalism that he, like Roscoe Pound decades earlier, calls "mechanical jurisprudence,"[8] Dworkin's version of coherence incorporates the unitary rationality of formalism and sometimes seems to draw deeply from metaphysical sources. The latter claim is potentially controversial, not least because Dworkin himself on occasion explicitly denies that his theory is metaphysical. But if there are many Nixons,[9] as Dworkin says, perhaps, in a different sense, there is more than one Dworkin. For notwithstanding his occasional self-description, elements of his theory do suggest the metaphysical props of formalism. For example, at times his theory of rights ultimately rests not on the Constitution, not even on notions embedded in the constitutional order, but on transcendental "political morality."[10] Note his claim that individual rights are moral

[5] *Southern Pacific Railway v. Jensen*, 244 U.S. 205, 222 (1917).

[6] Oliver Wendell Holmes, "The Path of the Law," 10 *Harv. L. Rev.* 457 (1897), at 478.

[7] Sotirios A. Barber, *On What the Constitution Means* (1984), at 13; and Barber, *The Constitution of Judicial Power* (1993), at 46–47, citing Michael Moore, "A Natural Law Theory of Interpretation," 58 *So. Cal. L. Rev.* 286 (1985).

[8] Ronald Dworkin, *Taking Rights Seriously* (1977, 1978), at 15–16.

[9] Id., at 131–132.

[10] See, for example, id., at 131–149.

rights, justified in a political theory of justice that is both temporally prior and ontologically superior to any particular political arrangement, agreement, or constitution.[11] On a strong reading of this view, constitutional theory is a subset of moral theory, which consists of principles that are true independent from the beliefs or practices of any particular person, society, or time.

Whatever the difficulty in describing Dworkin as metaphysician, however, clearly his theory embraces formalism's unitary reason. He contends that even the most difficult and divisive of legal and constitutional problems has a singular "right answer."[12] That a right answer does exist for every such problem is linked to the rationality of the moral foundation of law and Constitution. "[O]ur law," he says, is a "seamless web."[13] Dworkin's view of coherence is unabashedly heroic; indeed, he calls it "Herculean."[14]

I wish to challenge certain aspects of Dworkin's formalism without abandoning the idea of coherence itself. Specifically I wish to suggest that the American constitutional experience reveals the following lessons: First, at the level of mythic or constitutive narrative, from the very start of the constitutional order there were two prominent competing accounts of the Constitution—what it *meant* and what it *was*. Second, those accounts provided competing logical foundations for opposing claims concerning what the Constitution required with respect to slavery; those foundational accounts did not, however, *determine* an answer to questions related to slavery. In fact, within each account opposing claims with respect to slavery could be generated. Consequently, there was more than one constitutionally defensible "answer" to basic questions concerning slavery. Third, no rational way existed to adjudicate the correctness of one or another claim. The selection of any particular answer or approach to a given question was a function not simply of constitutional logic but of cultural choice. There was more than one rationality in the constitutional world.

II

The most basic disjunction in the American constitutional world revealed itself at the very founding of the order. It appeared in the debates between Federalists and Antifederalists over the ratification of the Con-

[11] Id., at 150–183.

[12] Id., at 81, 104, 291, 331 et seq.

[13] Ronald Dworkin, "No Right Answer?" in *Law, Morality, and Society* (Hacker and Raz, eds., 1977), at 58, 84.

[14] Dworkin, *Taking Rights Seriously*, supra note 8, at 81 et seq.

stitution. As proponents of ratification, the Federalists argued that the Articles of Confederation were incapable of meeting the needs of the new country. The Articles were inadequate, the account went, because the confederated form of politics denied the polity the means to invigorate commerce, inhibited the defense of the eastern third of the continent, stifled and embarrassed the country in its dealings with other nations, and otherwise endangered the stability and growth of the Union.[15]

The remedy for these deficiencies was a *national* commercial republic, properly crafted and exquisitely balanced. This remedy presupposed several things. First, the basic economic form was to be commercial capitalist; this was not, however, laissez-faire capitalism. Instead, and second, it required an energetic national political authority with the means not only to protect "private" property but also to underwrite the conditions for material prosperity. Third, to achieve this level of energy, the Federalists promoted a national government capable of exercising authority directly over the citizenry without suffering debilitating constraints from the states.

But if the federalist national government's authority over citizens was to be direct, the people's participation in making their laws was to be distinctly indirect. In important respects, representation was to be detached from the people. The reasons for this were complex but arose largely from a distrust of populism. To the Federalists, recent events in the states demonstrated that an exercised populace threatened the stability of the order, indeed threatened the public good itself.[16] The challenge was to find some way to constrain the effects of those passions that tended to breed instability and bad laws. Concerning that challenge, the Federalists displayed a decided ambivalence about the ability of text to constrain politics. Mere parchment barriers were not sufficient. Parchment could prescribe institutions and supply a rough set of functional parameters for their operation, but only institutional relations, properly conceived and constructed, could supply an enduring check on the excessive tendencies of people and government.

One could not guarantee the face of the future, however. At best, the Constitution could direct the institutional means by which future generations, through experimentation and innovation, could meet new challenges and hence make their own mark on the world. One prominent federalist metaphor for institutions of national government was that of the machine. According to that metaphor, the basic aim of the Constitu-

[15] On the federalist position generally, see Hamilton et al., *The Federalist* (1787–1788), especially nos. 10, 14, 15, 37, 39, 47–51, and 84.

[16] See Gordon S. Wood, *The Creation of the American Republic, 1776–1787* (1969), especially at 344–389; James Madison, "Letter to Thomas Jefferson" (October 24, 1787), in *Letters and Other Writings of James Madison*, vol. 1 (1865), at 343–358.

tion was to make "a machine that would go of itself."[17] Construct institutions with sufficient care, give them enough power to permit them their play, minimize or neutralize those passions that might cause friction and breakdown, and the future of the polity would be more secure than it would be without the new constitutional technology.

But who could authorize the creation of such a machine? And what manner of act was it to make a constitution? Federalists' answers to these questions implied that stepping into their constitutional world was indeed fateful. James Madison is an instructive source here, as he was present at the Convention in Philadelphia, was keenly aware of the theoretical and practical stakes, and spoke out of both sides of his mouth on these questions.

His notes of the Convention indicated that the ratification of the Constitution was an act of special significance requiring extraordinary authorization: "[T]he Legislatures [of the states] were incompetent to the proposed changes. These changes would make essential inroads on the State Constitutions, and it would be a novel & dangerous doctrine that a Legislature could change the constitution under which it held its existence. . . . [Consequently], ratification must of necessity be obtained from the people."[18] On this account, popular ratification was presupposed by the particular aims of *this Constitution*; however, the character of *any constitution* may have made special authorization necessary. A constitution on the one hand, Madison said, is different from a league or treaty on the other. Both are morally obligatory. But "[i]n point of *political operation*, there are two important distinctions in favor of [a constitution]." First, a law violating a constitution is "null & void," though a law violating a treaty might not be. Second, "a breach of any one article [of a treaty] by any of the parties, frees the other parties from their engagements. In the case of a union of people under one Constitution, the nature of the pact has always been understood to preclude such an interpretation."[19]

Again, on Madison's view, a constitution could claim this special status since it could trace its authority directly to "the people." But who were the people? According to the federalist account of the Constitution, they were a *national* people, "the People of the United States." In at least one respect this presented an historical difficulty, for the nation did not exist when the Constitution appeared on the scene, certainly not in any plausible institutional form. Federalists might finesse this diffi-

[17] See Michael Kammen, *A Machine That Would Go of Itself: The Constitution in American Culture* (1986).

[18] James Madison, *Notes of Debates in the Federal Convention of 1787* (Koch, ed., 1987), at 352.

[19] Id., at 353.

culty with one of two moves. First, they might claim that if the nation itself did not exist, the idea or possibility of nationhood did, as it had been given a certain ethical reality through Jefferson's Declaration of Independence and the shedding of blood, sweat, and tears in the Revolution. The Constitution simply exploited those common psychic bonds to establish a national institutional reality. Second, Federalists might claim that even if "the people" were not a national people when the Constitution was drafted, they were *created* as a national people through the very process of ratification—and they would be drawn ever more closely together through commercial and institutional practices that the Constitution would soon set in motion. Thus the Constitution would create the very people on whom it would rely for its authority.

On either account, the people attained a kind of mythic stature. In the first, they did so by virtue of their common association with an event of mythic, creative proportion. In the second, they did so because at ratification they were present, if at all, only as a constitutive fiction. Either way, as Cover's theory suggests, their mythic presence had distinct implications for the character of the Constitution, although Federalists themselves may have been but dimly aware of these implications at the time of the founding. The Constitution was emblematic of a special kind of political act. It was a "covenant."

Historically the notion of covenant carries deeply religious baggage. Its Sinaitic origins are unmistakable, its reformation in Christian hands no less so. Consequently some commentators suggest even today that a higher authority, specifically God, is essential to the establishment of covenantal relations.[20] If the American covenant traces its origins to the Revolution, this requirement presents fewer problems than if it arises strictly from the Constitution. After all, the Declaration of Independence invoked both "Nature's God" as authorizing the American people's new station "among the Powers of the Earth" and the "Creator" as endowing "inalienable Rights." But if the people were born with the Constitution, or if they alone authorized the Constitution without needing God's supervision or blessing, or if the Constitution significantly departed from substantial aims or presuppositions of the Revolution, then the religious connection was more difficult to sustain. For the ability to describe the Constitution as covenantal hangs on whether one could supply a secular conception of covenant. Rozann Rothman claims that the Federalists did rely on just such a conception, though not con-

[20] See, e.g., Daniel J. Elazar, "The Biblical Theory of Covenant: Biblical Origins and Modern Developments," in *Covenant, Polity, and Constitutionalism* (Elazar and Kincaid, eds., 1980), at 3, 11. See also Vincent Ostrom, "Hobbes, Covenant, and Constitution," in id., at 83.

sciously and perhaps in tension with certain noncovenantal, contractarian arrangements in the Constitution.[21]

But what distinguishes covenant, stripped of its religious content, from a contract or compact (akin, in Madison's terms, to a mere treaty)? Even in its secular form, covenant is no ordinary agreement. It is rather an agreement among parties that essentially transforms the status of the parties and their relations with one another. In other words, it aims at defining or creating "a people," such that these people are tied together, not as an aggregation of individuals but as a kind of community. They are obliged to one another, not by consent alone and certainly not by coercion but by mutual concern, respect, and fellow feeling and by some sort of common ethical commitment. In short, they are obliged to one another by their commitment to one another.

Thomas Hobbes's distinction between contract and covenant is instructive. "The mutuall transferring of Right," he said, is a contract. A covenant, on the other hand, is an agreement in which full performance is not achieved until sometime in the future.[22] This distinction implies two characteristics. First, the covenantal agreement is marked by a kind of trust or "faith" among the parties that is not present to the same degree in a contract. Second, a covenant's principal orientation is toward the future. It is of indefinite duration. In its most stringent iteration, it is presumed to be perpetual, or, if not perpetual, it cannot be terminated except by common consent. If covenantal, then, the Constitution was to be binding in an especially powerful way, with respect to both the manner in which it constituted and the longevity of the institutional relations it established. It left people differently situated toward one another than they had been before the founding.

In connecting covenant with federalist nationalism, I do not mean to imply that the idea of covenant was determined by federalist principles (or vice versa). Nor do I claim that Federalists consistently or consciously embraced the covenantal view. I do suggest, however, that a congeniality existed between the covenantal view of the Constitution and the federalist position concerning the Constitution's character and authority that made plausible the linkage of the two. Notwithstanding this congeniality, though, the idea of national covenant seems partially to contradict a position that Madison himself later adopted as part of his justification for ratifying the Constitution. In *The Federalist*, No. 39, he claimed that the authority of the Constitution derived from "the

[21] Rozann Rothman, "The Impact of Covenant and Contract Theories on Conceptions of the U.S. Constitution," in *Covenant, Polity, and Constitutionalism*, supra note 20, at 149 et seq.

[22] Thomas Hobbes, *Leviathan* (1651) (Macpherson, ed., 1968), at 192–193.

people, not as individuals composing one entire nation; but as composing the distinct and independent States to which they respectively belong." The Constitution was binding because of "the assent and ratification of the several States."

What is one to make of this contradiction? Madison's later position might well have been simply a tactical revision—made possible in part by the fact that he was writing under a pseudonym—that aimed at assuaging antifederalist anxieties over the nationalist dimensions of the proposed Constitution. The character of the contest for ratification in New York and the function of *The Federalist Papers* themselves lend credence to such a view.[23] But regardless of which view reflected Madison's genuine position, the national covenantal account was the one that made sense of certain antifederalist fears about the character of the proposed order and about the fatefulness of a decision to ratify the proposed Constitution. Moreover, it was the one that certain prominent nineteenth-century descendants of the federalist position would eventually adopt as their own.

As opponents of ratification, the Antifederalists were quite diverse, both geographically and in terms of material interest. The unsystematic character of their attacks on the proposed Constitution reflected this diversity. If unsystematic, however, the writings of the Antifederalists displayed a kind of nomic kinship that not only tied them to one another but also distinguished them from the Federalists. The Antifederalists opposed the Constitution precisely because they feared the federalist constitutional world. They feared that world because federalist commitments—to both values and interests—were so different from their own. Those fears mattered because the Antifederalists took seriously the authority of the federalist view of the Constitution; that is, the Antifederalists argued as though the nomic world of the Federalists *accurately described* the Constitution in many important respects. And where the stated aims of the Federalists did not comport with the antifederalist reading of the Constitution, that reading was predictably more dire than federalist commitments would openly acknowledge.

Of primary note is that with respect to the Articles of Confederation, the Antifederalists viewed as virtues many of what the Federalists described as defects. Thus the federalist agenda was, from the antifederalist perspective, a solution in search of a problem. Was political power

[23] See John P. Roche, "The Founding Fathers: A Reform Caucus in Action," 55 *Am. Pol. Sci. Rev.* 799 (1961). Roche argues that *The Federalist* was simply a political tract designed more to confine opposition by quieting fears than to explicate the proposed constitution and its projected constitutional order.

decentralized under the Articles of Confederation? That was as it should be. As self-conscious inheritors of the American revolutionary tradition, the Antifederalists distrusted power exercised from the center. Political power, they said, could safely reside only at the local or the state level, where it was closest to the people; the Federalists' willingness to embrace centralized power was a betrayal of the basic aims and principles of the Revolution.[24]

Both federalist and antifederalist political thought was "republican" in character; antifederalist localism, however, suggested a shading of thought, on matters both economic and political, that distinguished the two political theories. If the basic economic form for the Federalists was commercial capitalist, the antifederalist economic world was largely an agrarian republic of small farmers. If federalist theory required a national people, antifederalist theory implied that people could act as "a people" only in discrete communities. Federalists' distrust of popular passion led them to try to filter, and thus to inhibit, popular political activity and to promote a political system that did not depend on the robust presence of virtue. Antifederalists, on the other hand, embraced democracy, whose very function relied on direct connection with the people and whose success depended on the basic virtue of the common man. The federalist approach to change exalted experimentation and innovation, whereas the Antifederalists valued tradition and stability. If the prevailing federalist metaphor was mechanical, the Antifederalists' was organic.

The Antifederalists also had faith in the power of parchment to constrain politics, a sentiment that might seem curious or naive from our present perspective. Their faith, combined with their worries about the federalist aspiration for national power, led them to insist that the Constitution's failure to include a bill of rights was a fundamental, fatal defect. Some such guarantee was essential, they said, as a shield against the arbitrary actions of political institutions so remote from citizens' daily lives.

The federalist response to this criticism was uncharacteristically weak, perhaps because a more powerful response would have conceded more to antifederalist fears than seemed prudent of one who wanted the Constitution ratified.[25] Hamilton replied that the constitutions of several states also lacked a bill of rights. This, of course, did little to meet the

[24] On these and other characteristics of antifederalist thought, see Cecelia M. Kenyon, *The Antifederalists* (1985), including her useful introductory essay on "The Political Thought of the Antifederalists," in id., at xxi et seq.

[25] See Hamilton, *The Federalist*, No. 84 (1788).

antifederalist claim that power exercised closer to home was inherently more trustworthy and less needful of explicit limitation than power exercised more remotely.

Hamilton also argued that a bill of rights was inappropriate as it was inconsistent with the Constitution's basic character. Such provisions, he said, were historically "stipulations between kings and their subjects," an attempt to secure particular rights against a general presumption of royal prerogative. In contrast, the Constitution rested on quite other theoretical assumptions and performed a different political function. The Constitution's authority, said Hamilton, derived from "We the People"; the people did not need to reserve particular rights because under the Constitution they "surrender nothing, and . . . retain every thing." The Constitution's function, then, was simply to describe and to "regulate the general political interests of the nation." Its function, that is, was to describe the purposes for which governmental institutions might act and hence to establish the general contours of governmental power. To insert a bill of rights, he might have suggested, would transform the Constitution into something it was not: a mere contract that describes in legal detail the rights of people against a government they already controlled.

The remoteness and power of the proposed national government, however, may have painfully reminded Antifederalists of the British Crown. Notwithstanding the purported source of the Constitution's authority, the dangers inherent in the creation of such power necessitated particular, contractlike limitations against abuse. Thus the same general delegations of power that Hamilton extolled as consistent with the Constitution's essential character, the Antifederalists viewed with alarm as inconsistent with the very survival of people's rights.

Hamilton anticipated this objection with a third claim that grew out of his argument that a bill of rights ran contrary to the Constitution's very nature. Including such a bill in the Constitution, he said, would actually endanger rights, as it might supply unscrupulous men a pretext for reading the Constitution as delegating power that it does not delegate. For example, why include an explicit liberty of the press when the Constitution's description of powers contains no authority to regulate the press? Such a provision might tempt certain men to read the right in a quibbling, narrow, legalistic fashion, and in so doing to read it out of existence. The security of rights, he said, depends on "the general spirit of the people and of the government."

Of course the specter of unscrupulous, ambitious men and the suggestion that rights depended on the spirit of the government did little to assuage the antifederalist fear of governmental tyranny. In fact they reinforced Antifederalists' impulse to insist on textual authority for a concrete set of rights which they could assert against a dispirited or, worse, corrupt government.

Finally, Hamilton insisted that the Constitution already was "in every rational sense, and to every useful purpose, A BILL OF RIGHTS." What, he asked, does a bill of rights do? It "declare[s] and specif[ies] the political privileges of the citizens in the structure and administration of government," and it "define[s] certain immunities and modes of proceeding, which are relative to personal and private concerns." To these concerns the Constitution already explicitly spoke.

At this point Hamilton's argument had turned on itself. For if he could assert that the Constitution already expressly guaranteed certain rights of citizenship and personhood, and if he could claim that it did so without violating its character as a constitution or threatening the security of rights themselves, then the Antifederalists could plausibly argue that the specification of *additional* rights similarly would neither violate the Constitution's character as a constitution nor impair the security of rights. Thus the Antifederalists insisted on a bill of rights. The Federalists relented. The Constitution was ratified.

But a curious thing happened after ratification: The Antifederalists began to claim the Constitution as their own. In so doing they did not adopt a federalist theory of the Constitution. Instead, just as the antifederalist theory of republicanism informed the Antifederalists' critique of the Constitution before ratification, that same theory began to inform their understanding of the Constitution after ratification. Simply put, they began to read the Constitution through the lens of antifederalist political theory, in effect to make a new constitution through interpretation.

The text was sufficiently ambiguous to permit such an understanding. The procedure described in Article VII, by which the Constitution was ratified, permitted Antifederalists to embrace Madison's second account of the Constitution's authority; that is, although the Constitution rested on the authority of "the people," they were not a *national* people but people of *states*. "We the People of the *United States*" became "We the People of the United *States*." The shift in emphasis was subtle but significant. The people of the states, now united, formed a union. They did so not through covenant but by contract. Hence ratification did not alter but rather reinforced the basic, existing political identities and allegiances of the people.

This account of the authority of the constitutional order was not "mythic" in quite the same way as the national covenantal account. But perhaps it did not require an explicit present myth. For one thing, the authority of the antifederalist Constitution did not reside in a fictitious people, for the people were already members of ongoing political communities: the individual states. Consequently the function of the antifederalist Constitution was not deeply transformative. The Constitution did not aim at "making" a people in any thick sense of the word but instead rode aback a people whose political arrangements were substantially established. The Constitution certainly *revised* those arrangements. It was, to that extent, a new thing under the sun that therefore required at least an *account* of how it came to be. But its *myth* lay further back, in the very idea of "state" and of the "sovereignty" residing therein.

Besides Article VII and the Preamble, several other textual provisions bolstered the contractarian view of the Constitution. For example, one might have pointed to the crucial role of states in amending the Constitution under Article V. Senators were selected by established institutions of the states. The Electoral College gave special weight to majoritarian preferences *within* states, permitting each state to speak with a single voice in the election of the president and vice president. The very presence of the Bill of Rights, as Hamilton argued, invigorated the contractarian view of the Constitution, if it did not render the Constitution fundamentally incoherent. But one provision lent particular force to state-centered contractarianism: The Tenth Amendment noted that all "powers not delegated" to the national government were "reserved to the States respectively, or to the people." The Amendment's reservation was not without ambiguity, but later it did supply textual ammunition to an antifederalist reading of the Constitution.[26]

III

In the beginning neither the federalist nor the antifederalist account had much to say about slavery; however, the accounts would soon supply the ground on which battles over slavery would be waged. Stated most simply, the constitutional problem was the relation between the constituent "parts" (the states) and the "whole" (the national government) of the political world the Constitution ostensibly created. That the debate, so framed, eventually became a vehicle for addressing matters in which slavery was intimately implicated illustrates the malleability of constitutional discourse and the extent to which constitutional categories permit one to talk about things without naming, much less defining, them.

The dispute between South Carolina and the United States over Con-

[26] Even John Marshall would later implicitly endorse the antifederalist view, at least with respect to the scope of rights contained in the Bill of Rights. Those rights, he said, bound the national government, but did not constrain the states. *Barron v. Mayor and City Council of Baltimore*, 32 U.S. (7 Pet.) 243 (1833).

gress's tariffs of 1828 and 1832 aptly illustrated the persistence and seriousness of the divide between Federalists and Antifederalists.[27] Those tariffs protected certain raw materials that were of benefit to economic interests in the North and the West at the expense, said radicals in South Carolina, of the interests of Southern agriculture.[28] Relying on the constitutional theories of John C. Calhoun, South Carolina's newly elected legislature called a state convention to address the tariffs. Speaking for "the people of the State of South Carolina in Convention assembled," the convention adopted an "ordinance of nullification" declaring the tariffs "null, void, and no law, nor binding upon this State, its officers or citizens."[29]

Calhoun's justification for nullification—sometimes called interposition[30]—unapologetically relied on an antifederalist theory of the Constitution's authority. Because the Constitution had been ratified by the people of the states, those same people reserved the right to nullify, through state convention, any national law perceived to be inimical to their interests: "[I]t would [then] be the duty of the General Government to abandon the contested power, or to apply to the States themselves, the source of all political authority, for the power in one of the two modes prescribed in the Constitution [i.e., by amending the Constitution]." If the national government could obtain the consent of three-fourths of the states via the amending process, even the nullifying states would be bound to recognize its authority. Until then, the national government must refrain from enforcing the contested law anywhere in the nation.[31]

In his *Disquisition on Government* Calhoun later expanded on his justification in two ways—one constitutional, the other quasi-revolu-

[27] The controversy over the tariffs was not the only evidence of the division, nor should it be taken to suggest that the divide between Federalist and Antifederalist was identical to that between North and South, though the former division would ultimately and ambivalently be implicated in the latter.

[28] See Frederic Bancroft, *Calhoun and the South Carolina Nullification Movement* (1928), at 8–20, 117–118.

[29] Id., at 126–128, 120; South Carolina's Nullification of Tariffs of 1828 and 1832 (November 24, 1832), in *State Papers on Nullification* (1834; repr. 1970). The legislature, in calling the convention, and the convention, in adopting the ordinance, had relied heavily on Calhoun's "Exposition and Protest," drafted in 1828 in the wake of the first tariff. Calhoun, *The Works of John C. Calhoun*, vol. 6 (Cralle, ed., 1855), at 1. See also Calhoun's Letter to James Hamilton (August 28, 1832), in id., at 144, and his "Address on the Relation Which the States and General Government Bear to Each Other" (July 26, 1831), in id., at 59.

[30] Neither term should be confused with the more complex notion of "concurrent majorities," which Calhoun did not adopt until the late 1840s.

[31] Calhoun, *Works*, supra note 29, vol. 6, at 160–161, 172, 179–180. Bancroft, supra note 28, at 120–124.

tionary.[32] The constitutional justification aimed to articulate principles that a constitutional regime must presuppose if it is to avoid becoming one of unlimited powers, which spawns oppression, which in turn breeds "anarchy, the greatest of all evils." It relied on an Aristotelian hierarchy of social organization, beginning with the individual. In order for the individual to fulfill his nature, he must live in the society or community of other human beings. Similarly, society, to serve its function of permitting individuals to flourish, requires government. The problem is that government, if improperly constituted, will always deviate from its purpose and aggrandize the powers of its officers. This tendency is present even in a democracy, whose officers become beholden to a majoritarian faction (or some majoritarian combination of lesser factions) of the community. What can prevent a numerical majority from riding roughshod over the interests of the members of the minority party? Clearly suffrage alone cannot; neither can limited tenure for governmental officers or the separation of governmental powers, unless (in the latter case) each branch or department of government be granted a veto over the actions of the others; nor can the provision of standards in a written constitution unless some "organism" exists whose function and interest are to enforce the written limits and consequently to prevent oppression by the majority. That organism, of course, is the state.[33]

Calhoun's second justification implicitly recognized a Lockean right to withdraw from established government or at least from the decisions of such a government. It aimed at maintaining governmental legitimacy, however, by ensuring that government derive its authority from the consent of the governed, not only at the moment of the constitutional founding but also continually in its operation. Unlike Locke, Calhoun did not speak of a right of revolution in so many words. For one thing, he feared the prospect of anarchy that revolution might represent. For another, he argued that the right of a part of the community to nullify national legislation would effectively prevent the abuses that might undermine legitimacy and justify revolution.[34] Nullification, he said, "pre-

[32] Calhoun, *Disquisition on Government* (Cralle, ed., 1883). The *Disquisition* was originally published in 1851.

[33] Id., at 1, 8, 12–17, 22–24, 31, 34, 38. Calhoun's position on separation of powers looks similar to Jefferson's departmentalism. Jefferson, "Instruct[ions to] a Federal Prosecutor" (1807), in Murphy, Fleming, and Barber, *American Constitutional Interpretation*, 2d ed. (1995), at 306–308. Further, Jefferson's Kentucky Resolutions were part of the first attempt by a state to interpose itself against an act of the national government.

[34] In the *Disquisition*, Calhoun emphasized the constitutional grounding for his theory, but neither he nor others were reticent in 1832 to recognized its extraconstitutional ori-

vents all partial or local legislation [like the tariffs], and restricts its action to such measures as are designed for the protection and good of the whole. In doing this, it secures . . . the rights and liberty of the people, regarded individually; as each portion consists of those who, whatever may be the diversity of interests among themselves, have the same interest in reference to the action of the government."[35] But when all was said and done, the theoretical promise of Calhoun's theory was attenuated by its apparent powerlessness in the dispute over the tariffs. In the face of federal force, South Carolina accepted a compromise and backed down.[36]

The rhetoric of nullification cloaked the connection between the tariffs and slavery; however, as Wiltse points out, the doctrine of nullification was essentially Calhoun's "political defense of slavery": "Just as the industrial North and East required a government strong enough to levy and collect the import duties on which their prosperity was founded, so the South required a [central] government too weak to interfere with her system of labor."[37] And during the crisis itself, the Southern essayist and firebrand Robert Turnbull suggested that the squabble over tariffs demonstrated that economic interests, regional cultural identity, the Constitution, and slavery were intimately connected to one another. He argued that a fundamental conflict existed between the economic interests of the North and West on the one hand and the South on the other, that the conflict was inextricably tied to nationalism (i.e., the supremacy of national political authority), and that nationalism would ultimately lead to the abolition of slavery, which would mean the demise of Southern culture.[38]

In this way antifederalist constitutionalism, connected to slavery, became the vehicle through which many prominent Southerners pursued what they considered to be their interest. At the same time, to risk an alternative metaphor, it was a lens through which they perceived and understood their constitutional world. But its effectiveness depended

---

gins and revolutionary implications. George McDuffie, for example, argued that the right of nullification "flows from a higher source" than the Constitution. Bancroft, supra note 28, at 98.

[35] Calhoun, *Disquisition*, supra note 32, at 60.

[36] Congress facilitated the state's retreat by radically reducing the tariff's duties. Bancroft, supra note 28, at 134–138, 144, 156–157, 165–170; Andrew Jackson, "Proclamation by the President of the United States of America (December 10 1832), in *State Papers*, supra note 29, at 74. But see South Carolina's Ordinance of Nullification of the Force Act (March 18, 1833), in id., at 98.

[37] Charles M. Wiltse, *John C. Calhoun: Nullifier, 1829–1839* (1949), at 120.

[38] Bancroft, supra note 28, at 28–29, 47–48, 117–119.

partly on two expectations. The first was that slavery would continue to go without saying; the second, that there would be no substantial contrary view of the Constitution. The first would prove nondurable; the second, simply deluded.

IV

The contrary view, of course, was the federalist one. It did not die after ratification. One of the most able iterations of the federalist view came from John Marshall, most cogently in his opinion for the Supreme Court in *M'Culloch v. Maryland*.[39] Although he acknowledged at the outset that the case concerned the powers of "a sovereign state," he said that the Constitution had radically constrained the states. He rejected Madison's antifederalist claim that the Constitution's authority derived "not . . . from the people, but [from] the act of sovereign and independent states." According to Marshall, states might form a confederation or league, as was arguably the case under the Articles of Confederation, but they could not form a nation—"an effective government, possessing great and sovereign powers"—as was created under the Constitution. The present national government acquired its authority from the people, whose authority the Constitution itself acknowledged and who, acting in conventions, ratified the document. They ratified the Constitution not on behalf of the states but on their own behalf. No matter that the conventions were held within state boundaries, for where else could they have been held? "The government of the Union . . . is, emphatically and truly, a government of the people. In form and in substance it emanates from them. Its powers are granted by them, and are to be exercised directly on them, and for their benefit."[40]

The source of the Constitution's authority bore directly on its allocation of political authority. Because the national government lacked plenary powers, it could act only in those matters that the Constitution enumerated. "The government of the Union," however, was "supreme within its sphere of action." If the action of a state were to conflict with that of the national government acting pursuant to an enumerated power, the latter must prevail. The supremacy of the national government was sanctioned by the supremacy clause of Article VI and, more important, by the very nature of national government. The government of the Union, said Marshall, "is the government of all; its powers are

[39] 17 U.S. (4 Wheat.) 316 (1819). Marshall's nationalism presaged—perhaps inspired—Lincoln's almost four decades later. Albert J. Beveridge, *The Life of John Marshall*, vol. 4 (1919), at 293. Of course Marshall was not the only early proponent of nationalism.

[40] *M'Culloch v. Maryland*, supra note 39, at 400, 401, 403–405, 410.

delegated by all; it represents all, and acts for all. Though any one state may be willing to control its operations, no state is willing to allow others to control them. The nation, on those subjects on which it can act, must necessarily bind its component parts." And where the Constitution delegated to the nation the authority to act, it also implied the authority to act by any means the nation might deem "appropriate." The parts cannot control the whole.[41]

Despite *M'Culloch's* attention to the structure of political authority, Marshall's nationalism also had a distinctively economic cast. First, the case was essentially a dispute over the incorporation of a financial institution that had an important effect on the nation's economy.[42] Second, some of the Chief Justice's rhetoric—from his choice of constitutional categories for resolving the dispute (for example, that the case substantially implicated Congress's authority over commerce) to his interest in "the industry of the nation"[43]—pointed toward deeper economic concerns.

An even stronger indication of the extent to which matters of commerce were intimately bound up in Marshall's nationalism came five years later in *Gibbons v. Ogden*.[44] There Marshall argued that national authority over commerce was indispensable to the very life of the Constitution itself. The "[p]owerful and ingenious minds" who argued for an expansive conception of the sovereignty of states were essentially trying to "leave [the Constitution] a magnificent structure indeed, to look at, but totally unfit for use." Their theory was simply "not to be found in the constitution." Moreover, it was inconsistent with the Constitution, for it "would cripple the government and render it unequal to the objects for which it is declared to be instituted." On Marshall's account, if the Constitution did anything, it created a government with sufficient power to maintain a great commercial nation.[45]

Of course national supremacy over commerce did not necessarily imply national supremacy over slavery (although, as Berns notes, there were people who harbored such fears or hopes in 1787 and 1788).[46] But slavery lurked beneath the surface. For one thing, the timing of *M'Culloch* and *Gibbons* placed the cases in the midst of an intense national debate over slavery in the territories, a debate only temporarily muzzled

[41] Id., at 405, 409–420.

[42] See Bray Hammond, *Banks and Politics in America from the Revolution until the Civil War* (1957).

[43] *M'Culloch v. Maryland*, supra note 39, at 407.

[44] *Gibbons v. Ogden*, 22 U.S. (9 Wheat.) 1 (1824).

[45] Id., at 187–188, 190, 222.

[46] See Walter Berns, "The Constitution and the Migration of Slaves," 78 *Yale L. J.* 198 (1968). John Randolph, for one, believed that *M'Culloch*'s nationalism was in conflict with slavery's survival. Beveridge, supra note 39, at 308–309.

by the Missouri Compromise. For another, Marshall's nationalism was the constitutional embodiment of the same commercial ethos that would give rise to the tariffs of 1828 and 1832. In general, by the end of the 1820s, an array of issues—in favor of "slavery restriction, national banking, a protective tariff, and security of contract"—had coalesced under the umbrella of nationalism, while another array—favoring slavery, free trade, and state banking—had joined under localism.[47]

Further, Marshall himself in *Gibbons* had virtually invited people to draw an analogy between Congress's powers over commerce and slavery. He argued that at least one aspect of slavery—the international slave trade—was a part of commerce, power over which the Constitution withdrew from the states (except for the temporary ban in Article I, Section 9).[48] Granted, one might distinguish the authority to regulate international trade from the authority to regulate a domestic institution. But in Marshall's expansive reading of congressional power over even domestic commerce, a few Southerners as early as the 1820s were beginning to perceive a threat both to the market in slaves "among the several states" and to the very institution of slavery.[49] Marshall did not assuage these Southerners' fears when, in the early 1830s, he became a national vice president of the American Colonization Society.[50]

V

Whatever the implications of Marshall's nationalism and whatever its persuasive power within the polity, by the mid-1830s almost no one was prepared to argue that Congress had authority to regulate or abolish slavery in the states. One reason was that, despite tensions, Northern capital and Southern plantation were intimately tied to each other

[47] Beveridge, supra note 39, at 370.

[48] *Gibbons*, supra note 44, at 206–207, 216–217.

[49] Beveridge, supra note 39, at 420, 536. Robert Walsh had argued in 1819 that Article I, Section 9, embodied a compromise under which the South retained the temporary right to import and trade slaves; but he also claimed that the article delegated an immediate national power to restrict the expansion of slavery beyond the then present borders and an eventual national power to prohibit all trading in slaves, international and domestic. Berns, supra note 46, at 220–221. Walsh was not alone in his interpretation. Justice Johnson, sitting as Circuit Judge (and no Northerner), held unconstitutional a South Carolina statute regulating local aspects of the importation of slaves as inconsistent with Congress's "exclusive" power over commerce. *Elkison v. Deliesseline*, 8 Fed. Cas. 493 (D. S.C., 1823). One person went even further, arguing that after 1808 Congress possessed the power under the commerce clause to abolish slavery altogether. As of the early nineteenth century, however, Madison and almost every other prominent Southerner, disagreed on all points. Berns, supra note 46, at 201–202, 204.

[50] Beveridge, supra note 39, at 472–479.

under a constitution that partially embodied a compromise between the two.[51] Few citizens saw advantage in disturbing an arrangement that, whatever its vices, seemed to benefit both regions. Another reason, which is treated briefly below, had to do with the ethos of the country—including significant elements of antislavery thought—both on the constitutional status of slavery and blacks and on the nature of Union. Finally, as chapter 1 suggested, the constitutional text implied some protection for slavery. People might argue about the extent of that protection and about how content the framers were to agree to it, but certain provisions seemed, if euphemistically, to protect the institution.

Opponents of slavery, however, disagreed over the political strategy that followed from the position that slavery was constitutionally sanctioned. Early in the nineteenth century, antislavers tended to follow a strategy that was understandably unambitious. Let us call them "gradualists." Beneath their opposition to slavery lay a distinctly antifederalist understanding of the constitutional order. The gradualists' remedies tended to be legalistic (promoting judicial, instead of political, remedies), localized (relying heavily on state constitutions and statutes for legal theories), individualized (providing assistance to individual slaves instead of global assaults on the institution of slavery), and, predictably, gradualistic.[52] The strategy grew out of several considerations, all rooted in general sensibilities regarding slavery or in understandings of the distribution of national political authority.

First, to be opposed to slavery was not necessarily to be sympathetic to blacks and was certainly not to endorse human equality. National ethos, if in fact one existed on the question of slavery, was never deeply antagonistic to slavery, even up to the commencement of hostilities in 1861. Apart from declared abolitionists, most Northerners until at least the 1850s did not exhibit acute concern about slavery, and, in any event, very few were prepared at any time to dissolve the Union over the fate of a few million blacks. Especially before 1833, but afterward as well, many Americans who opposed slavery advocated sending freed blacks to colonies in Africa or the Caribbean.[53]

Second, the matter of emancipating slaves without breaking the federal treasury had to be resolved. This was a practical problem in that it implicitly acknowledged that slaveholders would never abandon their interests in slaves without some sort of fight or compensation. But it was also a *constitutional* problem to the extent that any political le-

[51] Staughton Lynd, *Class Conflict, Slavery, and the United States Constitution* (1967).

[52] William M. Wiecek, *The Sources of Antislavery Constitutionalism in America, 1760–1848* (1977), at 84–85.

[53] See Merton L. Dillon, *The Abolitionists: The Growth of a Dissenting Minority* (1974), at 19–20.

verage slaveholders might have was informed by an understanding of what the Fifth Amendment's general commitment to the protection of property amounted to and what its "just compensation" clause required. The fiscal commitment that immediate emancipation represented was, for most opponents of slavery in the early years of the century, too substantial to be viable. Thus some, like Jefferson and Marshall, supported schemes that would have emancipated slaves gradually.[54]

Third, and just as important, was a more general sense of what the Constitution permitted or required regarding slavery. There was a solid consensus that the regulation of slavery was exclusively the prerogative of each state within its boundaries and that the national government had no authority to regulate slavery in any state. Even into the 1850s this "federal consensus" persisted as the dominant theory of the constitutional status of slavery.[55] Textually grounded in one or more versions of the Tenth Amendment and perhaps the Ninth, the consensus served as a kind of antifederalist hedge against the logical tendency of Marshall's nationalism to swallow much of localism, at least where commerce was concerned.

The consensus effectively said this: It does not matter whether federalism or antifederalism accurately describes the character of constitutional authority; for, with respect to slavery, the polity will treat it as if it were purely local, not subject to regulation at the national level. In operation, it was a kind of implicit gentlemen's agreement that seemed to anticipate a restrictive version of what Calhoun would later call the doctrine of concurrent majorities: Where slavery was concerned, the nation cannot act because it cannot act in a manner consistent with the interests of all states (or even all regions). Hence, notwithstanding nationalism's putative threat to slavery, the federal consensus reduced the danger and therefore assuaged Southern insecurity. But it did not eliminate insecurity altogether.

One reason Southern insecurity persisted was that gradualism did not remain the sole strategy attractive to opponents of slavery. In 1833 a radical abolitionist association—the American Anti-Slavery Society—was founded on the principle that slavery was wrong and should be abolished everywhere immediately. The founding of the Society was the first significant public indication of cracks in the federal consensus.[56]

[54] Thomas Jefferson, "Letter to Jared Sparks" (February 4, 1824), in *Thomas Jefferson: Writings* (Peterson, ed., 1984), at 1484–1487; Beveridge, supra note 39, at 473–479.

[55] Wiecek, supra note 52, at 15–17, 276–277. Wiecek argues that the consensus was effectively dead by 1848, a victim of the Treaty of Guadaloupe Hidalgo. In fact the consensus seems to have survived the Treaty, which most directly implicated congressional authority over slavery not in the states but in the territories.

[56] See id., at 15–17, 85, 276–277.

Unlike the gradualists, the Garrisonian wing of the Society—including William Lloyd Garrison, Frederick Douglass, and Wendell Phillips—abjured political or legal action against slavery.

The justification for Garrisonian "non-resistance" was both theological and pragmatic, but it ultimately rested on a deeply nationalist understanding of the Constitution. This was a nationalism, however, that resisted Marshall's expansive invocation of the commercial republic. It certainly rejected the notion that Congress's power to regulate commerce conferred power to regulate slavery. At the same time, however, Garrisonian nationalism basically repudiated the idea of a federal consensus. The Constitution's commitment concerning slavery, said the Garrisonians, did not rely on mere informal consensus. The Constitution was, at its core, a proslavery covenant. It sustained slavery not as an antifederalist sop to the South but as a fundamental ethical commitment of the nation.

Ironically the most articulate proponent of such a reading of the Constitution was Frederick Douglass, a former slave who had purchased his freedom after escaping bondage in Maryland.[57] With William Lloyd Garrison, Douglass denounced the Constitution as "a covenant with death" and "a most foul and bloody conspiracy against the rights of three millions of enslaved and imbruted men."[58]

His denunciation of the Constitution was no cavalier dismissal, for it stemmed from his studied interpretation of the text.[59] In fact, in his early years, Douglass's interpretation was, by his own account, almost exclusively textual. He pointed, of course, to the three-fifths clause, the clause concerning the slave trade,[60] and the fugitive slave clause.[61] But he

[57] Frederick Douglass, *Narrative of the Life of Frederick Douglass, an American Slave* (1845), in *The Classic Slave Narratives* (Gates, ed., 1987), at 255–256, 319–320. The apparent incongruity of a former slave's interpreting the Constitution as a "proslavery compact" was not lost on Douglass. See his "Letter to Gerrit Smith, Esq." (January 21, 1851), in *The Life and Writings of Frederick Douglass*, vol. 2 (Foner, ed., 1950), at 149: "I am sick and tired of arguing on the slaveholders' side of this question, although they are doubtless right as far as the intentions of the framers of the Constitution are concerned."

[58] Douglass, in *Life and Writings*, supra note 57, vol. 1, at 40–41; Douglass, in id., at 379. Walter M. Merrill, *Against Wind and Tide: A Biography of William Lloyd Garrison* (1963), at 205.

[59] Douglass, *Life and Writings*, supra note 57, vol. 1, at 208–209, 274–275, 328–329, 362–367.

[60] Compare Douglass's reading of this clause (that it pertained only to congressional power over the *international* slave trade) with that of Robert Walsh and others (that it authorized congressional regulation of the *domestic* slave trade as well). Berns, supra note 46, at 221.

[61] Foreshadowing a line of decisions of the Supreme Court, Douglass claimed that the fugitive slave clause actually nationalized a slaveholder's right to own slaves.

cited other provisions as well. For example, Article I, Section 8, authorized Congress to "suppress insurrections," and Article IV, Section 4, authorized the United States to protect each state against "domestic Violence." Both provisions, he said, covered legitimate acts of rebellion by slaves.[62]

According to Wiecek, Douglass could have pointed to more provisions than these. Article I, Sections 2 and 9, required that "direct Taxes . . . be apportioned among the several States" as if each slave were three-fifths of a person. This requirement, Wiecek argues, was designed "to prevent Congress from laying a head tax on slaves to encourage their emancipation." Further, Article I, Sections 9 and 10, prohibited Congress and the states from taxing exports. The reason for this, says Wiecek, was "to prevent them from taxing slavery indirectly by taxing the exported products of slave labor."[63]

The pragmatic and theological conclusions that followed from the Garrisonians' constitutional observations went as follows: If the country were to be purified, the agents of purification must themselves be without taint. To pursue political and legal remedies, however, was to participate in the corrupt political system that maintained the evil institution of slavery. Hence to participate was to debase abolitionism. Pragmatically, given what Garrisonians perceived as the country's constitutional commitment to slavery and given the strength of the South in national political and legal institutions, the idea of transforming the constitutional beast from within was quixotic. The more realistic way to eliminate slavery was to transform the hearts and minds of individuals on the question of slavery. Of course that transformation could occur only outside the covenant with hell.[64]

Garrisonians were rarely explicit about such matters, but clearly an abolitionist transformation would have to follow one of two courses. In one case, it would have to achieve a virtually universal awakening of the American psyche. This would obviate the need for political action, for politics is necessary only when people either disagree about their interests or aspirations or are unwilling or unable to act on them with-

[62] Fehrenbacher argues, against Douglass, that the framers did not intend by these provisions to aim at insurrections by slaves. Don E. Fehrenbacher, "Slavery, the Framers, and the Living Constitution," in *Slavery and Its Consequences: The Constitution, Equality, and Race* (Goldwin and Kaufman, eds., 1988), at 1, 12. However, at least one framer seems to have considered that the provision might apply to slaves. See James Madison, *The Federalist*, No. 43 (1788).

[63] Wiecek, supra note 52, at 62–63.

[64] See Merrill, supra note 58, at 38–39; Garrison, "What Shall Be Done?" (July 30, 1831), in *Documents of Upheaval: Selections from William Lloyd Garrison's "The Liberator," 1831–1865* (Nelson, ed., 1966), at 10–11.

out coercion. In this way slavery, like Marx's bourgeois state, would simply wither away. Short of that, however, the abolition of slavery would ultimately have to depend on the antislavery movement's ability to convert its moral majority into an effective political majority that could enforce its will through democratic processes. Although Phillips seemed to acknowledge that this second, "political" alternative might follow from strategies of non-resistance and moral awakening, the rhetoric of most other Garrisonians included no reference to it.

VI

If most Garrisonians disavowed a political agenda, by 1840 another wing of the Society—"antislavery constitutionalists"—openly acknowledged that part of its aim was to achieve political and legal change.[65] Acting mainly through local antislavery societies (as the Garrisonians controlled the national Society), the constitutionalists revived a faith in political and legal reform that had been part of the creed of early crusaders against slavery. But the constitutionalists revised the earlier creed in at least three ways. First, although they were willing to take incremental victories where they could find them, their philosophical aim was slavery's immediate abolition. Second, although they did not eschew reform within states, their attention was primarily on change at the national level. Third, they argued that the Constitution itself permitted national political institutions to act against slavery. Some of them added one more tenet that suggested a distinctly abolitionist turn in national covenantalism: The Constitution was substantively committed not to sustaining slavery but to abolishing it.

The ingenuity with which antislavery constitutionalists assailed the constitutionality of slavery was impressive. For example, Alvan Stewart argued that the Fifth Amendment's due process clause authorized both Congress and the federal judiciary to abolish slavery everywhere, including any state, in the United States. That clause, he said, embodied a constituent principle of the common law. Indeed it was "but an enlargement of the language of Magna Charta— . . . neither will we pass upon him, or condemn him, but by the lawful judgment of his peers, or by the law of the land." At a minimum, said Stewart, due process required that every person claimed as a slave be entitled to vindicate his freedom through an indictment by a grand jury and the trial and judgment of a petit jury. Stewart conceded that the Constitution was an instrument of

[65] In this context "constitutionalists" simply denotes persons who were willing to rely explicitly on constitutional arguments in attacking slavery.

compromise between North and South. But the framers' compromise was this: In exchange for "*greater* security from his slaves' insurrections and flights," the slaveholder "agreed . . . upon a new definition of slavery" under which he abandoned claims to "vested rights of property in the slave" and agreed to have each slave's status as slave determined by due process of law.[66]

As Stewart acknowledged, if his reading of the Fifth Amendment were to hold, "there is not a slave at this moment, in the United States." Any slave could challenge his status by filing a petition for a writ of habeas corpus, which a federal judge should promptly issue. Short of waiting for the disposition of millions of petitions for habeas corpus, however, Congress could abolish slavery in toto by statute on the ground that during the forty-eight years since the Constitution's ratification, slaveholders "have never established their title to their alledged [*sic*] slaves by due process of law." Finally, and for the same reason, Northerners were no longer obliged to return any fugitive slave except where evidence existed that the requirements of due process had been satisfied.[67]

However unconventional was Stewart's reading of the text or his account of the framers' intentions, a greater problem for his theory was largely unconnected with the specifics of the Fifth Amendment. It had to do instead with the assumption, widely shared both at the founding and when Stewart was writing, that the Bill of Rights imposed limits only on the national government, not on the states.[68] Implicit in Stewart's treatment may have been a nascent theory of the primacy of national citizenship and of the fundamentality of certain rights across and within states. Such an extension of nationalist constitutionalism would not have been beyond the pale, but its incompatibility with prominent notions of both citizenship and the reach of the first eight amendments made a fuller articulation and justification desirable, if not essential.

Theodore Dwight Weld faced fewer such constraints when he argued a year later that Congress had authority to abolish slavery in the District of Columbia. Even so, his argument was fraught with textual gym-

[66] Alvan Stewart, "A Constitutional Argument on the Subject of Slavery," *The Friend of Man*, vol. 2, no. 18 (Utica, October 18, 1837), reprinted in Jacobus tenBroek, *Equal under Law* 281 (1965), at 282–287.

[67] Id., at 288–289, 294–295.

[68] See John Marshall's opinion for the Court in *Barron v. Mayor and City Council of Baltimore*, supra note 26. But see Justice Chase's opinion in *Calder v. Bull*, 3 U.S. (Dall.) 386 (1798). Ironically, and contrary to Marshall, Calhoun held a nationalist theory of the application of the Bill of Rights.

nastics and theoretical assumptions that challenged conventional understandings.[69]

Like Stewart before, Weld ultimately relied on the Fifth Amendment. Drawing on assumptions of liberal political economy, he argued that slaves had a property right in themselves and were deprived of their earnings without due process of law; thus Congress would actually *promote* the purposes of the Fifth Amendment (including the protection of rights in property) by abolishing slavery. Nor did the Amendment require compensation of slaveholders. For one thing, the "taking" of property (assuming slaves to be property) would not have been for a "public use." Because the Fifth Amendment required compensation only for takings for public use, there must be no compensation owing if the taking were not for public use. For another, the Fifth Amendment required only "just" compensation. Because slavery unjustly deprived slaves of their liberty and property, any compensation to slaveholders would have been unjust. Finally, because justice is the legitimate end of all governments (as affirmed in the Preamble), Congress not only was not prohibited from abolishing slavery in the District but was positively authorized to do so, perhaps everywhere.[70]

Both Stewart and Weld relied on implicit assumptions that slavery was morally wrong, that morality properly informed one's reading of the constitutional text, and that, apart from limits imposed by the Constitution itself, governments were not authorized to act immorally. But in challenging the constitutional foundations of slavery, no one integrated morality and law more systematically or comprehensively than did Lysander Spooner. He wove natural law and rights so tightly with textual exegesis that natural morality and constitutional text were virtually indistinguishable.[71]

For Spooner, "law is an intelligible principle of right, necessarily resulting from the nature of man." The obligations of law derive solely from the natural rights of individuals. Natural law and natural right are coextensive. Natural law is "the paramount law. . . . [T]here is, and can

[69] Theodore Dwight Weld, "The Power of Congress over Slavery in the District of Columbia," *The Anti-Slavery Examiner*, no. 5 (New York: The American Anti-Slavery Society, 1838), reprinted in *Equal under Law*, supra note 66, at 243, 244, 256–257, 275. Weld's argument that Congress was constitutionally authorized to abolish slavery in the District of Columbia was based in part on a problematically expansive reading of Article I, Section 8.

[70] Id., at 271–277. Moreover, Congress was authorized to abolish slavery in order to provide for the common defense and promote the general welfare, which were also purposes laid down in the Preamble. Id., at 278–279.

[71] Lysander Spooner, *The Unconstitutionality of Slavery* (1845, 1860).

be, correctly speaking, *no law but natural law*." Law is "the rule, principle, obligation or requirement of natural justice," and natural justice could not allow slavery.[72]

But the United States had a written constitution "which judicial tribunals actually recognize as authoritative." Therefore Spooner could not content himself with the proposition "that there can be no law contrary to natural right," however much he might think it true. He had to speak to the *constitutionality* of slavery and of ostensible laws upholding the institution. In order to speak to the question of constitutionality, he drew on what he called "ordinary rules of legal interpretation." The fundamental principle of interpretation was that "all language must be construed '*strictly*' in favor of natural right." Three rules followed from that principle. First, where language is susceptible of more than one meaning, the one consistent with justice and natural right is preferred. Second, a meaning that comports with natural right can be overridden by other language in the Constitution, but only if that language is explicit and its meaning unavoidable. Third, where the language itself can be construed to give an "innocent" meaning, "no *extraneous or historical evidence* shall be admitted" to give "an unjust or immoral meaning."[73]

With respect to the Constitution, euphemisms such as "person[s] held to service or labor" (in Article IV, Section 2), "all other persons" (in Article I, Section 2), the "migration or importation of such persons" (in Article I, Section 9), and "domestic violence" (in Article IV) did not refer to slaves or slavery. Instead "persons held to service or labor" referred to indentured servants, "all other persons" referred to aliens, "migration" referred to persons leaving one of the states, "importation" referred to any immigrant coming into the United States, and "domestic violence" referred not to slaves' insurrections but to any *unjustified* violence.[74]

If Spooner's attempts to wrest himself from the linguistic bondage of the Constitution's provisions purportedly sanctioning slavery were often belabored, his readings of its "positive provisions," those consistent with his version of liberty, were more plausible and direct. In speaking to citizenship, for example, he argued that "the Constitution made all 'the people of the United States' *citizens* under the government to be established by it." "The people," in whose name the Constitution was ordained and established, connoted all people "permanently inhabiting the United States, . . . [not simply] *white* people [or] . . . *free* people." The language was not restrictive. It implied "the whole people."[75]

[72] Id., at 5–15.
[73] Id., at 15–18, 58–59, 62.
[74] Id., at 67–89.
[75] Id., at 90.

Moreover, Article IV's guarantee of a republican form of government was a guarantee of liberty, not slavery. Unlike the language purportedly protecting slavery, Spooner said, Article IV was explicit and unambiguous. A republican government was essentially a commonwealth, the property of the whole people, "controlled by the combined will and power of the public," whose end was "the protection of the rights of all." Slavery and republican government could not stand together, for slavery nullified republican government. Further, the only way to secure a *national* republic was to ensure that every *state* also had a republican government, promoting "the rights of man," "liberty and justice," and freedom of contract.[76]

Calhoun would not have disagreed with Spooner's general insistence that republican government be a government of the whole people. However, he would have disputed the incompatibility of slavery with free government, for he and many other prominent Southerners were arguing (or would soon do so) that slavery was *essential* to maintaining free institutions of self-government. Similarly, Calhoun did not accept the argument of Spooner, Marshall, and others that the Constitution and nation were creations of the people as a whole rather than of the people of sovereign states. He also disagreed with the notion that the way to preserve liberty was through universal citizenship and individual rights. It was not that the rights of individual citizens were unimportant to Calhoun, but that the only way to ensure their protection was to preserve the *forms* of free government. Preserving the forms of free government required that the national government be constrained from legislating on matters on which *all* the constituent members of the national polity did not agree. Only concurrent majorities could achieve, in Spooner's words (but not with his meaning), "the protection of the rights of all." On Calhoun's terms, they ensured not that a part would control the whole but that the will of all the parts was adequately represented in the policies of the nation.[77]

The logics of Calhoun and Spooner were like mirrored opposites. Both supplied constitutional theories of nullification. But where Calhoun would have permitted state conventions to nullify national deci-

[76] Id., at 105–114.

[77] If one reason for the concurrent majority was that individuals had insufficient power to enforce their interests against a majority, it is not clear, given Calhoun's Hobbesian proclivities, why he would expect a national majority to be willing to yield even to a state's nullification of national legislation. Arthur Bestor argues that when all was said and done, state sovereignty's claim to protect minorities was essentially a sham. See his "State Sovereignty and Slavery: A Reinterpretation of Proslavery Constitutional Doctrine, 1846–1860," 54 *J. Ill. St. Hist. Soc.* 117 (1961), at 180. Although the theory of state sovereignty did serve other masters as well, I suspect that Bestor's position is overstated.

sions that were incompatible with local interests, Spooner would have had judges annul (usually local) decisions that did not cohere with the national application of principles of natural law and right. In Calhoun and Spooner, the Constitution had produced a pair of genetically oppositional theories that represented two deeply incompatible nomic constitutional worlds. The boundaries of Calhoun's world were defined by the connection of antifederalist localism to the preservation of slavery. Spooner's world, on the other hand, grew around the junction of federalist nationalism to abolition. For the first time, a definitive constitutional line began to separate the South from the North.

CHAPTER THREE

Interpretive Authority and Constitutional Division, Part I

I

I claimed in chapter 2 that a single Constitution could produce multiple coherent answers to constitutional questions. One reason for that capacity has to do with the basic character of constitutional authority and with the role of interpretation in the constitutional order. I argued that constitutional authority rests atop an account or myth of the origins of the order. A normative regime—a *nomos*—arises from that account. Although elements of that *nomos* may antedate the founding of the order, they receive their constitutional authority by virtue of their connection to the founding. Analytically, then, they follow from the Constitution, even if historically they precede it. In the beginning of a constitutional order, one can find its end.

Sometimes, however, more than one account can be generated. In such cases, each account will ground its own *nomoi*. We saw in chapter 2 how the Constitution of the United States accommodated competing accounts of its own origins: federalism and antifederalism. We also saw how those accounts generated competing responses to the problem of slavery. As it happens, however, neither account determined either response. For example, federalism was able to generate constitutional interpretations both abolitionist (Spooner) and proslavery (the Garrisonians). Similarly, antifederalism generated a proslavery interpretation (Calhoun), and we shall see in chapter 4 how it could also generate an abolitionist interpretation.

The mere fact of the availability of alternative accounts of the origins of the order cannot explain the simultaneous availability of disparate interpretations within a single account; however, the latter phenomenon might be explained in one of two other ways. First, perhaps one or more of the competing interpretations within a single account are incoherent or constitutionally indefensible. I reject this explanation where slavery was concerned. For although certain interpretations suffered deficiencies with respect to coherence or compatibility with constitutional standard, those deficiencies were usually no greater for any one interpretation than for another.

In the years before the Civil War, it sometimes did appear that certain interpretations were more congenial to a particular account of the founding than others. For example, we shall see in this chapter and the next that the localist antifederalist account proved a more durable foundation for proslavery interpretation than did the nationalist federalist account. And although abolitionist interpretations had a tough time taking firm root in either account, they ended up being most closely identified with federalist theories like those of Spooner. But those alliances were a function less of constitutional logic than of cultural and political contingencies that made certain affinities more plausible because they represented superior strategies for particular constitutional actors. In short, in light of certain conditions at any given time, disparate motives—including expectations, desires, hopes, and fears—impelled competing actors to attach to divergent accounts of constitutional origin. But different conditions in the polity or a different arrangement of motives could have easily impelled different connections between interpretations and foundational accounts.

We can see these considerations at work in a number of antebellum forms; three stand out. The first, which we shall see in this chapter, was Frederick Douglass's eventual gravitation toward a nationalist abolitionist interpretation of the Constitution. The second was the gradual tendency of decisions of the United States Supreme Court to embrace a nationalist proslavery interpretation, a tendency that, when consummated, would have explosive consequences for the polity. Third, in reaction to the evolving doctrine of the Supreme Court, there was the brief flirtation by Northern state courts, especially in Wisconsin, with a starkly antifederalist antislavery interpretation of the Constitution. As both the second and third concern the courts, we shall take them up in chapter 4.

None of these phenomena would have been visible except for the fact that the Constitution permitted a wide range of interpretive authority. This allocation of interpretive authority is the second, more plausible explanation for the emergence of opposing interpretations within a single account of origins. One reason for the distribution of authority grows out of the radical division of power that the Constitution instituted. But another, more basic reason returns to first principles of constitutionalism. Chapter 1 suggested that constitutionalism holds that a constitution can succeed in *regulating* a polity only if people—including both citizens and institutional actors—can fashion their behavior in accordance with constitutional standards. More fundamentally, a constitution can succeed in genuinely *constituting* a polity only if people—especially citizens—can construct their very identities by reference to the constitution. Similarly, this genuine constituting of a polity can occur only if citizens—perhaps in contrast with institutional actors—can reject the constitution.

Whether they are simply adapting their behavior to constitutional standards or attaching to, rejecting, or detaching from the constitution itself, people must be able to interpret the constitution. Usually their interpretation will be rough or incomplete. Sometimes it will be instrumental or pretextual. Nonetheless, if the constitution is to succeed, people must be able to generate some account of its meaning. And the abundance of motives and interpretive contexts—not to mention institutional functions—that are inescapable in the world make interpretive diversity unavoidable. But more than unavoidable, such diversity may be essential to the success of a constitutional order. On the other hand, it can also divide in ways that breed the failure of the order—not necessarily the failure to adhere to particular standards but the failure simply to survive. As I suggested in chapter 1, constitutionalism anticipates and embraces the possibility of this radical form of failure.

This chapter expands on this notion that the American Constitution necessarily implies a distribution of interpretive authority. Certainly the localism of the antifederalist account does so. But even a deeply federalist account must assume some such distribution. On either account, the distribution of authority has at least two consequences. First, interpretive authority is the site of competition within and among constitutional actors. Second, and as a direct result of this, constitutional battles are often not only about what constitution means but about who may say what it means, when, and why.

Even where interpretive authority is widely distributed, it may be possible—especially on a federalist account—to posit a hierarchy of interpreters above which sits a supreme, final authoritative interpreter. In the United States the Supreme Court has sometimes spoken as if it had supreme interpretive authority.[1] Frequently many in the polity have willingly acceded to the Court's claim to authority.[2] In chapter 4 I shall

[1] John Marshall's opinion for the Court in *Marbury v. Madison*, 5 U.S. (1 Cranch) 137 (1803), may imply some such claim, though one may read the opinion less ambitiously. For clearer claims to judicial supremacy, see *M'Culloch v. Maryland*, 17 U.S. (4 Wheat.) 316 (1819) (concerning federalism); *Cooper v. Aaron*, 358 U.S. 1 (1958) (concerning federalism); *United States v. Nixon*, 418 U.S. 683 (1974) (concerning the president); *Powell v. McCormack*, 395 U.S. 486 (1969) (concerning Congress); and "Statement of Laurence H. Tribe," U.S. Senate, Subcommittee on Separation of Powers, *The Human Life Bill: Hearings on S. 158*, 97th Cong., 1st Sess., vol. 1, 249–252.

[2] Others have not only resisted the Court's claims to supremacy but have laid similar claims on behalf of other institutions. For example, some have argued that ultimate interpretive authority resides in the legislature, usually meaning the Congress. See Justice Gibson's dissent in *Eakin v. Raub*, 12 Sergeant & Rawle (Sup. Ct. Pa., 1825); and *Katzenbach v. Morgan*, 384 U.S. 641 (1966). Others have contended that supremacy rests in the states. See the competing arguments of Thomas Jefferson, "Kentucky Resolutions" (1798), and James Madison, "Virginia Resolutions" (1799), both in *Documents of American History*, vol. 1 (Commager and Cantor, eds., 1988), at 178; John C. Calhoun, *A Discourse on the Constitution and Government of the United States*, in *Works of John C.*

consider the consequences of such a position with respect to slavery in the United States. There I shall also show that the functions and institutional position of courts—especially the Supreme Court—can generate peculiar approaches to constitutional problems; but the Court's claims to authority neither exhaust the meaning or range of the Constitution nor put constitutional problems to rest.

In the present chapter we shall take up the interpretive authority that certain nonjudicial actors asserted in response to problems associated with the presence of slavery in polity. We shall pay special attention to two such actors—Congress and society itself. In connection with those actors we shall see the following: First, when Congress acts, it cannot escape the constitutional dimensions of its role or the constitutional implications of its decisions, even when it tries to do so. Second, Congress's institutional makeup and function make it difficult for it to act in a decisive, coherent, principled manner, but neither disables it from doing so. Third, political culture grounds and influences the character of constitutional debate, even in institutions, like Congress, that possess a degree of autonomy. Thus Madison's claim that the structure of representation would permit Congress to filter passion and serve as a rational, reflective body is, in some circumstances, unsubstantiated. Fourth, however, even when Congress attempts to solve a problem in a manner that appears institutionally successful, it nonetheless can drive a wedge between political cultures and thus exacerbate systematic constitutional division. Finally this chapter will show that within Congress and across society, battles over the Constitution laid the foundation for the ultimate failure of the American constitutional order.

II

Given the emergence of Calhoun's and Spooner's positions by 1850, one might have imagined that the country was on the verge of a gigantic constitutional mitosis. But the time was not yet right for such a division.

Calhoun, vol. 1 (Cralle, ed., 1856), at 111; and the claims of the State of Wisconsin in *Ableman v. Booth*, 62 U.S. (21 How.) 506 (1859). Executives have often claimed not supreme, but concurrent authority, equal to that of other branches. See, e.g., Thomas Jefferson, "Instruct[ions to] a Federal Prosecutor," in *American Constitutional Interpretation* (Murphy, Fleming, and Barber, eds., 2d ed., 1995), at 306; Andrew Jackson, "Veto of the Bank Bill," in *Documents of American History*, vol. 1, (Commager and Cantor, eds., 1988), at 270; Abraham Lincoln, "First Inaugural Address—Final Text," in *The Collected Works of Abraham Lincoln*, vol. 4 (Basler, ed., 1953), at 262; and Franklin D. Roosevelt, "Speech of March 9, 1937 [on Reorganizing the Judiciary]," Senate Report No. 711, 75th Cong., 1st Sess., 41.

First, the genetic cleavages that seemed to anticipate cellular division were far more complex and less bipolar than an analysis of only Calhoun and Spooner might indicate. Second, the regional affinity for one gene—that of nationalism/localism—would eventually reverse itself, only to reverse itself again very shortly. And third, as of 1850 the subtle particulars of Spooner's and Calhoun's theories claimed few devoted adherents.[3]

Notwithstanding these constitutional considerations, in many respects Northerners and Southerners had always lived in different worlds, even more distinct culturally than geographically. Those differences were deeply rooted in the distinctive logics of their socioeconomic systems.[4] But as important as those differences were, they sometimes concealed cultural similarities, including the deeply significant symbols that tied the two regions together. Despite the immigration of huge numbers of Celts (notably including Irish Catholics), Germans, and others by mid-century, both cultures remained predominately Anglo-Saxon and Protestant, used the same language, occupied a contiguous territory, and shared basic customs and traditions. They had inherited the same legal system[5] and were parts of the same political system. With the exception of Native Americans, Hispanics (who largely resided in territories formerly held by Mexico), and of course blacks, Americans were, by today's standards, an ethnically homogeneous lot.[6]

From an economic standpoint, as disparate as the two economies were, the interests of capitalists and plantation owners were, more often than not, closely linked. As early as 1816 Calhoun had acknowledged that "agriculture, manufactures, [and] commerce" were integral parts of a larger economic order.[7] By the late 1850s Northern capitalists were

[3] Even among abolitionists, Spooner's ideas initially gained little currency. In 1847 Wendell Phillips criticized them as "logically absurd and self-contradictory," but his real concern may have been simply that they were unrealistic. Wendell Phillips, *Review of Lysander Spooner's Essay on the Unconstitutionality of Slavery* (1847), at 3–4. Calhoun's fears were certainly widely shared among Southerners and were intensifying, but his doctrine of concurrent majorities never gained a wide following in the United States. David M. Potter, *The South and the Concurrent Majority* (1972), at 8. The doctrine of nullification proved much more durable as an idea, though it has only infrequently found institutional expression.

[4] See Anne Norton, *Alternative Americas: A Reading of Antebellum Political Culture* (1986), at 64–96, 116–131.

[5] One should take seriously, however, Mark Tushnet's observation that the law produced by that system reflected the distinctive tendencies and contradictions of Northern and Southern societies. Tushnet, *The American Law of Slavery, 1810–1860* (1981).

[6] David M. Potter, *The Impending Crisis: 1848–1861* (1976), at 8, 13–14, 32.

[7] Frederic Bancroft, *Calhoun and the South Carolina Nullification Movement* (1928), at 3. In the 1840s, though, he changed his stance, finding common cause with Mike Walsh, a radical Northern labor leader (and later a Congressman from New York), based on a

usually quicker than their Southern brethren to recognize the confluence of interests, but the recognition persisted on both sides. As late as 1861, in the wake of several Southern secessions, the mayor of New York City argued that the city should secede from the State of New York and establish itself as "a *Free City*," in order "to preserve a continuance of uninterrupted intercourse with every section."[8] Capitalists were motivated by a belief that Northern commercial prosperity depended on Southern agriculture.[9] And despite what is sometimes considered their quasi-feudal characteristics, Southern plantations were participants in a unique form of "capitalist enterprise."[10]

Clearly, however, slavery was a source of regional division, if not economic then moral and cultural. In the face of slavery's divisive tendencies, national political institutions attempted to mitigate the forces of separation and to strengthen proslavers' sense of security. For example, between 1836 and 1844 Congress formally adopted gag rules restricting the receipt of petitions opposing slavery and instituted a ban against mailing abolitionist literature to the South. Within Congress, the only victories antislavery societies could claim were the eventual repeal of the gag rule in the House and a few heated floor debates concerning Congress's power over slavery.[11] Moreover, well into the 1850s the federal consensus continued to serve as a kind of constitutional security blanket. Though that consensus had ceased to command anything resembling universal support, neither antislavery societies nor the abolitionist movement posed a serious political threat to slavery, even on the eve of the Civil War, at least at the national level.[12]

But national institutions could not consistently forestall regional division or prevent questions about slavery from entering the public life of the polity. In one form or another, slavery was at stake in almost every significant debate in American national politics. By the 1850s debates

---

shared antagonism to capital. Arthur M. Schlesinger, Jr., *The Age of Jackson* (1945), at 408–409. For an account of the similarities that Walsh, like Marx, saw between slave labor and wage labor, see id., at 490–491.

[8] "Mayor Fernando Wood's Recommendation for the Secession of New York City" (January 6, 1861), in *Documents of American History*, supra note 2, at 374. Wood intimated that the city might also dissolve its ties to the United States, but the intimation is oblique.

[9] Potter, supra note 6, at 443–444.

[10] See Louis M. Hacker, *The Triumph of American Capitalism* (1940), at 124–127.

[11] Outside Congress, however, the gag rules were a public relations bonanza for the societies, enabling them to link slavery to the more popular issues of free speech and civil liberties. By one report, during only the first eighteen months of the gag rules, the number of petitions "increased from 23 to 300,000." Russel B. Nye, *Fettered Freedom: Civil Liberties and Slavery Controversy, 1830–1860* (1963), at 41–67.

[12] Potter, supra note 6, at 145.

over tariffs, banking, homesteading, the disposition of public lands, and the construction of a railroad to the Pacific—not to mention Cuba, the Gadsden Purchase, and the spoils of the Mexican War—became issues that divided North from South. If not always visible in those arguments, slavery lingered just beneath the surface.[13]

Another series of debates, however, brought slavery visibly to the fore. They grew out of the country's continental aspirations, aspirations that raised a thorny question: As the country expanded westward, what was to become of slavery in newly acquired territories? Congress assumed primary responsibility for addressing the question. But the manner in which it did so evinced three general characteristics. First, Congress turned to the question only when it was forced to do so—that is, as new territory became available for settlement or admission to the Union. Second, Congress's approach to resolving the issue was distinctly incremental. It never attempted to settle the matter for the entire continent for all time. Third, and following from the first and the second, congressional action was generally borne of compromise, not principle.

The reasons for Congress's approach were complex but two deserve mention. First, the function and operation of representative institutions in a large republican political system make it almost impossible for a sizable aggregation of people, representing a diverse range of interests and values, to agree both on a policy *and* on the reasons for acting. Of course one can generate reasons to justify a particular legislative action, and those reasons are frequently "public" in character. Usually, however, the reasons are diverse and tend to speak to local concerns. Hence there is often no single principle to explain why a legislative body adopts a policy and certainly no one explanation for why it fails or refuses to adopt a policy. Second, and related to the first, slavery was a sensitive issue, especially for this polity, and politicians, who harbored strongly pragmatic propensities in any event, tended to treat sensitive issues gingerly. Caution dictated a strategy not to "overfix" the dilemma of slavery, whose future was not clear and whose capacity to sow discontent was high.

The original states came to the Union with whatever institutions they had at the time. Under most accounts of the founding, those states had authority to create, maintain, alter, or abolish their domestic institutions independent of congressional authority, except, of course, where commerce among the several states or republican form of government was implicated. Even during the Revolution, however, the Continental Congress encouraged states to cede their western lands "for the common benefit of the United States." Those lands would be organized, settled,

[13] Id., at 145, 391–392.

and admitted as "distinct republican States," which "shall have the same rights of sovereignty, freedom and independence, as the other states."[14] Virginia's cession of its western lands after the Revolution recited the congressional language concerning the "sovereignty, freedom and independence" of the states to be formed from the territory.[15] But it did not speak of slavery. However, North Carolina's later cession of the territory south of the Ohio River did. It explicitly provided "that no regulations made or to be made by Congress shall tend to emancipate slaves." As Wiecek notes, Congress acquiesced in this and similar provisos by admitting slave states from the territories west of North Carolina, South Carolina, Georgia, and Florida.[16]

Later the Continental Congress adopted the Northwest Ordinance of 1787, formally organizing the territory northwest of the Ohio River.[17] For our purposes two aspects of the Ordinance stand out. First, it combined attributes of what we could later describe as federalism and antifederalism. On the federalist side, the "national" legislature was regulating territory belonging to the United States.[18] On the antifederalist side, the Ordinance described itself as establishing "articles of compact between the original states, and the people and states in the said territory." Given its early date, this self-description might carry little weight but for the fact that the Ordinance was repassed after the Constitution was ratified.[19] The second significant aspect of the Ordinance was this provision in Article VI:

> There shall be neither slavery nor involuntary servitude in the said territory, otherwise than in punishment of crimes, whereof the party shall have been duly convicted. Provided always, that any person escaping into the same, from whom labor or service is lawfully claimed in any one of the original states, such fugitive may be lawfully reclaimed, and conveyed to the person claiming his or her labor or service as aforesaid.[20]

[14] Resolution of Congress on Public Lands (October 10, 1780), in *Documents of American History*, supra note 2, at 119.

[15] Virginia's Cession of Western Lands to the United States (December 20, 1783), in *Documents of American History*, supra note 2, at 120.

[16] William M. Wiecek, *The Sources of Antislavery Constitutionalism in America, 1760–1848* (1977), at 102–103.

[17] Act of the Congress of the Confederation for the Government of the Territory of the United States, North-West of the River Ohio (July 13, 1787), in *Documents of American History*, supra note 2, at 128. The Territory consisted mainly of lands ceded by Virginia.

[18] In fact the term *national* in this context is a misnomer, as the political institutions of the central government under the Articles of Confederation were more confederated than national.

[19] Ordinance for the Government of the Territory North-West of the River Ohio, 1 Stat. 50–53 (August 7, 1789).

[20] Three years earlier with identical language, Jefferson had proposed that Congress

In fact slavery persisted in the Territory well into the nineteenth century, but in formal terms the Ordinance did mark the sectional division of the country. Eventually institutions and practices would catch up with language and ideas. The line of demarcation was the Ohio River; as the country expanded farther west, however, that line would not suffice. Arguments over the location or existence of the boundary would intensify as the unsettled portion of the continent shrank.

The first site of struggle was the territory acquired in the Louisiana Purchase. Missouri, which was part of that territory, began petitioning for statehood in 1817. But it would take Congress three years of intense conflict to devise a compromise. At the heart of the conflict was slavery. The Missouri Compromise admitted Maine as a free state and Missouri as a slave state, thus preserving the equal balance between slave and free states. It also prohibited slavery in the rest of the territory of the Louisiana Purchase north of 36°30′, which marked most of Missouri's southern boundary.[21]

The Compromise muted debates in Congress over the status and future of slavery for twenty-six years. But the old sore began to fester in 1846 over the anticipated acquisition of new territory from Mexico, against whom the United States had recently trumped up a war. David Wilmot, a member of Congress from Pennsylvania, introduced a bill to prohibit slavery outright in the Mexican territories. Wilmot's Proviso—which was identical to Article VI of the Northwest Ordinance—never passed the Congress, but its mere proposal provoked such strongly sectional responses that political parties ruptured over the issue.[22]

In response to the Proviso, members of Congress began proposing competing principles for resolving questions over slavery in the territories. William Wick, from Indiana, proposed extending the line of the Missouri Compromise west through the anticipated Mexican cession, presumably to the Pacific. Lewis Cass, of Michigan, proposed the principle of popular sovereignty, in which decisions about slavery would be left to the discretion of each territory, just as each state had authority to regulate slavery within its borders. Finally, John C. Calhoun pressed a nationalist theory of rights, insisting that Congress lacked authority to

---

exclude slavery from the land ceded by Virginia, but Congress defeated his proposal. See "Report of Government for the Western Territory" (April 23, 1784), in *Documents of American History*, supra note 2, at 121. On the history of slavery in the Territory after the adoption of the Ordinance, see Paul Finkelman, "Slavery and Bondage in the 'Empire of Liberty,'" in *The Northwest Ordinance: Essays on Its Formulation, Provisions, and Legacy* (Williams, ed., 1989).

[21] Potter, supra note 6, at 54–56.

[22] Id., at 23, 54; James M. McPherson, *Battle Cry of Freedom: The Civil War Era* (1988), at 52–54.

regulate slavery in the territories and that the territories themselves lacked authority to exclude slavery before they attained statehood.[23]

The search for a controlling principle was in vain, as all sides grew increasingly agitated. Moreover, the situation in the territories became more complicated. In 1848 Mexico signed the Treaty of Guadalupe Hildago, ceding California and the territory of New Mexico to the United States. Any chance for a reflective resolution of the disposition of those territories was destroyed by the discovery of gold in California's Sierra Madre and by the migration of settlers and the avaricious frenzy the discovery prompted. In the wake of the presidential election of 1848, in which the Democrats split in two and the new president betrayed proslavers by endorsing the admission of California, national politics seemed on the verge of a crisis.[24]

Southern radicals, some bent on disunion, called a convention of Southern states for June 1850. A deadlock in Congress over the disposition of the Mexican territories was finally broken in 1850 by compromise, but only under trying conditions that demonstrated the fragility of the solution. California was admitted as a free state; territorial governments were approved for New Mexico without restriction as to slavery; the slave trade in the District of Columbia was abolished, although slavery itself remained legal; interstate trade in slaves was declared to be beyond congressional authority; and a new fugitive slave law was enacted, making it easier for slaveholders to recover slaves.[25]

In the beginning, debates over the status of slavery in the territories had not been strictly a sectional issue. But the prevailing tendency, increasing rapidly through the 1850s, was a political division between North and South.[26] Northerners who wanted to restrict or prohibit the territorial expansion of slavery came to their position for a variety of reasons, two of which are especially pertinent here. Some, including most abolitionists, simply thought slavery was wrong for moral reasons or because it was incompatible with what they considered to be the country's fundamental precepts. Others, especially Freesoilers, were interested merely in keeping the territories open to the labor and enterprise of white settlers.[27]

[23] Potter, supra note 6, at 55–61.

[24] Id., at 1, 64–68, 72–88.

[25] Id., at 88–89, 90, 93, 95, 99, 106–109, 112.

[26] McPherson, supra note 22, at 52–54, 60–63, 117–118.

[27] Abraham Lincoln was one of the most prominent proponents of both positions. See, for example, *Political Debates Between Abraham Lincoln and Stephen A. Douglas* (1894), at 26–28, 31–33. Douglas, however, was probably the most systematic proponent of the latter position. See id., at 19–20. The sentiment was widely shared among whites. As one clergyman delicately put it, "I kem to Kansas to live in a free state and I don't want niggers a-trampin' on my grave." Potter, supra note 6, at 203.

Southerners who wanted slavery in some or all of the territories also did so for at least two reasons. Some, including those who advocated acquiring Cuba and other new territories, had no moral qualms whatsoever about slavery and were determined to establish an empire of slaveholders. Others, less imperial, were interested simply in maintaining a rough equilibrium between slave and free states.[28] Both positions were tied to the South's increasing sense of alienation from the rest of the country, an alienation fed by the apparently increasingly subordinate position of the South within the Union.

During the crisis over the admission of California, Calhoun died. But in his final speech to the Senate, he denounced three conditions that he said had undermined Southern political strength.[29] First, owing largely to the patterns of immigration, the dramatic increase in the population of the North compared with the far lower rate of increase in the South meant that the North could effectively control both the House of Representatives and the Electoral College. In addition, the compromises designating territories as slave or free had left a slave territory that was substantially smaller than the free territory. These trends, Calhoun expected, would reinforce the North's popular (and hence its political) advantage and would eventually translate into the admission of a greater number of free states than slave states, which would effectively give the North control of the Senate. With control over the national political apparatus, the North could dictate virtually all national policy.

Second, according to Calhoun, the North was already translating its political advantage into a "system of revenue and disbursements" that aimed to prop up Northern capital at the expense of Southern agriculture. Third, and sealing the first two trends, the national government now "claim[ed], and practically maintain[ed], the right to decide in the last resort . . . the extent of its powers." This "right" signaled the transformation of what had been a constitutional government, constrained by both practical and theoretical limits to its authority, into "a great national consolidated democracy," with no such limits at all. Under this consolidated democracy, argued Calhoun, the South was becoming an oppressed colony, much as the American colonies had been under British rule some eighty years before. Hence the problem of slavery was not simply an economic one. Nor was it strictly a matter of national policy, writ small. It also implicated, at the most fundamental level, the structure of the polity.[30]

Clearly, however, concerns about economics, politics, and constitu-

[28] McPherson, supra note 22, at 72, 115–116; Potter, supra note 6, at 16–17, 99–100.

[29] John C. Calhoun, "Address in the Senate of the United States, on the Subject of Slavery" (March 4, 1850) (Princeton University Microfiche Collection), at 2–4, 8.

[30] The Compromise of 1850 did little or nothing to remedy what Calhoun perceived to be the fundamental inequities of American constitutional structure.

tional structure would not have seemed so profound had Southerners not perceived a serious threat to their central values, interests, and culture. Further, regardless of the real similarities between Southern and Northern cultures and their modes of economic organization, people's *perceptions* of their situation were just as important as (and in some ways more than) the reality. So when George Fitzhugh drew parallels between Northern factories and Southern plantations in order to debunk critiques of slavery, he did so not to show the two regions' similarities but to emphasize their differences. He and others sought to extol what they perceived to be the virtues of Southern values, interests, and ways of life.[31] And at the center of all three, they argued, was slavery.

III

Calhoun's pessimism about the fate of the South gained some of its power from the Southern sense of a growing national opposition to slavery. In fact subtle shifts in American political culture outside the South during the 1850s had begun to confirm for some Southerners that their nagging insecurities were not imaginary. Justice Joseph Story had acknowledged growing opposition in certain Northern states to the Fugitive Slave Act as early as 1842 in *Prigg v. Pennsylvania*.[32]

Such a change may partly explain Frederick Douglass's gradual change of heart on the constitutionality of slavery. An increasingly receptive audience (outside the Supreme Court and the South) may have made not only moral arguments against slavery more viable but constitutional ones as well. Douglass had begun to express doubts about his prior position as early as 1849. He had come to the conclusion, he said, that if "strictly construed," the Constitution "is not a pro-slavery instrument."[33] Take the fugitive slave clause, for example. Douglass reasoned that if "a man from another country should read that clause . . . with no other knowledge of the character of American institutions," the reader would never imagine that it applied to slaves.[34]

[31] See George Fitzhugh, *Sociology for the South, or the Failure of Free Society* (1854), in *Slavery Defended: Views of the Old South* (McKitrick, ed., 1963), at 34–48; Edmund Ruffin, *The Political Economy of Slavery; or, the Institution Considered in Regard to its Influence on Public Wealth and the General Welfare* (1857), at 5–10; James Henry Hammond, "Speech on the Admission of Kansas" (March 4, 1858), in *Slavery Defended: Views of the Old South* (McKitrick, ed., 1963), at 123–124.

[32] 41 U.S. (16 Pet.) 536 (1842), at 621.

[33] Douglass, Letter to C. H. Chase, *The North Star* (February 9, 1849), in *The Life and Writings of Frederick Douglass*, vol. 1 (Foner, ed., 1950), at 352.

[34] Douglass, "The Address of Southern Delegates in Congress to their Constituents," *The North Star* (February 9, 1849), in *Life and Writings*, supra note 33, vol. 1, at 354–357.

But it made no sense, he said, to read the Constitution in such a literal way, for the Constitution was not a divine but a very "human" instrument; therefore it "must be explained in light of those maxims and principles which human beings have laid down as guides to the understanding of all written instruments . . . emanating from human beings." Those maxims included not simply its framers' intentions, which were bad enough, but also "common sense," which must acknowledge, apart from theoretical niceties, the brute facts pertaining to the circumstances that gave rise to the instrument. "The Constitution is not an abstraction. It is a living, breathing fact, exerting a mighty power over the nation of which it is the bond of Union." Despite its linguistic ambiguity, despite the framers' fear to speak the name slavery and reveal their "moral deformity," the Constitution was "radically and essentially pro-slavery, in its fact as well as in its tendency."[35]

Douglass "demand[ed] the immediate dissolution of the American Union, as required by liberty and the law of the living God." That law, "unchangeable and eternal," superseded the Constitution and existed "above all earthly statutes." It prohibited slavery even if the Constitution did not.[36] In prescribing disunion, Douglass had a great deal of company among abolitionists after the Mexican War.

Ironically he justified his continued resistance to antislavery constitutionalism in an eloquent, poignant defense of written constitutions and constitutional processes. Antislavery constitutionalists, he said, advocated that the national government ought to abolish slavery. "The question is not, however, what a government ought to be, or to do, but what the government of the United States is authorized to be, and to do, by the Constitution of the United States." Antislavery constitutionalism had two perverse tendencies, he said. The first was to quell people's impulse to abolish the Constitution and government of the United States and to replace them with a constitution and government that better served "the ends of justice." The second was to conflate the Constitution with what government said it meant. This latter doctrine, he said, would

> make[ ] the government superior to, and independent of, the Constitution, . . . without which the government is nothing better than a lawless mob, acting without any other or higher authority than its own convictions or impulses as to what is right or wrong. If this doctrine be sound, it is a mere farce to have a written constitution at all; for if the government can override and violate its Constitution in one point, it may do so in all.—There is

[35] Douglass, "The Constitution and Slavery," *The North Star* (March 16, 1849), in *Life and Writings*, supra note 33, vol. 1, at 361–363, 366. See also Douglass, Letter to Gerrit Smith (May 21, 1851), in id., vol. 5, at 183.

[36] Douglass, supra note 34, at 360.

> no limit, or safety, or certainty. If it can abolish slavery in violation of the Constitution, because it conflicts with the moral sentiments of the majority, the same may be done in other cases for the same reason. . . . [A]nd government will merely be the voice of an ever-shifting majority, be that good or evil.[37]

But Douglass's doubts and aspirations were getting the better of him. After wrestling with himself for years, in 1851 he publicly abandoned his long-standing commitment to a proslavery account of the Constitution's meaning. In doing so, he renounced history and intentionalism as interpretive modes and embraced a union of textualism and natural rights that clearly derived from Spooner. The only practical solution to reconciling the "conflicting and irreconcilable intentions" of the framers regarding slavery, he said, was to adopt two rules of construction. First, "the Constitution is the record of its own intention." Second, "[w]hen such an outrage [as slavery] is meant to be perpetrated, the intention must be expressed with irresistible clearness. There must be no ambiguity about it."[38]

Douglass's new account of the Constitution's meaning and his old one were motivated by an identical moral impulse—the abolition of slavery. What had changed was his sense, both theoretical and practical, of constitutional possibility. The theoretical possibility had to do not only with what one might read the Constitution to mean but also with the potential of having one's meaning ratified by the polity. Calhoun's fear had become Douglass's hope: that an antislavery majority was emerging in the North and, if in the North, then (for practical purposes) in the country.

In discovering an allegiance to Constitution and country, Douglass was breaking intellectually with his long-time friends and allies, the Garrisonians.[39] But even those sympathetic to the Garrisonian gospel

[37] Douglass, "Comments on Gerrit Smith's Address," *The North Star* (March 30, 1849), in *Life and Writings*, supra note 33, vol. 1, at 374–377.

[38] Douglass, "Is the United States Constitution for or against Slavery?" *Frederick Douglass' Paper* (July 24, 1851), in *Life and Writings*, supra note 33, vol. 5, at 194–195, 198–199. That Douglass viewed his new position as grounded not simply in a newly found rule of construction but also in a theory of natural rights was apparent from his Jeffersonian account of its "eternal" foundation: "That every man has a right to be free, needs no proof. It is self-evident." Douglass, Speech Delivered to Church Congregation at Harveysburg, Warren County, Ohio (May 1852), in id., at 223. See also Douglass, "The U.S. Constitution Anti-Slavery," *Frederick Douglass' Paper* (June 24, 1853), and "Slavery Unconstitutional," *Frederick Douglass' Paper* (February 1, 1856), both in id., at 284–285, 373–376.

[39] Garrison, who suffered from an abiding self-righteousness, considered Douglass's transformation nothing short of apostasy. He ridiculed and ostracized Douglass, who stuck to his guns with tenacity and dignity. Douglass, "The Anti-Slavery Movement,"

(apart from Garrison himself) began to reread the political climate. For example, while continuing on one level to adhere to non-resistance, Wendell Phillips began on another plane to acknowledge the potential for political change. "[I]f we look back twenty years," he said, "we can see a change in public opinion; yes, we can see a great change." And that change portended political consequences. But unlike Douglass, Phillips did not view those consequences as constitutional in character, at least not directly. In fact they were anticonstitutional: "[N]o law . . . can abide one moment when popular opinion demands its abrogation. The government is wrecked the moment the newspapers decree it. . . . Mr. Webster says we live under a government of laws. He was never more mistaken. . . . We live under a government of men—and morning newspapers." A revolution was approaching, said Phillips, but neither in the rarefied realm of constitutional discourse nor at the end of the barrel of a gun. "Revolutions are not made: they come. A revolution is as natural a growth as an oak. It comes out of the past. Its foundations are laid far back."[40]

What Phillips did not acknowledge (whether he recognized it or not) was that the natural and irresistible changes he foresaw were possible only if they were "constitutional" in some sense. For the Constitution was a source of the political structure and an embodiment of some of the very values that permitted such change and rendered it sensible. Implicit in Phillips's prediction, then, was an assumption that the reconstitution of the country would occur through normal constitutional processes, which allowed space for moral argument outside politics, permitted newspapers a relatively free hand in trying to shape public opinion, and translated opinion into policy by institutions of representative government.[41]

But newspapers and antislavery societies were not the only vehicles for changing opinion on slavery. In 1852 Harriet Beecher Stowe published *Uncle Tom's Cabin*, a novel depicting the plight of slaves in as vivid and heart-wrenching a manner as had yet been presented. Stowe said she was moved to write the book by debates over the various bills that became the Compromise of 1850. At that time, she "heard, with perfect surprise and consternation, Christian and humane people actually recommending the remanding [of] escaped fugitive slaves into slavery, as a duty binding on good citizens." Her aim was to demonstrate

---

Speech Delivered to the Rochester Ladies' Anti-Slavery Society (January 1855), in *Life and Writings*, supra note 33, vol. 2, at 351–352. On the breach between Douglass and Garrison, see Foner's essay in id., vol. 1, at 53–55.

[40] Wendell Phillips, "Public Opinion," Speech Before the Massachusetts Anti-Slavery Society (January 28, 1852), in *Speeches, Lectures, and Letters* (1891), at 35.

[41] Id., at 36, 44–45, 50.

that slavery was so horrific that "such a question could never be open for discussion."[42]

Stowe imagined among her audience not simply Northerners but also "you, generous, noble-minded men and women, of the South." But clearly the more receptive audience lay in the North. *Uncle Tom's Cabin* was a huge seller by nineteenth-century standards. In her introduction to the 1878 edition, Stowe noted that "[t]en thousand copies were sold in a few days, and over three hundred thousand within a year; and eight power-presses, running day and night, were barely able to keep pace with the demand for it." By 1862 the book would sell more than two million copies around the world.[43]

IV

Few copies of *Uncle Tom's Cabin* were sold in the South.[44] But the reaction there was swift, strong, and far out of proportion to the few copies sold there. It was also far from what Stowe might have hoped. In a scathing review published within nine months of the novel's release, George Frederick Holmes lambasted the book.

First, he said, it falsely portrayed slavery. But second, even if its depictions of slavery's brutality and Uncle Tom's "virtues, misfortunes, and martyrdom" resembled actual occurrences in the South, the lesson Stowe inferred from them, that slavery should be abolished, was defamatory. That message "is absolutely fatal to all human society—to all social organization, civilized or savage, whatever. It strikes at the very essence and existence of all community among men, it lays bare and roots up all the foundations of law, order and government. It is the very evangel of insubordination, sedition, and anarchy, and is promulgated in support of a cause worthy of the total ruin it is calculated to produce." In short, Lockean natural rights would lead to a Hobbesian war. But slavery was not simply necessary for warding off anarchy. It was also a positive good for slave and society. The condition of the slave, both "morally and materially," was "infinitely superior" to that of laborers anywhere else in the world (including the North). Moreover, slave labor was the only system "in which the interests of the labourer and the employer of labour are absolutely identical, and in which the reciprocal sympathies of both are assured."[45]

[42] Harriet Beecher Stowe, *Uncle Tom's Cabin, or Life Among the Lowly* (1852; repr. 1965), at 445–446.

[43] Id., at xxi, 446; McPherson, supra note 22, at 88–89.

[44] Potter, supra note 6, at 143 n. 44.

[45] George Frederick Holmes, "Uncle Tom's Cabin," 18 *Southern Literary Messenger*

Whether incited by *Uncle Tom's Cabin* or not, in the decade following its publication Southerners produced a torrent of literature defending slavery. Slavery had long had its vocal proponents,[46] but in the early 1850s they became increasingly intense, defensive, and prolific. Significantly the literature was rarely constitutional in character but addressed most of the propositions (and a few more) that Holmes had touched on: The survival of Southern civilization was at stake in the debates over abolition;[47] slavery was essential to the economic prosperity of the entire nation;[48] slavery was the foundation for all successful societies through the ages;[49] Southern slavery was a positive good—more moral, humane, productive, and conducive of good social order than Northern capitalism;[50] blacks were inherently inferior to Indo-Europeans, both as a society and as individuals, and were therefore naturally subservient;[51] God, through scripture, had sanctioned slavery.[52]

The literature was often strident, sometimes arrogant, even defiant in tone. But its character frequently belied its purpose, for most defenders of slavery were attempting to justify the institution, not only to the South but to the rest of the country. The fear, said George Frederick

---

721 (1852), in *Slavery Defended*, supra note 31, at 99, 100–102, 104–105, 107–108, 109–110.

[46] In *The Peculiar Institution: Slavery in the Ante-Bellum South* (1956), at 134, Kenneth M. Stampp notes that proslavery arguments were already being propagated in the early nineteenth century. Stampp traces commerce in such arguments to Nat Turner's rebellion in 1800. Id., at 133.

[47] Hammond, supra note 31, at 122; John C. Calhoun, "Speech on the Reception of Abolition Petitions" (February 6, 1837), in *Slavery Defended*, supra note 31, at 13; Ruffin, supra note 31, at 3–5, 13; Henry Middleton, *Economical Causes of Slavery in the United States and Obstacles to Abolition* (1857), at 9–10, 30–49.

[48] Ruffin, supra note 31, at 4, 23; Middleton, supra note 47, at 1, 4–6, 8, 10–19; David Christy, "Cotton Is King; or, Slavery in the Light of Political Economy" (1860), in *Cotton Is King, and Pro-Slavery Arguments* (Elliott, ed., 1860), at 33–34, 55–60, 215–226; Hammond, supra note 31, at 121–122.

[49] Hammond, supra note 31, at 122; Calhoun, supra note 47, at 13; Ruffin, supra note 31, at 3–5.

[50] Fitzhugh, *Sociology for the South*, supra note 31, at 34–37, 40–48; Fitzhugh, "Southern Thought—Its New and Important Manifestations," 23 *De Bow's Review* 337 (October 1857).

[51] Fitzhugh, *Sociology for the South, or the Failure of Free Society* (1854), in *Ante-Bellum* (Wish, ed., 1960), at 88–95; Ruffin, supra note 31, at 10, 15–20, 22; Middleton, supra note 47, at 8, 20–25, 27–29; Calhoun, supra note 47, at 13; Christy, supra note 48, at 215, 216; Josiah Nott, *Types of Mankind* (1857), at 49–50, 52–53, 298; Josiah Nott, *Indigenous Races of the Earth* (1857).

[52] Thornton Stringfellow, "The Bible Argument: or, Slavery in the Light of Divine Revelation," in *Cotton Is King*, supra note 48, at 461, 463–473, 478–490; Stringfellow, *Slavery: Its Origin, Nature, and History, Considered in the Light of Bible Teachings, Moral Justice, and Political Wisdom* (1861).

Holmes, was that *Uncle Tom's Cabin* would "awaken rancorous hatred and malignant jealousies between the citizens of the same republic, the fellow countrymen whose interest and happiness are linked with the perpetuity of a common union."[53] The very activity of defending slavery often grew from an impulse to make the institution comprehensible to those with whom Southerners shared economic interests and a social, cultural, intellectual, and religious heritage, but, most important, who were fellow members of a common polity.

There was a growing sense, however, that slavery was becoming more peculiar and less comprehensible to many outside the South. Consequently slavery's defenders were increasingly talking to themselves, preaching only to the converted.[54] Besides, the very need to defend slavery, even to discuss it in justificatory terms, must have seemed ominously significant to its proponents who had for so long sought to insulate it constitutionally by insisting that it go without saying.

V

By the 1850s slavery went anything but without saying. Beneath the formal compromises, national politics was beginning to unravel. The Whig Party was disintegrating. The Democratic Party was losing its broad geographical base as the party came increasingly under the sway of proslavery elements. New partisan movements—from Free Soilers to Barnburners, Constitutional Unionists, Southern Righters, Know-Nothings, the American Party, the North American Party, and the Liberty Party—were forming and dying with startling frequency. In some respects this activity signified a healthy democratic vigor, but it also pointed toward an emerging crisis for the constitutional order.

Disputes centered mainly on the territories and consistently implicated two issues: the character of territorial sovereignty and the status of slavery. As had been the case with the tariffs some thirty years earlier, the impetus for the debate was an issue that seemed on the surface to have little to do with slavery—the extension of a railroad to the Pacific.

Stephen Douglas coveted a route that would run through his state of Illinois, which meant it would probably also run through the Kansas Territory. But he faced two problems. First, he had to find a way of

[53] Holmes, supra note 45, at 101.

[54] There were exceptions. For example, Fitzhugh, who ratcheted a defense of slavery from a Marxist critique of industrial capitalism, was read fairly widely in the North and even traveled there. In addition, defenders such as Calhoun and Hammond, who were politicians in the national arena, often had audiences consisting of more than simply Southerners. But these were exceptions that proved the rule.

ameliorating resistance to the route from Southerners, who predictably favored a Southern route. Second, he had to find an acceptable standard for organizing the territory. His solution (partially his, at any rate) was enacted in 1854 as the Kansas-Nebraska Act. That Act embraced popular sovereignty as the standard for determining when territories would be admitted as states and expressly repealed the Missouri Compromise as "inconsistent with the principle of nonintervention by Congress with slavery in the States and Territories."[55]

The consequences, political and constitutional, were substantial. First, because the Act repealed a formula under which neither Kansas nor Nebraska could have been admitted except as free states, many opponents of slavery viewed it as a vehicle for extending slavery into *all* the territories. In fact adherents of popular sovereignty had supported it for a variety of reasons, most having nothing to do with the expansion of slavery. But if the equation of the Act (and Manifest Destiny) with slavery's expansion were exaggerated, it was not entirely unfounded.[56] It provoked a political upheaval among abolitionists and others who were worried about the expansion of slavery.[57]

The second consequence of the Kansas-Nebraska Act was to exacerbate tendencies that were already leading to the demise of the existing system of parties. By 1856 the Whigs had all but died,[58] and the Democrats, who in the early 1850s had been the only party that could genuinely claim a national constituency, suffered huge losses in the North while gaining an increasingly firm hold on the South. "Know Nothings"—anti-Catholic nativists who exploited fears that immigrants would undermine the position of "natives" in capitalism's market for labor—were making substantial inroads in the North. They eventually merged with the Republican Party, recently organized around a vaguely defined opposition to slavery.[59]

[55] Potter, supra note 6, at 145–167, has an excellent and detailed account of the adoption of the Act. See also Harold W. Hyman and William M. Wiecek, *Equal Justice under Law: Constitutional Development, 1835–1875* (1982), at 165.

[56] The fracas over the Ostend Manifesto and the potential seizure of Cuba lent credence to fears of imperial slavery. Potter, supra note 6, at 180; McPherson, supra note 22, at 108–109.

[57] Potter, supra note 6, at 167–176. On the heels of the adoption of the Kansas-Nebraska Act, Garrison delivered a speech at an Independence Day rally in Framingham, Massachusetts. After speaking calmly, almost quietly, he paused, held up a copy of the Fugitive Slave Act, and burned it. One by one he burned other documents, until he had only one left. Finally, he held it up for display, identified it as the Constitution, and burned it too. Walter M. Merrill, *Against Wind and Tide: A Biography of William Lloyd Garrison* (1963), at 267–268.

[58] McPherson, supra note 22, at 125–126.

[59] Potter, supra note 6, at 231–241; McPherson, supra note 22, at 170–201. The alli-

In the presidential election of 1856 two other parties—the American Party and the North Americans—nominated candidates for president. James Buchanan, the Democrat, won the election, but did not win a majority of the free states—the first time an elected president had failed to do so since 1828, the year of the tariff that precipitated the crisis over nullification.[60]

In his inaugural address Buchanan focused on the question of slavery in the territories. That issue, he said, did not present an ordinary political question but a fundamental problem that had engendered animosities and "geographical parties." Those forms of factionalism endangered slaveholders and threatened "the very existence of the Union." The solution was to apply the principle of popular sovereignty to the territories and to "leave the people thereof perfectly free to form and regulate their domestic institutions in their own way." The national government was obliged only to "secure to every resident inhabitant the free and independent expression of his opinion by his vote." Buchanan was unconcerned about when and how the people of a territory might decide to permit or prohibit slavery: by territorial legislature or by constitutional provision when petitioning for statehood. That issue was a minor one, he said, and besides was "a judicial question, which legitimately belongs to the Supreme Court of the United States, before whom it is now pending, and will, it is understood, be speedily and finally settled."[61] The Supreme Court, he suggested, must limit the Congress strictly to its expressly delegated powers.[62]

---

ance would have seemed incongruous only if one understood Republicanism to have been motivated by a strong moral aversion to slavery. In fact Republicans often displayed a curious combination of racism and xenophobia. Norton, supra note 4, at 224. Many abolitionists remained suspicious that Republicans' aim was simply to save the territories for settlement by "*white* men." Frederick Douglass, "The Danger of the Republican Movement," Speech before the First Nominating Convention of the Radical Abolition Party (May 28, 1856), in *Life and Writings*, supra note 33, vol. 5, at 386.

[60] Potter, supra note 6, at 241, 262, 265; McPherson, supra note 22, at 153–157.

[61] James Buchanan, "Inaugural Address" (March 4, 1857), in *The Works of James Buchanan*, vol. 10 (Moore, ed., 1910), at 105–110. His invocation of the Supreme Court was a veiled reference to the Court's review of *Dred Scott v. Sandford*. Having corresponded with Justices Catron and Grier and Chief Justice Taney about *Dred Scott*, Buchanan, by the time of his inauguration, knew something of what the Court's holding would be on at least one of the central issues of the case. See Don E. Fehrenbacher, *The Dred Scott Case: Its Significance in American Law and Politics* (1978), at 312–314.

[62] Buchanan, supra note 61, at 111. Although he would have applauded Buchanan's sympathy for slavery and his notion of a strictly limited national government, Calhoun had opposed popular sovereignty (in favor of a national right to own slaves) as a constitutional device for resolving disputes over the status of slavery in the territories. Moreover, he deeply distrusted the federal judiciary as the institutional enforcer of constitutional limits on the national government. On the latter, see Calhoun, "Address on the Relation

In Kansas popular sovereignty was not proving to be the panacea Buchanan had hoped it would be. Instead the territory was the scene of rigged elections and widespread violence. Two separate governments, each commanding its own army, claimed authority to govern. Drawing recruits from the local antislavery militia in Lawrence and christening them the "Army of the North," John Brown found five proslavery settlers living near Pottawatomie Creek and hacked them to death with broadswords. After three referenda (two marked by fraud), Kansans could not agree on a state constitution. In a territory where an overwhelming majority did not care a whit about slaves, slavery had become the most important wedge dividing the people.[63]

In Congress circumstances were only slightly less crazed. Senator Charles Sumner of Massachusetts, incensed over events in Kansas, spent two days in May 1856 delivering a vitriolic speech on the floor of the Senate. Preston Brooks, member of Congress from South Carolina and nephew of one of the senators Sumner had castigated, assumed responsibility for retribution. He walked onto the floor of the Senate and beat Sumner senseless with a walking cane. Radical Southerners rejoiced, while many moderate Northerners were convinced that proponents of slavery had gone mad.[64]

For both radical camps the political struggle over slavery and the territories was increasingly an all-or-nothing proposition. Proponents of slavery were becoming expansionist, even imperialist in their outlook.[65] Some radical opponents of slavery were growing more and more nationalist in their rhetoric about its abolition. Frederick Douglass, now a constitutionalist, advocated a Union in which slavery was destroyed. His language illustrated how easily the moral rhetoric of an abolitionist critique of the Constitution could be converted to the agenda of an antislavery constitutionalism:

> How can you form a more perfect Union with slavery? Only by abolishing the Free States, entirely. There is no such thing as a perfect Union while we have both Liberty and Slavery! They are as opposite as light and darkness—as Heaven and Hell; and there can never be a real Union formed between the two. The only union that can be formed between them, is a

Which the States and General Government Bear to Each Other," in *Works*, supra note 2, vol. 6, at 69–72.

[63] Potter, supra note 6, at 199–203, 291–327; McPherson, supra note 22, at 150–153, 162–168.

[64] McPherson, supra note 22, at 149–150.

[65] See, e.g., William W. Freehling, *The Road to Disunion: Secessionists at Bay, 1776–1854* (1990), at 22, 458.

union of struggle between them, for the death of one or the other. Liberty must either cut the throat of Slavery, or have its own cut by Slavery.[66]

Any middle ground capable of accommodating the radical camps on both sides of the constitutional divide was eroding rapidly. And increasing numbers of people were making their way into those camps.

The two sides were not mirrored opposites, however. For example, while slavery was the only political issue worth talking about for true believers among the radical abolitionists,[67] many Southerners, both radical and unionist, continued to search for a language that both expressed their growing insecurity and avoided any direct talk about slavery.

But the quarrel over Kansas suggested that the disjunction between North and South extended beyond differences between their respective radical camps. More broadly it was a function of a growing breach between Northern and Southern political cultures. Even for people who remained near the center or were willing to compromise on the manner in which slavery would exist in the Union, it was becoming more difficult to agree on a procedure or arrangement that would resolve differences over substantive values.

[66] Douglass, "The Danger of the Republican Movement," supra note 59, at 389.

[67] See, e.g., Wendell Phillips's account of a meeting between William Lloyd Garrison and Reverend Lyman Beecher: "The reply of [Beecher] was, 'Mr. Garrison, I have too many irons in the fire to put in another.' My friend [Garrison] said, 'Doctor, you had better take them all out and put this one in, if you mean well either to the religion or to the civil liberty of our country.'" Wendell Phillips, "Philosophy of the Abolition Movement," Speech to the Massachusetts Antislavery Society (January 27, 1853), in *Speeches, Lectures, and Letters* (1894), at 130.

CHAPTER FOUR

Interpretive Authority and Constitutional Division, Part II

I

In contrast with the passion and disarray in Congress and society, the courts typically were models of stability and reason. I wish to turn the discussion now to courts—particularly the Supreme Court. It may seem odd in our time that a book dealing with issues of constitutional interpretation and meaning has deferred for so long any systematic treatment of courts. Recall, for example, Ronald Dworkin's claim that problems of constitutional meaning are basically problems of principle, and problems of principle are distinguishable from problems of policy. The latter are not *constitutional* in any serious sense of the word. They are problems of politics, writ small. Their proper analytical mode is consequentialist, and their proper institutional forum is the legislature.[1]

On the other hand, constitutional problems—problems of principle—are not susceptible to treatment by consequentialist analysis, according to Dworkin. Fundamentally they are problems of right (and thus of duty). They are penetrable only by deontological method. Hence constitutional problems are not simply rational in character but exhibit a particular kind of rationality. The tasks of discerning and applying constitutional principle are genuinely heroic, requiring a Herculean capacity. Dworkin's prototypal hero, his Hercules, is the judge.[2]

But if chapters 2 and 3 have established anything, it is that judges were not the only actors on the constitutional stage in nineteenth-century America, at least where slavery was concerned. Other, lesser mortals—including members of Congress, citizens, and even noncitizens (in the case of Frederick Douglass)—actively participated in debates over questions of constitutional moment. Strangely they were not oblivious to constitutional principle, and they acted as if they were entitled to participate in constitutional discussion. Far from being the *only* constitutional actors in the nineteenth century with regard to slavery, courts

[1] Ronald Dworkin, *Taking Rights Seriously* (1977, 1978), at 81 et seq.

[2] Id., at 105–130.

were probably not even the most *important* constitutional actors of the time. In practice, interpretive authority was widely dispersed.

Nonetheless, institutional practices may well have demonstrated that there was more to Dworkin's claims than might first meet the eye. For whatever the way that *individuals*—as citizens, noncitizens, or members of Congress—might have talked about the Constitution, when Congress acted *as an institution*, it frequently did so in a peculiar way. It was peculiar, that is, when measured against the standard that constitutional judgment be principled, whether we think of principle as "integrity" in Dworkin's thick sense or as "coherence" in a somewhat thinner sense.[3] Congress acted by embracing a series of compromises that seemed as a group to rest on no common principle whatsoever, other than a common motive of defusing the explosive issues arising from slavery and territorial expansion. Chapter 3 offered explanations for this institutional tendency. But if the tendency were peculiar as a constitutional strategy, it was nonetheless pronounced and persistent.

Courts, on the other hand, were different. In saying this, of course, one must be humble in the face of diversity. For then as now, there were courts and there were Courts. There were state courts of various stripes and inclinations; there were lower federal courts; and there was the Supreme Court of the United States. It would take us beyond the scope of this study to survey comprehensively the positions of all these courts on questions pertaining to slavery, even were we to limit the inquiry strictly to constitutional questions. Instead this chapter focuses on the Supreme Court in order to exploit a comparison of the styles of Court and Congress as constitutional actors.

The Supreme Court's approach to constitutional problems was methodologically distinctive precisely because it exhibited a great deal of principled coherence or integrity. One reason the justices were able to pursue this approach was that their institution was autonomous from Congress and from other political actors. At times its autonomy seemed to border on insularity. Of course this appearance was in some ways deceiving, as the Court's autonomy has never amounted to complete independence. One could rehearse Hamilton's arguments in *The Federalist*, No. 78, on the various limits to the power of courts. But there were and are other limits to the Court's authority and independence, subtler than those Hamilton admitted.

For one thing, justices are almost always political actors before they

[3] Dworkin, *Law's Empire* (1986), at 176 et seq. In Dworkin's hands, "integrity" is similar but not identical to his earlier notion of "articulate consistency." See Dworkin, supra note 1, at 86–90. Articulate consistency is essentially consistency over time across cases. This is distinct from both internal coherence and consistency with fundamental principles of fairness and justice. Integrity embraces all three notions.

are appointed to the Court. In the mid-nineteenth century, for example, Roger Brooke Taney had had a long and distinguished political career before Andrew Jackson nominated him as Chief Justice to replace John Marshall in 1836. (Jackson had previously nominated Taney as Associate Justice, but the Senate rejected the nomination.) Although Taney had a deserved reputation as an antifederalist states' righter, as Jackson's Attorney General he presided over the nationalist repudiation of South Carolina's attempt to nullify the tariffs of 1828 and 1832. Then in 1833, as newly appointed Secretary of Treasury, Taney presided over Jackson's dismantling of the Second Bank of the United States. Among the other justices who sat when the Court decided *Dred Scott v. Sandford*, all but one had had substantial experience in national, state, or local politics before their appointments to the Court.[4] When a president, with the advice and consent of the Senate, appointed a member of the Court, he was appointing a person who typically had a modicum of political skill and a fairly refined pragmatic sense of the possibilities for, limits to, and implications of political action.

These considerations suggest another limitation on the Court's autonomy: Justices are nominated by presidents who have their own political agendas and who nominate with those agendas fully on their minds, if not on their lips. One can overstate the extent to which presidential motives constrain judicial action, for American history is replete with examples of justices who have disappointed their nominators. But it would be a mistake to underestimate either the ideological sensibility that often justifies an appointment (from the president's standpoint) or the sense of loyalty that pertains even among politicians. Of course the public lives of justices are frequently longer than those of the presidents who nominate them, but the habits engendered by ideological predisposition and reinforced by gratitude or loyalty can outlive the political conditions that generated an appointment.

Another constraint on the Court is Congress's tremendous authority over the federal judiciary. The Senate's power over confirmation and Congress's power to establish—and apparently to disestablish—federal courts affect indirectly the manner in which the Court's pronouncements are executed, as both powers can influence the identities of the very persons who serve as judges. Still indirectly, Congress controls the salary of justices, though Article III of the Constitution says that the salary cannot be diminished as long as the justice sits. More directly, Congress controls the jurisdiction of the Court. Although Justice Mar-

[4] *Oxford Companion to the History of the Supreme Court of the United States* (Hall, ed., 1992), at 116–117, 129–130, 211–212, 216–217, 349–350, 541–542, 583–584, 857–859, 920–921.

shall transformed this limitation into a judicial power in at least one case, for many less innovative justices the mere possibility that Congress might contract federal jurisdiction is an inchoate weapon that can inhibit novel or zealous judicial action. Finally, Congress has authority to impeach sitting justices, though, for the most part, experience has shown this to be a mere parchment power.[5]

Notwithstanding these limits on the Court's power, its autonomy is real. The crucial component of this autonomy, which Hamilton took pains to justify, was what we have come to know as lifetime tenure but which the Constitution calls tenure "during good Behavior." If institutional authority in republican governments resides somewhere in the balance between accountability and autonomy, the tenure of justices strikes the balance more strongly toward the latter where the Court is concerned. Consequently the Court is in many ways strategically insulated from some of the crasser predations and manipulations of other institutions (and of the people).

One factor that seems to animate this insulation—and is another source of the Court's autonomy—is the normative idea captured by the notion "rule of law." One conception of rule of law having rhetorical power in the United States holds, among other things, that when the ruler or state acts coercively (and perhaps noncoercively as well), it should act in a manner consistent with established rules and principles. According to this conception, rule of law is more than an idea, for it requires certain institutional arrangements for its realization. A component of those institutional arrangements is a judiciary partially independent of "politics." The judiciary must be independent from politics, the account might go, because courts are among the most visible and active institutions through which the state exercises coercive power. The judiciary's independence is designed to ensure that when the state acts coercively through courts it acts reflectively, with reason, consistently with the rules laid down, and always according to law. To the extent that the polity is committed to some notion of rule of law, its courts must be partially independent from other, political institutions.

Nor, as a source for judicial autonomy, should we overlook judicial review, the judicial power to tell other institutional actors what not to do or, more radically, what to do. This power did not originate with *Marbury v. Madison*,[6] of course, but it did find enduring if convoluted expression in that case. On Marshall's account, judicial review is an

[5] Constitution of the United States, Articles I and III. Concerning the congressional power to disestablish courts, see the Senate's debates over the repeal of the Judiciary Act of 1801, in *Annals of Congress*, 7th Cong., 1st Sess. (1802), at 27–183.

[6] 5 U.S. (1 Cranch) 137 (1803).

attempt to realize in institutionally enforceable terms the notion that the Constitution itself effectively binds even the state. It is an attempt to bring a form of rule of law to bear on the state through the Constitution. At its inception, judicial review may well have been a consequence of judicial autonomy and not a cause. In operation, however, it can reinforce the independence of the Court when used wisely. In the early nineteenth century, the Supreme Court used the power sparingly, especially against Congress. But if the power were exercised rarely, it was nonetheless present, lying about, in the words of Justice Jackson in a different context almost a century later, "like a loaded weapon."[7]

Even if one conceded the Supreme Court's autonomy, why did it adopt an approach so characterized by a norm of coherence and fidelity to principle? In *The Federalist*, No. 78, Hamilton had suggested a somewhat different question: How can we be sure that the Court will act consistently with rule of law? His answer rested mainly on the simultaneous weakness and autonomy of the institution, which we have already considered. But institutional weakness and autonomy do not adequately explain why the Court's approach to constitutional questions would differ so from Congress's. Hamilton may have sensed this, for he attempted to patch the hole with the following claim: The "integrity," "moderation," "knowledge," and "skill" of those chosen as justices would bind them to the rules laid down. Whatever we might think of these characteristics as political virtues, they have proven consistently weak where matters of state and power are involved. What more, if anything, might explain the differences between Court and Congress?

On one account, the difference lies in the nature of the judicial function. Simply, it is part of what courts, including the Supreme Court, do: they identify law, interpret it, apply it to facts presented in cases, and offer reasons for the result in a case. If the Court does not do these things, it is not doing what is required of judges under the popular American version of rule of law; therefore its action to that extent is illegitimate from the standpoint of the norms that attach to the enterprise of judging. As with the virtues of character and competence that Hamilton proposed, however, such norms might be weak. Judges' habits can be powerful constraints, but they cannot guarantee fidelity to reason or law. And what happens if a judge simply lacks the requisite habits? The powers of competing institutions can check the predilections of judges, but institutions frequently fail to employ their countervailing powers; even when they use them, they can be ineffective.

Perhaps, though, the marriage of judicial function to rule of law is more powerful than we might imagine. In *Marbury v. Madison*, Mar-

[7] *Korematsu v. United States*, 323 U.S. 214 (1944), Jackson, J., dissenting, at 246.

shall solemnized the wedding in the following syllogism: (1) It is the job of judges to "say what the law is" and to apply it in cases; (2) Unless it be an absurdity, which Marshall presumed it was not, the Constitution is law; (3) Therefore, the Court must apply the Constitution in cases that come before it.[8] (Marshall generated another syllogism to explain why the Constitution was *supreme* law, but that aspect of Marshall's argument is not relevant here.)

Part of the power of Marshall's syllogism resides in its simplicity, its public comprehensibility. Comprehensibility would not matter much but for the fact that the ideas expressed in the syllogism are fundamental to a description of the constitutional order and are partially constitutive of the order's authority. Those attributes matter, in turn, because they are built into expectations that people—"the people"—have about the character of the regime that claims constitutional authority and the behavior of certain actors who are part of that regime. Those expectations are important for two reasons. First, the regime itself rhetorically engenders or promotes them. Second, the authority of judicial action depends not simply on the fact that the actor who performs it holds a particular office but also in some manner on the comprehensibility and acceptability of the action itself among the various audiences of the court. This consideration is especially pertinent to the Supreme Court. Its audiences include not only the parties to the litigation at bar but also other institutions and even the people at large. If people do not care about or pay attention to what the Court does, the consequences of a departure from norms of rule of law are minimal. But when crucial members of an attentive audience withdraw their acceptance from the Court, the institutional costs can be substantial. In the worst cases, the Court's very authority can collapse.

In this way, then, the marriage of judicial function to a kind of rule of law is reinforced by the institutional interest of justices. If ideas alone can sometimes be weak, when they attach to self-interest they can acquire great power.

In this chapter I illustrate these themes through an examination of the Supreme Court's approach to certain problems pertaining to slavery. My claims, in part, are these: First, the manner in which the Court exercised constitutional judgment differed from that in which Congress did. Second, the difference between the two was basically that the Court's approach demonstrated a superior attachment to rationality or principle. Third, the rationality of judicial function was manifested in three ways. Justices' actions tended to be internally coherent. They were largely consistent with decisions over time, though sometimes intense

[8] *Marbury v. Madison*, supra note 6.

dispute arose over the content and direction of precedent within the Court. And they were grounded in one of the two "mythic" accounts of the constitutional founding: federalism and antifederalism. Fourth, however, the evolving logic of judicial decision was sometimes cloudy because of the incremental manner in which the justices received and decided cases. For one thing, the Court was (and is) constitutionally required to wait for cases to come to it before it could rule. For another, and for reasons of both prudence and principle, the Court usually confined itself to rules and principles that were essential to resolving the issues of the case at hand. But if the Court were acting incrementally, its method nonetheless differed from Congress's. Fifth, because of the murkiness of the trajectory of the Court's decisions, the substantive logic of prior decisions could lead to surprising results. Sixth, those results had consequences that threatened not only the authority of the Court but the survival of the political order. Seventh, however, those consequences were compatible with ideas and practices that followed from the notion that the Constitution is law.

This chapter departs in two respects from a focus on the Supreme Court. Section IV briefly considers cases from state courts and lower federal courts that illustrate the growing resistance to slavery in parts of the Northeast and the old Northwest. These disputes arose over the rendition of fugitive slaves. Section V takes up a battle between the Supreme Court of the United States and the courts of Wisconsin, also over the question of rendition. The constitutional significance of these cases has less to do with the scope and operation of Article IV's fugitive slave clause than with the realignment of federalism and antifederalism with respect to slavery and with the political and constitutional consequences of that realignment.

II

In the first fifty years after the constitutional founding, the Supreme Court considered a number of cases pertaining to slavery. Many of the cases involved criminal prosecutions or the forfeiture of sailing vessels under one or more acts of Congress prohibiting various aspects of the international slave trade.[9] But most of the cases addressed strictly ques-

[9] Act of March 22, 1794 (prohibiting the trading of slaves from the United States to foreign ports); Act of May 10, 1800 (amending the Act of 1794); Act of March 2, 1807 (prohibiting the importation of slaves into the United States after January 1, 1808); and Act of April 20, 1818 (amending the Act of 1807). The cases were *Adams v. Woods*, 2 Cranch 336 (1805); *United States v. Schooner Sally*, 2 Cranch 406 (1804); *Brigantine Amiable Lucy v. United States*, 6 Cranch 330 (1810); *Josefa Segunda*, 5 Wheat. 338

tions of state law. These cases typically involved manumissions[10] or other questions related to ownership,[11] but three concerned claims for damages for the loss of slaves or for fraud committed by an agent in the sale of slaves.[12] Aside from the cases related to the slave trade, only one implicated an issue of national law, though in the end the Court disavowed jurisdiction in the case, letting the decision of Missouri's Supreme Court stand.[13]

None of the decisions explicitly raised constitutional questions about the status of slavery. A small number did involve sojourners, that is, slaves who resided temporarily in a state, country, or territory that prohibited the importation of slaves, but who then returned to a domicile that permitted slavery.[14] This type of case would eventually become deeply significant because of the question it implied about conflicts of laws: Which law would determine the status of the sojourner—that of the slave state or the "free" state? Any resolution of the question would require a national rule, perhaps a constitutional one, but none of the cases concerning sojourners before 1840 grappled deeply with potential conflicts of laws.[15]

There were indications, however, that the Court might not be able to avoid the constitutional dimensions of problems pertaining to slavery much longer. One of the earliest intimations arose in a case decided not by the Supreme Court but by Justice Story, sitting as Circuit Judge:

(1820), companion cases at 10 Wheat. 312 (1825), and 3 Pet. 57 (1830); *The Mary Ann*, 8 Wheat. 380 (1823); *The Emily and the Caroline*, 9 Wheat. 381 (1824); *The Merino*, 9 Wheat. 391 (1824); *The St. Jago de Cuba*, 9 Wheat. 409 (1824); *The Antelope*, 23 U.S. (10 Wheat.) 66 (1825), companion cases at 11 Wheat. 413 (1826), and 12 Wheat. 546 (1827); *The Plattsburgh*, 10 Wheat. 133 (1825); *United States v. Gooding*, 12 Wheat. 460 (1827); *United States v. The Ship Garonne*, 11 Pet. 73 (1837).

[10] *Scott v. Negro London*, 3 Cranch 324 (1806); *Scott v. Negro Ben*, 6 Cranch 3 (1810); *Mima Queen v. Hepburn*, 7 Cranch 290 (1813); *Negress Sally Henry v. Ball*, 1 Wheat. 1 (1816); *Negro John Davis v. Wood*, 1 Wheat. 6 (1816); *Mason v. Matilda*, 12 Wheat. 590 (1827); *LeGrand v. Darnall*, 2 Pet. 664 (1829); *Lee v. Lee*, 8 Pet. 44 (1834); *M'Cutchen v. Marshall*, 8 Pet. 220 (1834); *Fenwick v. Chapman*, 9 Pet. 461 (1835); *Wallingsford v. Allen*, 10 Pet. 583 (1836).

[11] *Spiers v. Willison*, 4 Cranch 398 (1808); *Ramsay v. Lee*, 4 Cranch 401 (1808); *Brent v. Chapman*, 5 Cranch 358 (1809); *Auld v. Norwood*, 5 Cranch 361 (1809); *Wood v. Davis*, 7 Cranch 271 (1812); *Williamson v. Daniel*, 12 Wheat. 568 (1827).

[12] *Beverly v. Brooke*, 2 Wheat. 100 (1817); *Boyce v. Anderson*, 2 Pet. 150 (1829); *Owings v. Hull*, 9 Pet. 607 (1835).

[13] *Menard v. Aspasia*, 5 Pet. 505 (1831).

[14] *Negress Sally Henry*, supra note 10; *Lee v. Lee*, supra note 10; *United States v. The Ship Garonne*, supra note 9.

[15] For a wide-ranging account of problems of conflicting laws over slavery in the United States in the nineteenth century, see Paul Finkelman, *An Imperfect Union: Slavery, Federalism, and Comity* (1981).

United States v. La Jeune Eugenie.[16] The case was a diplomatic nightmare, involving the U.S. Navy's seizure of a French vessel that was flying a French flag, sailing off the coast of Africa, and headed for a French colony. The officer in charge of the U.S. ship claimed that the French vessel was engaged in the slave trade and therefore had violated laws of the United States and "the general law of nations."

Story deftly avoided applying acts of Congress to the case; but, as if anticipating Lysander Spooner, he held that the international slave trade was "repugnant to the great principles of Christian duty, the dictates of natural religion, the obligations of good faith and morality, and the eternal maxims of social justice." In short, it violated basic principles of natural law. Consequently, he said, it also violated the law of nations. A nation might establish a contrary policy through explicit positive law, but "[n]o nation has a right to infringe the law of nations so as thereby to produce an injury to another nation." Story said he was duty-bound as a judge in this case "to consider the trade an offence against the universal law of society." Indeed a "claim founded on . . . any . . . act, which in the general estimation of mankind, is held to be illegal or immoral, might, I presume, be rejected in any court on that ground alone." "[T]his doctrine is neither novel nor alarming[, for] it stands on principles of sound sense and general policy, and, above all, of moral justice."[17]

Perhaps the passion and directness of Story's opinion convinced abolitionists that courts might be excellent forums for a constitutional assault on the domestic institution of slavery. Whatever the stimulus might have been, in 1838 a committee of the New England Anti-Slavery Society suggested that the Society commit itself to testing the constitutionality of slavery by taking one or more cases to the U.S. Supreme Court.[18]

Notwithstanding the committee's optimism, there were hints before the 1830s that the Supreme Court would not be open to abolitionist arguments from natural law. In 1825 in *The Antelope*, Chief Justice Marshall wrote an opinion for the Court that starkly contrasted with Justice Story's approach. Like *La Jeune Eugenie*, *The Antelope* arose out of problems pertaining to the slave trade. Technically the Court's opinion spoke to the narrow evidentiary question of whether possession of slaves might count as proof of ownership, but Marshall's opinion, like Story's, swept beyond the narrow question to address the larger

[16] 26 Fed. Cas. 832 (D. Mass., 1822), at 846 (Story, sitting as Circuit Judge).

[17] Id., at 840, 842, 846, 847.

[18] For a survey of abolitionist efforts in the Supreme Court, see William M. Wiecek, "Slavery and Abolition before the United States Supreme Court, 1820–1860," 65 *J. Am. Hist.* 34 (1978), at 40.

issue of slavery's place in "higher law." Marshall conceded that the slave trade might sometimes be inconsistent with natural law, but he insisted that natural law did not govern judicial obligation. The law of nations was binding, he said, but the slave trade was perfectly compatible with that law. The trade was universally upheld by "[t]he Christian and civilized nations of the world" and was therefore unlawful only if specifically renounced in positive law by authoritative legislative action.[19]

The conflict between Story and Marshall suggested that a larger battle over the content of law and the character of judicial duty might be brewing within the Court. Two cases—*Menard v. Aspasia* and *The Amistad*—faintly intimated that the Court might be willing to embrace Story's approach and some of its abolitionist implications.

Menard[20] was an action by a woman named Aspasia for false imprisonment. Her mother had been a slave, born in the mid-eighteenth century in the Northwest Territory when it still belonged to the French. Virginia eventually acquired that part of the Territory by conquest and later ceded it to the United States. Sometime after 1787, the year Congress adopted the Northwest Ordinance, Aspasia was born. She was raised there in bondage until 1821, when Menard bought her and moved her to Missouri. She then sued, claiming she was free under the Northwest Ordinance.[21]

Menard argued that she was still a slave. The subtle details of his position are not important, but the gist of his argument was this: In 1818 Congress admitted Illinois into the Union "on an equal footing with the original States in all respects whatever." Although the Constitution of the new state incorporated Article VI of the Northwest Ordinance, which prohibited slavery in the Territory, Menard claimed that the Ordinance applied only prospectively. It could not extinguish vested rights to property. Thus Aspasia's mother remained a slave even after the Ordinance, and so Aspasia was a slave because the status of offspring followed the condition of the mother. The logical corollary of Menard's claim was that neither the Ordinance nor state law could extinguish vested rights in property, including slaves.[22]

The Supreme Court of Missouri disagreed; because Aspasia was free in the Territory and the State of Illinois, the Court held, she carried that status with her into Missouri, even though Missouri was a slave state. On a writ of error, the Supreme Court of the United States, through Justice M'Lean, held that the Court lacked jurisdiction because the case

[19] *The Antelope*, 10 Wheat. 66 (1825), at 114–115, 120–122, 124–125.

[20] *Menard v. Aspasia*, supra note 13.

[21] Id., at 511–512.

[22] Id., at 512–513.

did not raise a question under the Constitution, treaties, or statutes of the United States. Had the courts of Missouri ruled *against* Aspasia, he said, then there would have been a live federal question. Implicit in these claims were two notions, both derived from Story's theory. First, title to slaves was strictly a matter of local law. Second, liberty was a fundamental national value, binding on the nation's courts and implicit in the Supreme Court's jurisdictional authority.[23]

The Amistad, decided in 1841, concerned the status of "cargo"—forty-nine blacks being carried from one Cuban port to another—who rose up, killed the captain, seized the ship, and made their way to Long Island. The United States and two Cubans prosecuted a libel action seeking to have the mutineers turned over to the Cubans as slaves. The blacks claimed that they were not slaves but had been kidnaped in Africa. As in *The Antelope*, the basic issue was narrowly evidentiary: Could the blacks attempt to prove that papers documenting the ownership of slaves were fraudulent? Justice Story, writing for the Court, held that they could, but, taking a swipe at Marshall, he made a fleeting nod to "eternal principles of justice."[24]

In the wake of *La Jeune Eugenie*, *Menard*, and *The Amistad*, abolitionists may well have thought they were about to witness the birth of a new *nomos* of antislavery constitutionalism, sanctioned and enforced by the nation's highest legal tribunal. But *The Amistad* would be the last unambiguous legal triumph for abolitionists in federal courts for more than twenty years. Only one year later, Justice Story himself would unwittingly preside over the abortion of antislavery constitutionalism from the jurisprudence of the Supreme Court. His instrument would be a case involving a problem, that of fugitive slaves, that would become an increasing irritant in the Court. It was not that the polity as a whole was deeply concerned about fugitives, though certain individuals in parts of the polity were. Fugitives troubled the polity because the cases through which they came to the Court pitted state against state and states against the nation.[25] The doctrines laid down in these cases would pave

[23] Id., at 514–517.

[24] *United States v. Libelants and Claimants of the Schooner Amistad*, 40 U.S. (15 Pet.) 518 (1841), at 587–597.

[25] The complete list of cases involving fugitive slaves is as follows: *Prigg v. Pennsylvania*, 41 U.S. (16 Pet.) 539 (1842); *Jones v. Van Zandt*, 46 U.S. (5 How.) 215 (1847); *Strader v. Graham*, 10 How. 82 (1851); *Norris v. Crocker*, 13 How. 429 (1851); *Moore v. Illinois*, 14 How. 13 (1852); *Ableman v. Booth*, 21 How. 506 (1859). After the 1830s the Court's cases concerning the slave trade slowed to a trickle and then stopped: *United States v. Morris*, 14 Pet. 464 (1840); *The Amistad*, supra note 24. Between 1840 and 1860 the great majority of the Court's cases involving slavery continued to implicate questions of state law: *Groves v. Slaughter*, 15 Pet. 449 (1841); *Williams v. Ash*, 1 How. 1 (1843); *Rhodes v. Bell*, 2 How. 397 (1844); *Adams v. Roberts*, 2 How. 486 (1844); *Miller v. Herbert*, 5 How. 72 (1847); *Rowan*

the way for *Dred Scott v. Sandford*, a case involving not a fugitive but a sojourner. In their own way, then, fugitive slaves helped precipitate the failure of the order.

III

Prigg v. Commonwealth of Pennsylvania involved a slaveholder's remedies in retrieving a fugitive slave from a free state.[26] Margaret Morgan had been a slave in Maryland. She escaped to Pennsylvania in 1832. Five years later her owner appointed Edward Prigg to apprehend her and carry her back to Maryland. Prigg found Morgan and prevailed upon a state magistrate in Pennsylvania to issue a warrant for her arrest; but, when a state constable arrested her and brought her before the magistrate, the latter refused to take further cognizance of the case. Prigg then seized Morgan and her children, one of whom had been born in Pennsylvania, and took them back to her owner in Maryland.[27] For Prigg, however, this was not the end of the story. Pennsylvania had enacted a "personal liberty law" making it a crime to take "any negro or mulatto," either "by force and violence . . . [or] by fraud or false pretenses," from Pennsylvania with the intention of delivering that person into slavery. For taking Morgan to Maryland, Prigg was indicted and convicted of violating the statute.[28]

He appealed to the Supreme Court, where John Marshall no longer sat but Joseph Story remained. Sensing an opportunity, Story wrote the opinion of the Court, but the Court was deeply divided. (There were seven separate opinions in *Prigg.*) Story renewed his claim that slavery was strictly a creature of local (positive) law. As precedent, he cited *Somerset v. Stewart*,[29] an eighteenth-century English case that addressed the circumstances under which a slaveholder could legally recover a slave who had fled to another country. Lord Chief Justice Mansfield had

---

v. Runnels, 5 How. 134 (1847); *Simms v. Hundley*, 6 How. 1 (1848); *Harris v. Runnels*, 12 How. 79 (1851); *Bennett v. Butterworth*, 12 How. 367 (1851); *Amis v. Myers*, 16 How. 492 (1853); *Wanzer v. Bennett*, 17 How. 584 (1854); *Vigel v. Naylor*, 24 How. 175 (1860). Most of the cases that did not involve fugitives were routine. One that was not was *Dred Scott v. Sandford*, 60 U.S. (19 How.) 393 (1857).

[26] 16 Pet. 539 (1842).

[27] Id., at 608–609.

[28] Id., at 608–609. On the nascence of personal liberty laws, see William M. Wiecek, *The Sources of Antislavery Constitutionalism in America, 1760–1848* (1977), at 150, 156–159; Thomas D. Morris, *Free Men All: The Personal Liberty Laws of the North, 1780–1861* (1974).

[29] *Somerset v. Stewart*, 98 English Reports 499 (1772), cited in *Prigg v. Commonwealth of Pennsylvania*, supra note 26, at 611–612. For an excellent discussion of the holding and doctrinal implications of *Somerset*, see Wiecek, supra note 28, at 20–39.

held in *Somerset* that the question of the status of international fugitive slaves was to be resolved by the law of the forum (the place to which the slave fled), not by the law of the slave's domicile (the place from which the slave fled). Hence, if the forum jurisdiction had no positive law supporting slavery, the slaveholder could not legally recover the (former) slave. Viewed through the lens of *Somerset*, *Prigg* would have simply represented a problem of comity. Because Pennsylvania did not recognize by positive law the institution of slavery, Morgan would have been considered free. Pennsylvania, then, presumably could have protected her against forcible detention and her return to a slave state.

Two considerations, one constitutional and one statutory, gave the status of fugitive slaves in the United States a national dimension: the fugitive slave clause in Article IV and the Fugitive Slave Act of 1793. Regarding the former, Story had this to say:

> Historically, it is well known that the object of this clause was to secure to the citizens of the slaveholding States the complete right and title of ownership in their slaves, as property, in every State in the Union into which they might escape from the State where they were held in servitude. The full recognition of this right and title was indispensable to the security of this species of property in all the slaveholding States; and, indeed, was so vital to the preservation of their domestic interests and institutions, that it cannot be doubted that it constituted a fundamental article, without the adoption of which the Union could not have been formed.[30]

This "fundamental article" authorized every slaveholder through self-help "to seize and recapture his slave, whenever he can do it without any breach of the peace or any illegal violence."[31]

But self-help might not be sufficient to recapture a runaway slave. Consequently the Constitution did not stop "at the mere recognition of the right," for it also implied the "means by which [the right] might be . . . enforced in cases where it did not execute itself." Hence the Fugitive Slave Act, which guaranteed the services of the courts of the United States in aid of rendition. By presenting proof of ownership to the courts, the owner could remove the slave with the help of federal officers. The Act also imposed a civil penalty on anyone who might "obstruct or hinder" the owner in seizing or removing the fugitive.[32]

National authority, said Story, was exclusive. When Congress adopted the Fugitive Slave Act, it preempted state action, even state action that

[30] *Prigg v. Commonwealth of Pennsylvania*, supra note 26, at 611.

[31] Actually, there was some disagreement over the source of the remedy. Story claimed that self-help was simply a common-law remedy attendant to the existence of a legal right in property of any sort. Taney, however, argued that the source of the remedy was constitutional, located textually in Article IV's fugitive slave clause. Id., at 613, 626.

[32] Id., at 613–618.

aimed at supporting the national statute. Such a result was supported not only by the fundamentality of the fugitive slave clause but also by the supremacy clause of Article VI. On this issue Story maintained only a plurality, as three concurring justices argued that states through legislation might support, but not hinder, the recovery of fugitive slaves. In fact one of the three, Chief Justice Taney, argued that states were *obliged* to assist in the recovery of fugitives.[33] But if Taney and his two colleagues disagreed with Story's claim about preemption, they did not dispute Story's bottom line. The right to recover fugitive slaves, Story emphasized, was "a new and positive right, independent of comity, confined to no territorial limits, and bounded by no State institutions or policy." Article IV's "true design was to guard against the doctrines and principles prevalent in the non-slaveholding States, by preventing them from intermeddling with, or obstructing, or abolishing the rights of the owners of slaves." Its method was a uniform national policy.[34] Thus the Fugitive Slave Act of 1793 was constitutional and Pennsylvania's personal liberty law was not.

Justice M'Lean, who had spoken for the Court in *Menard*, dissented in *Prigg*. Despite Story's nominal adherence to *Somerset*, his dictum that the states need not enforce the Fugitive Slave Act, and his insistence that his opinion in *Prigg* was a "triumph of freedom," it was not surprising that antislavery constitutionalists took little solace in the opinion.[35]

Nevertheless antislavery constitutionalists continued to press constitutional claims in the courts. Salmon P. Chase, an Ohio attorney strongly opposed to slavery, chose *Jones v. Van Zandt* as a vehicle for pressing another broad assault on the Fugitive Slave Act of 1793.[36] Jones, a slaveholder in Kentucky, had sued Van Zandt under the Act for harboring or concealing fugitives from labor. Chase, representing Van Zandt, tried to resurrect and extend M'Lean's opinion in *Menard*. He argued that the Act was unconstitutional, that it violated the Northwest Ordinance of 1787, and that it was incompatible with the requirements of natural right.

The Supreme Court, through Justice Woodbury (who had replaced

[33] Id., at 627, 634, 656.

[34] Id., at 611, 623, 624.

[35] William W. Story, ed., *Life and Letters of Joseph Story*, vol. 2 (1851), at 392. In his detailed analysis and critique of Story's opinion in *Prigg*, Paul Finkelman says the opinion was "an extreme proslavery opinion" whose proslavery implications Story intended and actively supported. Finkelman, "Story Telling in the Supreme Court: Prigg v. Pennsylvania and Justice Joseph Story's Judicial Nationalism," 1994 *Sup. Ct. Rev.* 247 (1994). I suspect the evidence on both points is ambiguous, but clearly the *logic* of *Prigg* was both nationalist and potentially proslavery, as *Dred Scott v. Sandford* would demonstrate fifteen years later.

[36] 5 How. 215 (1847).

Story), dismissed with dispatch every one of Chase's claims. The constitutionality of the Fugitive Slave Act had been resolved correctly, said Woodbury, in *Prigg*. The Northwest Ordinance similarly did not bar the recovery of fugitives or the imposition of penalties. Article VI of the Northwest Ordinance implied that slaveholders in states subsequently admitted to the Union—in those that were not "original states"—could not enforce a right to reclaim slaves who fled to the Northwest Territory. The fugitive slave clause of Article IV of the Constitution contained similar language. Neither provision was ever interpreted literally, however, and in *Van Zandt* the Court held that the territories were obliged to follow national rules concerning the disposition and status of fugitive slaves, from wherever they fled.[37] Finally, the Court summarily rejected the contention that it was bound by natural right. The institution of slavery "is a political question, settled by each State for itself; and the federal power over it is limited and regulated by the people of the States in the Constitution itself, as one of its sacred compromises."[38] Though Woodbury rhetorically embraced both nationalism and localism, it was not clear the two could stand together, at least not as Woodbury held them on this terrain.

Prigg and *Van Zandt* clearly boded ill for fugitive slaves. But what principles might apply in a case where the slaves were technically not fugitives? *Strader v. Graham*[39] presented such a case in 1851. Graham, a slaveholder in Kentucky, regularly hired out two of his slaves to perform as minstrels in Ohio. On one trip the slaves boarded a steamship in Louisville, as they had done several times before, but this time, on arriving in Cincinnati, they fled to Canada. The owner was never able to recover them because, under *Somerset*, the slaves became free once they entered Canada, where slavery was illegal. Graham sued the owners and captain of the steamship in state court under a Kentucky statute that rendered the owners and operators of such ships liable to a slaveholder for damages arising from the loss of a slave. Graham won at trial and in the Kentucky Supreme Court, so the defendants ratcheted up a federal claim to justify invoking the jurisdiction of the U.S. Supreme Court. They argued that because the slaves had gone to Ohio at the instance of the owner, they were not fugitives subject to the "fundamental article"; therefore the principles of *Somerset* ought to apply.[40]

Taney, who may have morally opposed slavery (he freed his own slaves), wrote for the Court. Although localist in tenor, his opinion inti-

[37] Id., at 229–231.

[38] Id., at 231.

[39] 10 How. 82 (1851).

[40] Id., at 83–93.

mated a nationalist doctrinal lever that turned *Somerset* completely on its head. "There is nothing in the Constitution of the United States," he wrote, "that can in any degree control the law of Kentucky upon this subject. . . . It was exclusively in the power of Kentucky to determine for itself whether their [the slaves'] employment in another State should or should not make them free on their return." Thus the Supreme Court was without jurisdiction in the case.

Nor did the Northwest Ordinance's prohibition of slavery give the law of Ohio special force in this case. Congress, said Taney, "could not restrict the power of States within their respective territories; nor in any manner interfere with their laws and institutions; nor give this court any control over them." Thus the Ordinance ceased to have force as each state carved from the territories was admitted to the Union. To hold otherwise would place Ohio and the rest of the states drawn from the Northwest Territories "in an inferior condition as compared with the other States, and subject their domestic institutions and municipal regulations to the constant supervision and control of this court." The Ordinance, on Taney's terms, was incompatible with the legitimate expectations of settlers in the territories. People migrated into the territories "upon the faith that . . . [the Constitution's] protection and benefits would be extended to them, and that they would . . . be admitted into the Union upon an equal footing with the old States."[41]

Had there been any doubt before, it was clear after *Strader* that the abolitionist promise of M'Lean's dicta in *Menard v. Aspasia* was either dead or mortally wounded. Despite *Strader's* rhetoric of localism and "judicial restraint," it was beginning to appear that a majority on the Court was prepared to apply localism and jurisdictional limits only in the service of a deeper principle: the protection of slavery. The gloss that *Moore v. Illinois* added to *Prigg* in 1852—that states had concurrent power with Congress to regulate the recovery of fugitive slaves as long as they *protected* property in slaves—reinforced a tendency toward nationalizing the right to own slaves.[42] The law of slave states had begun to take on an extraterritorial force independent of the sanction of the fugitive slave acts. Even in a case that one might have expected to be resolved by principles of *Somerset* or of competition, Taney enforced the law of a slave state as primary.[43]

[41] Id., at 93–97.

[42] *Moore v. Illinois*, 14 How. 13 (1852), at 19.

[43] Article IV's full faith and credit clause was a weak vehicle for resolving disputes over conflicts of laws, for it provided no substantive guidance concerning which law to apply ceteris paribus. The privileges and immunities clause was a potential vehicle for achieving substantive direction in cases of conflict, but questions about who had what privileges made its application problematic. On these and other questions related to comity in state and federal courts in the antebellum years, see Paul Finkelman, supra note 15.

IV

Given the nationalist trajectory of the Court's decisions, it should not have been surprising that state and local officials—even judges—in the North were increasingly called on to help render fugitive slaves to their masters. That alone was worrisome to abolitionists like Wendell Phillips and Henry David Thoreau. But the fact that documentation supporting the relationship between master and slave was often thin, sometimes fraudulent, only intensified the concern.[44] The surrender of Thomas Sims in 1851 and the rendition of Anthony Burns in 1854 were only two of the more prominent instances involving the rendition of fugitives. Both incidents occurred in Massachusetts and both required the participation of state judges.[45] The incidents raised a number of issues that folded neatly into a practical constitutional question for abolitionists: How could "conscientious" Northerners and Northern states remain committed to Union while simultaneously avoiding complicity in slavery?

Phillips's twofold answer revealed his gradual adoption of an antislavery constitutionalist approach and signaled a move toward a localist strategy for resisting slavery. First, he retreated from the position that slavery should be abolished immediately, arguing that "[t]he cause of three millions of slaves, the destruction of a great national institution, must proceed slowly; and, like every other change in public sentiment, we must wait patiently for it."[46]

Second, however, officials and citizens should resist without delay the return of fugitives to bondage. But how and by what authority should they do so? In a speech before a committee of the Massachusetts legislature, Phillips argued that Judge Loring, who had issued a warrant for the arrest and return of Anthony Burns, should be removed from the bench. Phillips's justification evoked shades of Calhoun's theories of state sovereignty and nullification. In rendering Burns, Judge Loring "acted in defiance of the solemn convictions and settled purposes of Massachusetts." Those convictions were partially expressed in a state statute, adopted in 1843, prohibiting state judges from granting certificates to render fugitives under the Fugitive Slave Act of 1793. That statute was binding, said Phillips, notwithstanding the Supreme Court's

[44] Kenneth M. Stampp, *The Peculiar Institution: Slavery in the Ante-Bellum South* (1956), at 74, 94, 258.

[45] See Harold M. Hyman and William M. Wiecek, *Equal Justice under Law: Constitutional Development, 1835–1875* (1982), at 153–155, for a discussion of Sims, Burns, and other cases involving the rendition of fugitive slaves. See also *Thomas Sims's Case*, 61 Mass. (7 Cush.) 285 (1851).

[46] Wendell Phillips, "Sims's Anniversary," Speech at the Melodeon (April 12, 1852), in *Speeches, Lectures, and Letters* (1894), at 78.

later decision in *Moore v. Illinois*. Further, Congress's adoption in 1850 of a new fugitive slave act that greatly restricted procedural protections available to fugitive slaves was of no effect in Massachusetts, for a resolution approved by the legislature and signed by the governor had nullified (before the fact) the Fugitive Slave Act of 1850:

> *Resolved*, That . . . we hold it to be the duty of [Congress] to pass such laws only in regard thereto as will be sustained by the public sentiment of the Free States, where such laws are to be enforced, and which shall especially secure to all persons, whose surrender may be claimed as having escaped from labor and service in other States, the right of having the validity of such claim determined by a jury in the State where such claim is made.
>
> *Resolved*, That the people of Massachusetts, in the maintenance of these their well-known and invincible principles, expect that their officers and representatives will adhere to them at all times, on all occasions, and under all circumstances.[47]

Phillips mocked Loring's contention that he owed a superior obligation to the Constitution of the United States (presumably as interpreted by the Supreme Court). If Loring sincerely believed himself obliged as a judge to recover fugitive slaves, said Phillips, he should recuse himself from the case or resign his office.[48]

With Phillips, Thoreau agreed that any officer who was incapable of doing justice in his official capacity should "resign his office, and get his living innocently." But he was persistently pessimistic about the prospects of internal reform through politics or law. Unlike Phillips, Thoreau continued to rely not on state law or a constitutional theory of state sovereignty but on nature and a theologically grounded higher law as the sources for civic duty. Consider the following passages from his essay "Slavery in Massachusetts":

> [E]ach inhabitant of the State [should] dissolve his union with [the state], as long as she delays to do her duty.[49]

> The law will never make men free; it is men who have got to make the law free. They are lovers of law and order who observe the [higher] law when government breaks it. . . . Whoever can discern truth has received his com-

[47] Phillips, "Removal of Judge Loring," Address to the Massachusetts Legislature's Committee on Federal Relations (February 20, 1855), in *Speeches*, supra note 46, at 182–183.

[48] Id., at 201–202.

[49] Thoreau, "Slavery in Massachusetts" (1854), in *Walden and Other Writings by Henry David Thoreau* (Howarth, ed., 1981), at 673–675.

mission from a higher source than the chiefest justice in the world who can discern only law. He finds himself judge of the judge.[50]

Show me a free state, and a court truly of justice, and I will fight for them if need be.[51]

In the United States and Massachusetts of the mid-1850s, however, Thoreau's brooding transcendentalism judged Constitution, laws, and demos all to be corrupt and contemptible.

Thoreau's frustrations were understandable. The wheels of politics often grind slowly, especially in the eyes of people of strong moral conviction. Even when the engine of change in political institutions and culture is running, however, law often serves as a brake on change. For although law is partly a function of politics and often reflects changes in political institutions and culture, it also plays a distinctly conservative role. One reason is that it is the very character and function of law, if not to nail down solidly certain aspects of human relations, then at least to constrain those relations and mark the boundaries within which they may occur. Another reason relates to the character of legal culture, especially the cultures of judges and the legal profession. As often as not, lawyers and judges act as conservators of existing arrangements. Tocqueville was tempted to describe the role as constitutional, in the sense that the legal aristocracy—employing the magic of legal method and motivated partly by a desire to protect its exalted place in society—helps promote an orderliness and reflection that keep democratic institutions from destroying both themselves and the constitutional order.[52]

But whatever the autonomy of law from politics, there is an institutional vehicle for importing political and moral commitments into law and thus opening it to the winds of political and social change. That vehicle is the jury.[53] Most personal liberty laws implicitly acknowledged the political content of jury verdicts by purporting to guarantee to captured fugitives a trial by jury as a condition of their return to slavery. Phillips argued that a jury in Massachusetts would never return a fugitive to slavery but even if one rendered such a verdict, "a Governor . . . would never dare to sign the warrant, until he had secured passage on board a Cunnard steamer."[54] Phillips may have been mortgaging hope to buy off his fear, but he seems at least to have accurately identified a

[50] Id., at 669.

[51] Id., at 676.

[52] Alexis de Tocqueville, *Democracy in America*, vol 1, part 2, ch. 8 (Meyer, ed., 1969), at 263–270.

[53] Of course juries can also end up reinforcing political and social stasis, not to mention unappealing prejudice.

[54] Phillips, "Sims Anniversary," supra note 46, at 81.

trend (whatever its cause) in the split between Northern and Southern legal cultures.

In 1851 the federal government went so far as to prosecute a white citizen of Pennsylvania for treason for helping to prevent the recapture of a fugitive slave. The trial judge noted that organized Northern resistance to enforcement of the fugitive slave acts would amount to a practical nullification not only of the acts but of the Constitution itself: "And . . . if individuals or state legislatures in the North can succeed in thwarting and obstructing the execution of this article of our confederation, and the rights guaranteed to the South thereby, they have no right to complain if the people of the South should treat the constitution as virtually annulled by the consent of the North, and seek secession from any alliance with open and avowed covenant breakers." The judge instructed the jury that Hanway was probably guilty of aggravated riot and murder; however, because there was no evidence that he was a member of an abolitionist society—such societies advocated "a traitorous resistance" to the execution of the fugitive slave acts and "promulgate[d] doctrines subversive of all morality and all government"—the court directed that he was not guilty of treason. The jury returned a verdict of not guilty.[55]

By 1854 the national government abandoned attempts to prosecute those who had tried to prevent the capture of Anthony Burns who had fled slavery in Virginia—this time the prosecution would have been not for treason but for violating the fugitive slave acts—because of what it viewed as the impossibility of getting a jury to convict in Massachusetts. In contrast, in the case of the *Wanderer* in 1858, juries in Georgia acquitted all defendants accused of violating the prohibition against the slave trade. Some said the acquittals were in deliberate defiance of the evidence. To many observers these cases were elements of a game of tit-for-tat in which law, through juries, had become indistinguishable from politics.[56]

Juries aside, there were other episodes of Northern resistance to the enforcement of fugitive slave laws throughout the 1850s, episodes that may have supplied further evidence of a growing disjunction between the constitutional cultures of North and South. In one case from Indiana arising under pre-1850 law, a slaveholder was unable to recover his slave through self-help remedies approved under *Prigg* because of the

[55] *United States v. Hanway*, 26 Fed. Cas. 105 (No. 15,299) (E.D. Pa., 1851), at 122–123, 124, 128–129.

[56] James M. McPherson, *Battle Cry of Freedom: The Civil War Era* (1988), at 120, 103.

resistance of a mob, a local sheriff, and a county judge.[57] More frequently after the adoption of the Fugitive Slave Act of 1850, state officials, often armed with warrants from state judges and aided by white citizens and free blacks, overtly and sometimes violently challenged federal officers who, with warrants from U.S. District Courts, were attempting to capture fugitives.[58] In these latter cases state officials actually jailed federal marshals. One marshal was jailed three times, another twice. In order to secure their release, the marshals had to petition federal courts under a special federal statutory procedure for habeas corpus, which ironically had been adopted to reinforce federal authority in the crisis over South Carolina's attempt to nullify the tariffs.

If these instances of official and civic resistance to the recovery of fugitive slaves were philosophical descendants of Thoreau's transcendentalism, they also bore an uncanny resemblance to John C. Calhoun's constitutional theories. And the federal judges who were being called on to confront officials and judges in Pennsylvania and Ohio did not flinch at describing the resistance as interposition and nullification. Not surprisingly federal judges univocally insisted on obedience to the laws of the nation. "Any other principle must lead to anarchy in its worst form, and result in the speedy overthrow of our institutions." It would undermine not simply national authority, they said, but law itself.[59]

Judge Leavitt in *Sifford* acknowledged "a deep-seated hostility to the fugitive-slave act of 1850 throughout most of the free states. I am also aware that there is among the people of Ohio an almost unanimous sentiment in opposition to slavery." Citizens, he said, taking aim at Thoreau, might express disapproval of laws, but they were not permitted to "resist the execution of a law" simply because they considered it "unjust or inexpedient." The consequence of resistance "would be, that every man, being a law unto himself, and acting under some vague notion of a higher law, would choose for himself what laws he would obey." He warned that such rampant individualism would "undermine the foundations of the social fabric. . . . As an unavoidable sequence, the bands of that union, which has been so potent for good in our country, so instrumental in its rapid advance to prosperity and great-

[57] *Norris v. Newton*, 18 Fed. Cas. 322 (No. 10,307) (D. Ind., 1850). The owner was able to procure an award of damages in a civil suit under the Fugitive Slave Act of 1793 against three members of the mob.

[58] *Ex Parte Jenkins et al.* (three cases), 13 Fed. Cas. 445 (No. 7,259) (E.D. Pa., 1853); *Ex Parte Robinson* [Robinson I], 20 Fed. Cas. 969 (No. 11,935) (S.D. Ohio, 1855); *Ex Parte Robinson* [Robinson II], 20 Fed. Cas. 965 (No. 11,934) (S.D. Ohio, 1856); *Ex Parte Sifford*, 22 Fed. Cas. 105 (No. 12,848) (S.D. Ohio, 1857).

[59] Robinson II, supra note 58, at 969.

ness, would be dissolved. In this event, a future would be presented which none could contemplate without the deepest horror."[60]

V

Another set of cases, commenced in Wisconsin, highlighted the curious strength of coupling antislavery constitutionalism with a theory of states' rights. These cases also indicated that decisions of federal courts did not consistently enjoy a presumption of legitimacy. Predictably the cases arose out of attempts to recover a fugitive slave. A slave escaped from Missouri to Wisconsin. Pursuant to the Fugitive Slave Act of 1850, the owner procured the services of a deputy U.S. marshal to recover the slave. But a state judge in Wisconsin issued a writ of habeas corpus ordering the deputy marshal to produce the slave. The officer ignored the writ; within hours, however, a mob gathered, forced its way into the jail, and liberated the slave.[61]

The owner was then arrested under a warrant issued by a Wisconsin judge for assault and battery against the slave. The owner petitioned the federal court for the District of Wisconsin for a writ of habeas corpus. After a hearing, that court ordered him released, holding that "[t]he law under which the [slave] was apprehended, is a law of the United States, adopted in pursuance of the constitution, and must be enforced."[62]

Next the U.S. marshal for Wisconsin arrested Sherman Booth, a newspaper editor who had been in the mob that liberated the slave, for violating the Fugitive Slave Act of 1850 by "assisting and abetting" the slave in escaping from governmental custody. Booth filed a petition, not in a federal court but with Justice Smith of the Wisconsin Supreme Court, for a writ of habeas corpus. He argued, among other things, that his arrest was improper because the Fugitive Slave Act of 1850 was unconstitutional. Justice Smith ordered the marshal to produce Booth for a hearing. The marshal, unlike his deputy before him, did not ignore the writ. After a hearing Smith ordered Booth released.[63]

Smith's opinion rested partly on the fact that the warrant had been issued by a U.S. commissioner, not a judge who could trace his authority to Article III of the Constitution. "[T]he States will never submit to the assumption, that United States commissioners have the power to hear and determine upon the rights and liberties of their citizens, and

[60] *Ex Parte Sifford*, supra note 58, at 112.

[61] *United States ex rel. Garland v. Morris*, 26 Fed. Cas. 1,318 (No. 15,811) (D. Wis., 1854).

[62] Id., at 1318–1319.

[63] *In re Booth*, 3 Wis. 1 (1854), at 2–6.

issue process to enforce their adjudications" unchecked by the power of state courts. Ultimately, said Smith, there was no conflict between state and federal judicial authority in this case because the warrant was not issued by a federal judge.[64]

But the facile assertion that commissioners were not judges was insufficient. It was weak not only because a state court was setting itself up against a federal judicial officer of some authority, but also because it was setting itself up as arbiter of the constitutionality of a federal statute concerning a matter which the U.S. Supreme Court in *Prigg* had declared to be exclusively within federal control. Consequently Smith needed to supply a theory of the character and distribution of constitutional authority between states and the nation.

An officer of a state, said Smith, just as an officer of the United States, took an oath to support the Constitution of the United States. But the former, unlike the latter, was "bound by a double tie," for he also took an oath to support the constitution of his state. "Our system of government is two-fold, and so is our allegiance." This system of dual allegiance was not a threat to the constitutional order. In fact it made the order more secure. "[E]very State officer who is required to take [dual oaths] . . . was designedly placed by the federal Constitution itself as a sentinel to guard the outposts as well as the citadel of the great principles and rights which it was intended to declare, secure and perpetuate. . . . [T]he last hope of free, representative and responsible government rests upon the State sovereignties, and fidelity of State officers to their double allegiance."[65]

But what of the claim of Judge Leavitt and others that confusion, disunion, and anarchy would follow if states reserved such constitutional authority? Smith turned those claims on their heads. The real threat to the nation, he said, arose from the opposite tendency, for federal encroachment on the authority of states "naturally leads to consolidation, consolidation to despotism, and ultimate anarchy, dissolution and all its attendant evils." In the constitutional order, then, states served as institutional vehicles for enforcing "a perfect conformity" to the Constitution and for ensuring that "the general government [did not] become the sole judge of its own powers." But states were not simply appropriate vehicles for accomplishing these ends. They were essential. "Without the States there can be no Union."[66]

As for the distribution of authority over the return of fugitive slaves, Smith first argued dubiously that the Constitution denied Congress any

[64] Id., at 9–11.
[65] Id., at 22–23.
[66] Id., at 24–25.

authority whatsoever to legislate on the matter.[67] But even if Congress had some authority over fugitives, Smith said the Constitution forbade Congress to act as it had in the Fugitive Slave Act of 1850. For one thing, the fugitive slave clause itself required that a fugitive be "delivered" only "up on Claim" of the master. The Act of 1850 permitted the recovery and return of slaves without the master's filing a formal claim. For another, the Fifth Amendment provided that no person could be deprived of his liberty "without due process of law." Fugitives, as citizens of the State of Wisconsin while they resided within its borders, were entitled to a trial before they could be returned to slavery. Again, the Act of 1850 denied such a right. If slaves were not persons within the purview of the Constitution, then the Fifth Amendment's protections applied at least to those free blacks who were not fugitives from labor but who were nonetheless at risk of losing their freedom through a summary proceeding. But who was free and who was a slave could not be settled without a hearing. Thus, regardless of whether slaves were persons for constitutional purposes, the Constitution required that due process be observed in the rendition of alleged fugitives.

Even were the Constitution silent on the matter, such a requirement would be mandated as consistent with "the first principles of natural law," the laws of "the civilized world," and "a fundamental condition of all civil governments."[68] Smith ordered Booth released and fired a parting antifederalist salvo worthy of John C. Calhoun: "Let the Free States return to their duty . . . and be faithful to the compact, in the true spirit in which it was conceived and adopted, . . . [or else] there will be no peace for the State or the Nation, but . . . agitation, acrimony and hostility will mark our progress, even if we escape a more dread calamity, which I will not even mention."[69]

Later the same year, the United States again attempted to prosecute Booth for the same ostensible violation of the Fugitive Slave Act of 1850. This time the government tried to meet the Wisconsin Supreme Court's objections by having the warrant issue from a U.S. district judge rather than a commissioner. Again Booth petitioned the Wisconsin Supreme Court for a writ of habeas corpus. This time, however, the Wisconsin court denied the petition, holding that the action was properly resting in a court of ostensibly competent jurisdiction and that the state court would not presume that the federal court would fail to resolve the constitutional questions competently.[70]

[67] Id., at 28–32.

[68] Id., at 37–42.

[69] Id., at 48. On a writ of certiorari, the Wisconsin Supreme Court affirmed Smith's decision and ordered Booth released. Id., at 49, 64–70.

[70] *Ex Parte Booth*, 3 Wis. 145 (1854), at 146–159, 150–155. Justice Smith concurred,

Predictably the U.S. district court disagreed with the Wisconsin Supreme Court's resolution of the case. It held the Fugitive Slave Act to be constitutional, found Booth and a co-defendant guilty of violating the Act,[71] and sentenced them to a fine and imprisonment. Both defendants petitioned the Wisconsin Supreme Court for a writ of habeas corpus, which the court promptly issued. After a hearing the state court ordered the defendants released from jail.[72] When the U.S. Supreme Court granted a petition by the United States for a writ of error, the Wisconsin Supreme Court directed its clerk to disobey the U.S. Court by refusing to make a return on the writ.[73]

VI

The dispute in Wisconsin set the stage for a showdown between the highest courts of a state and the nation over the festering problem of fugitive slaves. Presumably it also portended a constitutional resolution of the problem. But the Supreme Court's decision in *Dred Scott v. Sandford*[74] in 1857 made the ultimate disposition of *Ableman v. Booth*[75] two years later almost anticlimactic.

There is a common perception that *Dred Scott* appeared on the scene like a bolt from the blue (or a flash from the fires of hell), unbidden, unprecedented. In fact the logic of the decision had long been one of the possible logics of the constitutional order. It was foreshadowed by decisions of the Supreme Court stretching back for more than a decade. As Wendell Phillips might have put it, *Dred Scott* came out of the past; its foundations were laid far back.[76]

Dred Scott had been a slave, owned by Dr. Emerson, a physician in the U.S. Army, who lived in the slave state of Missouri. In 1834 master and slave moved from Missouri to a federal military post at Rock Island, Illinois, a free state. Two years later they moved to Ft. Snelling in the Louisiana Territory, north of 36°30′, which the Missouri Compromise had demarked to separate free territory from slave. While at Ft. Snelling, Emerson bought another slave named Harriet. Scott and Har-

---

noting that although the Wisconsin court had earlier declared the Fugitive Slave Act of 1850 unconstitutional, its decision was not an acquittal and therefore did not bar a subsequent prosecution.

[71] By this time the case was a twin prosecution of Booth and John Rycraft.

[72] *In re Booth and Rycraft*, 3 Wis. 157 (1855), at 158–173, 175–176, 186, 190, 211.

[73] *United States v. Booth*, 59 U.S. (18 How.) 476 (1856), at 477–478.

[74] 19 How. (60 U.S.) 393 (1857). Sanford's name was misspelled in the style of the case.

[75] 21 How. (62 U.S.) 506 (1859).

[76] Wendell Phillips, "Public Opinion," Speech Before the Massachusetts Anti-Slavery Society (January 28, 1852), in *Speeches*, supra note 46, at 35–37.

riet married, with Emerson's permission, and had two children, one born on a steamboat on the Mississippi River (apparently north of 36°30′), the other born in Missouri after the family returned there with Dr. Emerson in 1838.[77]

After Emerson died in 1843 Scott sued in a Missouri state court, alleging that he was free, having resided in a free state, and that he and his family were free, having resided in a free territory.[78] In a long line of cases the Missouri Supreme Court previously had held that when a slave went to a free state or territory at the voluntary instance of his owner and not as a fugitive, the rules of comity of *Somerset* would apply; that is, a slave's temporary residence in a free state or territory legally served to emancipate the slave.[79] In Dred Scott's case, however, the Missouri Supreme Court reversed itself.[80]

Scott then filed an action in trespass *vi et armis* (roughly, assault and battery or false imprisonment) in the U.S. Circuit Court for the District of Missouri. In the absence of a federal question Scott was forced to allege diversity of citizenship as the jurisdictional basis for the suit—that Scott was a citizen of Missouri, and Sanford, who was Emerson's successor in interest, a citizen of New York. Sanford filed a plea in abatement, alleging that the court lacked jurisdiction because Scott, "a negro of African descent," was not a citizen of the State of Missouri. The court rejected Sanford's plea and went on to hear the merits of the case; ultimately, though, it directed a verdict in favor of Sanford (which logically implied that Dred Scott was still a slave).[81]

When Scott petitioned the U.S. Supreme Court for a writ of error, the two principal legal issues were arcane questions of pleading and jurisdiction, but they implicated questions of great constitutional moment. First, regarding Sanford's plea in abatement, was Dred Scott a citizen for purposes of diversity of citizenship? If he was not a citizen, was it by

[77] *Dred Scott v. Sandford*, supra note 74, at 431–432.

[78] Don E. Fehrenbacher, *The Dred Scott Case: Its Significance in American Law and Politics* (1978), at 246, 248–250. Fehrenbacher rejects the popular misconception that *Dred Scott* was a contrived or "made" case. Id., at 267–276.

[79] See *Dred Scott v. Sandford*, supra note 74, at 550–552, 602, citing inter alia: *Winny v. Whitesides*, 1 Mo. 472 (1824) (residence in Illinois for three to four years); *LaGrange v. Chouteau*, 2 Mo. 20 (1828) (residence in Northwest Territory); *Julia v. McKinney*, 3 Mo. 270 (1833) (residence in Illinois); *Rachel v. Walker*, 4 Mo. 350 (1836) (residence for one year at Ft. Snelling in Louisiana Territory); *Wilson v. Melvin*, 4 Mo. 592 (1837) (residence for one month in Illinois). See also *Menard v. Aspasia*, supra note 13. See also Fehrenbacher, supra note 78, at 252–253.

[80] See *Dred Scott v. Sandford*, supra note 74, at 552–554, citing *Dred Scott v. Emerson*, 15 Mo. 576 (1852).

[81] *Dred Scott v. Sandford*, supra note 74, at 393–400; Fehrenbacher, supra note 78, at 270–274.

virtue of his being a Negro or his being a slave? Second, was it proper for the court to reach the substantive issues in the case? If so, had Scott become free by virtue of his residence in Illinois (under the law of the State of Illinois) and/or had he and his family become free by virtue of their residence in the Northern territory of the Louisiana Purchase (under federal law)?[82]

Taney marshaled an effective majority on both basic questions and on all subsidiary questions except one, on which he sustained a plurality.[83] His opinion was issued and reported as "the opinion of the court." Moreover, as Fehrenbacher notes, the other members of the Court, public officials throughout the nation, and the public at large—whether supporters or critics of the decision—consistently treated Taney's opinion as the opinion of the Court.[84] Consequently I, too, shall treat Taney's opinion as emblematic of the Court's holding, if not entirely of its members' sentiments.

The Chief Justice insisted that his decision was localist, that the national government could not interfere with decisions of states to resolve questions about how to deal with Negroes, slaves, or the institution of slavery.[85] There is a certain accuracy to that self-portrait. He did argue that Congress, certainly a national institution, had but limited authority to act where slavery was concerned. But other aspects of his opinion belied his insistence.

On the first set of questions, concerning whether Dred Scott was a citizen, a truly localist decision might have connected national citizenship with (if not derived it entirely from) state citizenship. Instead Taney separated the two. A citizen of a state, he said, was not necessarily a citizen of the United States. This distinction was important because it implicated who was entitled to protection and recognition under the Constitution. According to Taney, "the people" identified in the Preamble were synonymous with "citizens." Only those who were citizens of states (technically there was no nation) at the time the Constitution was ratified became citizens of the United States. Citizenship became nationalized as the birthright of their posterity and as the statutory right of

[82] Apparently no one—in pleadings, arguments, or opinions—addressed the possibility that Scott's older child was free because the child was born in a free territory. All seem to have problematically assumed—as did the court and parties in *Prigg v. Pennsylvania*, supra note 26—that the child's status was inherited from the parents, regardless of where the child was born.

[83] Taney did not hold a majority on the question of why Scott was not a citizen. Taney had argued that Scott was not a citizen because he was a Negro, not simply because he was (or had been) a slave. But see Kenneth M. Stampp, *America in 1857: A Nation on the Brink* (1990), at 97.

[84] Fehrenbacher, supra note 78, at 333–334.

[85] *Dred Scott v. Sandford*, supra note 74, at 426.

naturalized aliens. Negroes, he said, were not, nor were intended to be, included as citizens at the time of the founding. Even the language of the Declaration of Independence was not inconsistent with slavery. If it were, the framers of that document and the makers of the country's independence would have been the objects of undying ridicule as "incapable of asserting principles [ ]consistent with those on which they were acting." The founders were not stupid, he implied, and public opinion during both the Revolution and the constitutional founding understood that Negroes were property, were to be separated from whites, and were not guaranteed any rights by the Declaration or the Constitution.[86]

After the founding (before it, in some places), slavery had died out in certain states. Indeed, some states had conferred citizenship on Negroes. Taney contended, however, that in states where slavery had died, it had done so for climatic and economic considerations, not moral or constitutional ones. Even in free states, regulations persisted enforcing the subordination of Negroes and their separation from whites. Besides, echoing Story's opinion in *Prigg*, Taney said that the slaveholding states would never have entered the Union if they had imagined it would be possible to count Negroes among the nation's citizens. In fact the states had ceded to the national government in the Constitution the power of naturalization because "[n]o state was willing to permit another state to determine who should or should not be admitted as one of its citizens, and entitled to demand equal rights and privileges with their own people, within their own territories." Taney dismissed out of hand the possibility, suggested in dissent by Justice M'Lean, that there might be a hierarchy of citizenships and that although Negroes might not possess all rights (such as the right of suffrage), they might still be considered citizens with other limited rights (including the right to sue and be sued). For the Chief Justice, constitutional citizenship was unitary and national.[87]

Public opinion may have changed in Europe or even in the United States on the question of slavery, but such a change did not mean, Taney claimed, that the Court should construe the Constitution more liberally than was intended when it was "framed and adopted." If the document is unjust, it may be amended to remove the injustice. Otherwise it must stand as it did in the beginning. "Dred Scott was not a

[86] Id., at 404–410.

[87] Id., at 412–418, 422–423, 530–533. Although the notion of hierarchical citizenship seems outmoded today, remnants of it linger in constitutional restrictions on access to certain national governmental offices and elsewhere.

citizen of Missouri within the [original] meaning of the Constitution of the United States."[88]

On the second set of questions, concerning whether any or all of the Scotts were freed by virtue of temporary residence in a free state or free territory, a truly localist decision might have embraced either *Somerset* or a theory of comity under which each state or territory regulated slavery within its borders, with no local law preferred over another. One possible source for such a theory was the full faith and credit clause of Article IV of the Constitution. Under such a theory, if a conflict developed among laws, it was simply the price of dispersed authority.

One problem with this theory—at least with respect to the territories—was that Article IV seemed to delegate authority over territorial governments to Congress.[89] But Taney resisted congressional authority over the territories for two reasons. The first was a strained, unconvincing linkage of constitutional text to the framers' intentions. Article IV, he said, referred only to territory owned by the several states at the time of the adoption and ratification of the Constitution. The clause, then, was intended to refer "to a particular thing" held by "the several confederated States as common property" and not to any territory that the United States might come to own or control at some future time.[90]

The second reason, which informed the first, rested on a theory of the character of government in general and, more specifically, of governmental authority under the Constitution. The confederation that was established at the end of the Revolution "was little more than a congress of ambassadors, authorized to represent separate nations, in matters in which they had a common concern." Under the Articles of Confederation, the separate states, or perhaps the people within them, were sovereign.

> But when the present United States came into existence under the new government, it was a new political body, a new nation, then for the first time taking its place in the family of nations. It took nothing by succession from the Confederation. . . . And as the several States would cease to exist in their former confederated character upon the adoption of the Constitution, and could not, in that character, again assemble together, special provisions were indispensable.[91]

[88] Id., at 426–427.

[89] "The Congress shall have power to dispose of and make all needful Rules and Regulations respecting the Territory or other Property belonging to the United States."

[90] *Dred Scott v. Sandford*, supra note 74, at 432–438.

[91] Id., at 434, 441.

This covenantal theory of the founding was in one respect more nationalist even than Marshall's. For Taney, although the people of the states were the source of national authority, after the founding the sovereign states retired into the sky.[92]

The counterintuitive consequence of their retirement was not an expansion of national legislative power, however. Although the national legislature the states created was to exercise supreme authority within the scope of the powers granted it "throughout the dominion of the United States," it was also to be "restricted" to those enumerated powers "delegated to it by the people of the several states." Congress, Taney said, clearly had constitutional authority to provide for the organization, settlement, and government of the territories. But its authority, even to pursue those ends, was limited. Its control was confined to converting territories into states. It was specifically limited by those rights of person and property that were, "in express and positive terms, denied to the general government." Take the Fifth Amendment's due process clause, for example. Unlike abolitionist constitutionalists and Justice Smith of the Wisconsin Supreme Court, Taney did not read into the Fifth Amendment a charter of liberty for slaves. Instead he saw it as a guarantee for citizens who might migrate to the territories that they could not "be ruled as mere colonists" but retained rights of person and property, including the right to own slaves.[93]

In one swift move, the Chief Justice had resurrected Mr. Menard's claims of twenty-six years before. The Constitution explicitly recognized the right of property in slaves, said Taney. "This is done in plain words—too plain to be misunderstood." Consequently the Missouri Compromise was unconstitutional, and Dred Scott and his family had not been emancipated when they resided in the Northern portion of the Louisiana Purchase.[94]

Scott was also a slave, said Taney, despite having lived in Illinois. The operative precedent was *Strader v. Graham*, which established the law of the home state as controlling. In fact, under *Strader*, the law of the slave state would almost always be the "home" state, and therefore controlling. In Dred Scott's case, the (new) law of Missouri kept him a slave.[95]

Although Taney had used the language of comity, he had effectively nationalized the question of slavery in free states and territories for fugi-

[92] Cf. James Bradley Thayer, who years later (and somewhat closer to Marshall) had the *people* retiring to the sky. Thayer, "The Origin and Scope of the American Doctrine of Constitutional Law," 7 *Harv. L. Rev.* 129 (1893).

[93] *Dred Scott v. Sandford*, supra note 74, at 447–449.

[94] Id., at 451–452.

[95] Id., at 452.

tives and nonfugitives alike. He could have limited his holding to covering only those slaves who had left a slave state but later returned. Doing so would have mitigated controversy, covered the facts of the case, and been sensitive to considerations of comity (if not consistent with *Somerset*). But the Chief Justice tried to settle the matter using a broad constitutional principle that logically threatened to swallow the very possibility of maintaining a state without slavery. In the guise of limiting national political authority, he wrote a nationalist constitutional decision that employed an expansive constitutional right to own slaves. The rhetoric of limited national political authority was truly a guise, for in order to protect the constitutional right on Taney's terms, national institutions were obliged to act to enforce it.

Two years later Taney would author an opinion in *Ableman v. Booth* that placed the U.S. Supreme Court firmly at the forefront of enforcing that right.[96] Thus, although *Dred Scott* and *Ableman* embodied a curious proslavery revision of John Marshall's nationalism, the courts of Wisconsin and abolitionists elsewhere were actively employing John C. Calhoun's theory of nullification to oppose slavery. The constitutional world had indeed turned upside down—at least for a time.

[96] As Taney put it in *Ableman*, his purpose was simply "to protect and guard the rights of all." *Ableman v. Booth*, supra note 75, at 517.

CHAPTER FIVE

Lincoln, Douglas, and the Illusion of Division

I

Dred Scott gave proslavers in the South more than they might ever have dared hope for: a national constitutional formula, sanctioned by the Supreme Court, that virtually demolished boundaries for containing slavery. In doing so, however, *Dred Scott* ironically posed three interrelated problems both for the Union and for slavery in the Union.

First, it undermined the localist constitutionalism that Calhoun had argued was the ultimate protection for slavery, for in important respects it placed the constitutional fate of not simply fugitives but also the institution itself in the nation's hands. In 1860, insensitive to the possibility that he was putting at risk the doctrine of popular sovereignty which he had embraced in his inaugural address four years earlier, Buchanan endorsed *Dred Scott*'s recognition of a constitutional right to own slaves "independent of Congress, or of the State Legislature, or of the Territorial Legislature."[1] As long as crucial institutions of the national government were largely controlled by men like Buchanan who were sympathetic to slavery, proslavers might well feel secure.

But a right is secure only as long as either the institutional means exist for its enforcement or a widely shared ethos supports it (which, in a polity having democratic elements, may amount to the same thing). These institutional means are a function not only of the structure of political authority but of the content of these institutions as well. In other words, they are also a function of the people (and consequently the values) that fill them. What might happen, then, in a national government run by people less sympathetic than Buchanan to slavery, or even unsympathetic?

Second, *Dred Scott* helped to fracture the Democratic Party into two separate parties: the Northern Democrats and the Southern Democrats.[2]

[1] Quoted in Herbert W. Fisher, *Considerations on the Origin of the American War* (1865), at 39–40.

[2] For a detailed account of the implications of *Dred Scott* among Democrats (and others), see Kenneth M. Stampp, *America in 1857: A Nation on the Brink* (1990), at 100–109. Stampp holds that *Dred Scott* was politically inconsequential for Democrats in the

This internal division would not have been considered a serious threat to the South had the alternative party been the Whigs. But by the mid-1850s the Whigs were all but dead—victims of sectional division. The Republicans, on the other hand, were emerging as the country's second party by the late 1850s. The primary reason for the split in Democratic ranks was that *Dred Scott* posed different problems and opportunities for Northern Democrats than it did for Southern Democrats. Before *Dred Scott*, popular sovereignty had, to varying degrees and for different reasons, satisfied many Northern as well as Southern Democrats. As late as 1857 Douglas's position, embracing the sovereignty of states and territories to establish and maintain for themselves such institutions as they saw fit, was widely accepted in the Party, helping to give the Democrats a solid lock on the national government.

After *Dred Scott*, as the battle over the admission of Kansas demonstrated, those northern Democrats, especially Douglas, who gamely tried to avoid explicitly opposing the Court's decision while at the same time holding onto popular sovereignty, were branded as backstabbers by Southern proslavers. The Southern repudiation of Douglas's stance revealed a growing insecurity in and alienation from the rest of the Union that had deep emotional roots. But the Southern response was also oddly "rational," if one took seriously the inevitability of Northern control of the national political apparatus. What better way to mitigate the antislavery tendencies of a "national democracy" than to embrace a constitutionally protected national right to hold slaves? The weaker the prospect for institutional checks on Northern control of the nation's policies, the stronger the Southern insistence on parchment rights and on largely symbolic victories on territorial questions. Hence Southerners could move from relative comfort with Douglas's popular sovereignty in 1857, to distress at the same position in 1858, to insistence on what Fehrenbacher calls "full acknowledgment of slaveholding rights" in 1859.[3]

But they probably could not have made the jump to secessionism in 1860–61 without some equivalent countervailing response to *Dred Scott* in the North. Thus the third way the Court's decision helped provoke schism was to convert the question of slavery from one resolved by a series of compromises among political actors to one settled by constitutional principle. Even political compromise presupposed a kind

---

short term. In contrast, I argue that the *longer-term* consequences for sectional division (and for Democratic political success) were substantial.

[3] Don E. Fehrenbacher, *The Dred Scott Case: Its Significance in American Law and Politics* (1978), at 449–484.

of constitutional principle, as it rested on assumptions about the allocation of constitutional authority, but as chapters 3 and 4 pointed out, the principle underlying the congressional strategy of compromise was of a different order than was the principle of *Dred Scott*.

The conversion to constitutional principle had two consequences. First, in disposing of compromise as a way of resolving disputes, *Dred Scott* destroyed any centrist ground capable of accommodating those who had the keenest interests in the issue of slavery in the territories. Among the most important of those interested parties were whites who wanted the territories for themselves. Second, by explicitly raising the status of slavery to a national and constitutional level, *Dred Scott* focused attention on slavery in a way that abolitionist pamphlets could never have done. Ironically, then, the case gave more to abolitionists than they might have dared hope: an almost perfect device for arousing opinion in the North.

The reaction to the decision in the North, like the Southern reaction to *Uncle Tom's Cabin*, was swift and strong. One indication of the degree of attention the ruling received was the presence of an impressive market in unofficial pamphlets containing the justices' opinions. In the vanguard of the reaction against *Dred Scott* were antislavery and Republican newspapers. Preachers, pamphleteers, and commentators of various stripes joined the fray. Their attacks tended to be vitriolic and inflammatory and pursued one or both of two tactics: to castigate the Court as an institution and the place of judicial review in the pantheon of constitutional values or to criticize the substance of what the Court had done.[4]

The latter tactic had several versions. Some radical abolitionists denounced in moral terms the racism of Taney's opinion; such denunciations, however, did not typify the reactions of white Northerners, most of whom cared little about citizenship for blacks, still less about racial equality. Many Northerners and probably most Republicans were undoubtedly concerned about slavery (or slavery's extension). Taney's opinion had lent legitimacy to Northern fears of a national slave empire. But the political consequence of the attacks on *Dred Scott* by the antislavery press—and the intensity of feeling they aroused—were far too powerful to have rested on the strength of moral claims alone. Whatever the moral impulses that drove Northern opinion, they clearly were linked to Northern perceptions of self-interest. These perceptions in turn were colored by considerations of race. Consequently most

[4] Charles Warren, *The Supreme Court in United States History*, vol. 2 (rev. ed., 1947), at 279, 302–309, 315, 317–319, 327–329; Fehrenbacher, supra note 3, at 417, 421–428, 439–443.

white Northerners and probably most Republicans sustained an aversion to slavery coupled with an antipathy toward blacks.[5]

The psychic roots of such a division are easy enough to discern. But the politician's job of walking the line of division was more difficult. As Southerners before had searched for a way to express their insecurity but speak not of slavery, Republicans in Congress and elsewhere now searched for a language that would permit them to talk about slavery but not about blacks. A surprising number began to incorporate various versions of constitutional localism—the right of a state to resist decisions of national institutions that threatened their interests—into their rhetorical arsenals.[6] In the North that strategy kept the right silences while exploiting the proper fears. No moderate politician in the country capitalized on those fears more adroitly than Abraham Lincoln.

II

The forum that permitted Lincoln to seize the national stage on *Dred Scott* was a series of speeches and debates with Stephen Douglas in 1858. The occasion was the Illinois Legislature's impending decision to fill one of the state's seats in the United States Senate. The debates are widely considered to have been among the finest examples of political exchange in the country's history, focusing attention on slavery and on the constitutional implications of *Dred Scott* in a way that illuminated two distinctive, even polar, positions on the issues. Certainly they provided an impressive display of political oratory. But one remarkable aspect of Lincoln's and Douglas's positions was not their difference, but their similarity. That they could have been interpreted as radically different views on the question of slavery stems from their distinctive premises as well as from the capacity of partisan political rhetoric to generate the illusion of difference (and consequently of choice) in order to disguise profound similarity.

The claim that there was not a great deal of difference between Lincoln and Douglas is controversial. James G. Randall promoted it several years ago,[7] but it fell into disrepute as Lincoln gained a decided reputation in recent years as a statesman who envisioned and achieved a new beginning for the political order. Garry Wills's excellent book describes Lincoln's Gettysburg Address as a "refounding." On Wills's account, however, the Address was not an entirely original or transformative re-

[5] Fehrenbacher, supra note 3, at 429, 432–435.

[6] Warren, supra note 4, at 333–336, 345–348; Fehrenbacher, supra note 3, at 433.

[7] James G. Randall, *Lincoln the President: Springfield to Gettysburg* (1945), at 104–128. See also Randall, *Lincoln the Liberal Statesman* (1947), at 175–179.

founding but recaptured what Lincoln considered the basic ideas of the original founding at the time of the Revolution.[8] James M. McPherson, among the more enthusiastic of Lincoln's present-day admirers, goes further and argues that Lincoln was a "revolutionary statesman," who successfully prosecuted the "Second American Revolution," a revolution both ideological and social in character.[9] Even Lincoln's latter-day conservative detractors have joined the bandwagon. Willmoore Kendall, for example, saw in Lincoln the author of a new regime, dedicated to radical propositions that went far beyond anything the original founders instituted or imagined.[10] M. E. Bradford, too, insists that Lincoln's war was nothing short of a "second founding" that effectively repudiated the principles of the original founding.[11]

Some scholars claim that we need not wait until the Civil War, and certainly not until Reconstruction, for evidence of Lincoln's distinctive, revolutionary qualities. Harry Jaffa, for one, paints a detailed portrait of a radically disparate Lincoln and Douglas. The latter, Jaffa suggests, was a proponent of ancient liberty, the unrestricted liberty of a people to govern themselves. Lincoln, on the other hand, even by 1858, had inherited the mantle of Socrates and become the embodiment of modern liberty and natural right. "[T]he Lincoln-Douglas debates," says Jaffa, "are justly regarded as the greatest in American history, although in a deeper sense they constitute as well a unique episode in the history of free government in the Western world." The debates, he says, were "an intellectual and moral contest of the highest order of which democratic politics admits."[12]

Of course some dissidents dispute both the novelty of Lincoln's politics and the significance of the debates, but their numbers are dwindling.[13] At the risk of raging against wind and tide, I wish here to take

[8] Garry Wills, *Lincoln at Gettysburg: The Words That Remade America* (1992), at 90–147. Walter F. Murphy makes a similar claim about the Reconstruction Amendments. Murphy, "*Slaughter-House*, *Civil Rights*, and Limits on Constitutional Change," 32 *Am. J. Jurisprudence* 1 (1987).

[9] James M. McPherson, *Abraham Lincoln and the Second American Revolution* (1991), at vii–viii, 23–42.

[10] Willmoore Kendall, *The Conservative Affirmation* (1963), at 249–252.

[11] M. E. Bradford, *Remembering Who We Are: Observations of a Southern Conservative* (1985), at 23, 48, 66, 143–156.

[12] Harry A. Jaffa, *Crisis of the House Divided: An Interpretation of the Issues of the Lincoln-Douglas Debates* (1959, 1982), at 19–37.

[13] See, for example, T. Harry Williams, "Lincoln and the Radicals: An Essay in Civil War History and Historiography," in *Grant, Lee, Lincoln, and the Radicals: Essays on Civil War Leadership* (McWhiney, ed., 1964), at 92–117; and Norman A. Graebner, "Abraham Lincoln: Conservative Statesman," in *The Enduring Lincoln* (Graebner, ed., 1959), at 67–94. Both Williams and Graebner insist that Lincoln was fundamentally conservative and not a radical, as most now claim. David Donald attempts to reject the

up camp with the dissidents in some respects. Specifically I shall argue the following: First, the debates between Lincoln and Douglas demonstrated that the Supreme Court's pronouncements in *Dred Scott v. Sandford* did not dispose of the issues in the case. On the contrary, the decision provoked discussion and reaction the intensity and direction of which Taney could have but dimly imagined. Second, in an attempt to win election to the United States Senate and to preempt Douglas's capturing Free Soilers and Republicans, Lincoln embarked on a rhetorical campaign to demonstrate decisively the great distance that lay between Douglas and himself. Although Lincoln lost the election, he succeeded in driving a wedge between Douglas and both the Free Soilers and the Republicans. On many accounts, he also succeeded in demonstrating the differences between the two men. Third, one reason the division between Lincoln and Douglas appeared so substantial was that the two operated from divergent foundational myths. Lincoln, the Federalist, opposed Douglas, the Antifederalist. Fourth, notwithstanding this basic difference, Lincoln and Douglas arrived at conclusions that were substantially similar on almost all significant issues. To borrow Robert Cover's term, competing foundational myths generated almost identical *nomoi*—or at least policies—with respect to the expansion of slavery in the territories. The differences between Lincoln and Douglas, then, were more apparent than real. But they disguised a deeper and more ominous division, that between the Antifederalist Douglas and those Southern proslavers who were increasingly insisting on national enforcement of the national rights contained in *Dred Scott*.

III

Although some of his fellow Republicans were moving toward localism as a response to *Dred Scott*, Lincoln's deepest instincts were nationalist. The full extent and implications of his nationalism were not clear before the Civil War, but there were hints of his commitments in the early years of his political career.[14] His devotion to Union—sometimes described as

dichotomy of "radical" and "conservative" altogether, claiming instead that Lincoln was a pragmatist. At bottom, however, Donald's claim rests on the conclusion that Lincoln was not ideologically innovative. David Donald, *Lincoln Reconsidered: Essays on the Civil War Era* (1961), at 57–71, 128–143.

[14] See, for example, his "Address Before the Young Men's Lyceum of Springfield, Illinois" (January 27, 1838), in *The Collected Works of Abraham Lincoln*, vol. 1 (Basler, ed., 1953), at 108 et seq. There he begins to work out the connection between the ideas of nation and perpetuity: "As a nation of freemen, we must live through all time, or die by suicide." Id., at 109.

"mystical"—is familiar. But Douglas was a unionist, too, and a committed one. What distinguished Lincoln from Douglas was the constitutional theory that supported his attachment to Union.

Lincoln was a Federalist. He could trace his pedigree through Daniel Webster to John Marshall.[15] Indeed one can find in Marshall some of the sentiments—sometimes the very language—that later animated Lincoln's rhetoric. Both were advocates of free labor and commerce. Both expressed moral antipathy toward slavery, but neither insisted on policies to oppose it. Both imagined that the people were constitutive of the republic. In fact one can hear distinct echoes of Marshall's opinion in *M'Culloch v. Maryland* in Lincoln's invocation of "government of the people, by the people, and for the people" in 1863.[16] More important, they shared a commitment to the idea of nation. Marshall located the commencement of nationhood in the ratification of the Constitution. Lincoln pushed the founding further back, at least as far as the Revolution. But both contended that the character of the country was fundamentally transformed at a crucial historical moment from an aggregation of states to the home of a national people.

By Lincoln's time, however, the home was threatened from within, and the source of the threat on his view was the question of slavery's place in the territories and the nation. In June 1858 in a speech at Springfield, Lincoln decided to fire his initial shot across Douglas's bow. The shot was self-consciously bold:

> "A house divided against itself cannot stand." I believe this government cannot endure permanently half slave and half free. I do not expect the Union to be dissolved; I do not expect the house to fall; but I do expect it will cease to be divided. It will become all one thing, or all the other. Either the opponents of slavery will arrest the further spread of it, and place it where the public mind shall rest in the belief that it is in the course of ultimate extinction, or its advocates will push it forward till it shall become alike lawful in all the States, old as well as new, North as well as South.[17]

Under ordinary circumstances, evocation of the biblical house divided might have been attributable to rhetorical excess. *Dred Scott*, however, gave Lincoln's claims analytical bite.

Thus Lincoln's suggestion that "we may, ere long, see . . . another Supreme Court decision, declaring that the Constitution of the United

[15] Garry Wills perceptively and persuasively makes the connection to the constitutional theory of Webster. Wills, supra note 8, at 122–133.

[16] Lincoln, "Address Delivered at the Dedication of the Cemetery at Gettysburg—Final Text" (November 19, 1863), in *Collected Works*, supra note 14, vol. 7, at 22–23.

[17] Lincoln, Speech in Springfield June 16, 1858), in Lincoln and Douglas, *Political Debates Between Abraham Lincoln and Stephen A. Douglas* (1894), at 7.

States does not permit a *State* to exclude slavery from its limits," might have seemed plausible in the wake of *Dred Scott* and the Supreme Court's decisions on slavery earlier in the decade. "Welcome or unwelcome, such a decision is probably coming, and will soon be upon us, unless the power of the present political dynasty shall be met and overthrown."[18]

Lincoln would later advocate resisting *Dred Scott* within national political institutions, specifically the Congress, more notably the Senate. A judicial decision, he said, even on a constitutional issue, was binding only on the parties to the particular dispute.[19] Still later he would tie his position on this issue to the people: "[I]f the policy of government, upon vital questions, affecting the whole people, is to be irrevocably fixed by decisions of the Supreme Court, the instant they are made, in ordinary litigation between parties, in personal actions, the people will have ceased, to be their own rulers, having, to that extent, practically resigned their government, into the hands of that eminent tribunal."[20]

So framed, Lincoln's position parted company with Marshall's in two important respects. First, Marshall and Lincoln disagreed over the scope of the Supreme Court's authority. On this point, however, they did not disagree over the bindingness of the Court's decisions, at least in a given case. Moreover, Lincoln had an abiding faith in rule of law and abhorred the dangers of "mob rule."[21] Second, and more significant for considerations of federalism, Lincoln's approach to slavery seemed even more nationalist than Marshall's had been. After all, Marshall's Union could rest secure in the knowledge that the federal consensus would limit slavery's ability to disrupt the nation's affairs. Lincoln seemed to be suggesting in his opening salvo in Springfield that the problem of slavery required a national solution. As it happened, however, Lincoln held a localist card up his sleeve, one that would, like the federal consensus, trump nationalism where slavery was concerned. He would wait to play this card, but when in play, it would permit Lincoln to retain title to the national house, permitting localism to enter through the back door without letting Calhoun sit on the front porch.

In contrast with Lincoln, Douglas's inclinations were decidedly antifederalist. He exhibited two sets of traits that underscored those proclivities. First, his economic sympathies tended to be mildly agrarian, though it is not clear whether his agrarianism was a matter of principle,

[18] Id., at 11.

[19] Lincoln, Speech at Chicago (July 10, 1858), in id., at 29.

[20] Lincoln, "First Inaugural Address—Final Text" (March 4, 1861), in *Collected Works*, supra note 14, vol. 4, at 262, 268.

[21] One can see this faith and aversion very early, in his "Address Before the Young Men's Lyceum," supra note 14, at 110–112.

an expedient bow to Southern interests in his own party, or simply a concomitant of his attention to territorial expansion. Second, and more important, his theory of politics—encapsulated in the idea of popular sovereignty—had plainly antifederalist roots. Douglas had a deep faith in the people's capacity for self-government. That capacity was best exercised, he said, at the local level, at the level of states and territories. His democratic localism was an expression of a longstanding antifederalist distrust of centralized power: The nation should not interfere with the decisions of localities concerning the institutions and policies they required.[22]

None of this is to suggest that Douglas was not a Unionist. He was an avid Unionist. But, except for one passion, he was not a nationalist. The passion was for territorial expansion. "I would make this an ocean-bound republic," he said. And his entire political career bore witness to his devotion to establishing a continental republican empire. Nonetheless localism was essential to making and sustaining that empire, and the people of the states thus became the constituent actors of the polity.[23]

In securing reelection to the Senate, Douglas faced two challenges. They grew out of his commitments to localism and expansionism, on the one hand, and the problems that slavery presented to both, on the other. First, he wanted (and needed) to hold onto popular sovereignty as the principle for organizing and incorporating the territories. Consistency was a virtue, even for a politician. Second, he needed to adopt a rhetorical strategy concerning slavery and *Dred Scott* that would minimize alienating Southerners.[24] This problem was important because Douglas nurtured presidential ambitions that could not be realized without the aid of Southern Democrats. These challenges were remarkably similar to those he had confronted in getting congressional approval of his route for a transcontinental railroad. But in 1858, unlike in 1854, he could not achieve both goals simultaneously.

He solved the first problem easily enough. He simply invoked his long-standing commitment to popular sovereignty.[25] "If there is any one principle dearer and more sacred than all others in free governments, it is that which asserts the exclusive right of a free people to form and adopt their own fundamental law, and to manage and regulate their

[22] Damon Wells, *Stephen Douglas: The Last Years, 1857–1861* (1971), at 55–80. See also Glen Huron Seymour, *An Analysis of the Political Principles of Stephen A. Douglas* (Ph.D. diss., Department of History, University of Illinois, 1929).

[23] Robert W. Johannsen, *Stephen A. Douglas* (1973), at 162, 158–185.

[24] Douglas was keenly aware of the potential use of the debates as a national forum, but the risk of the forum was far greater for him than for Lincoln.

[25] Stephen A. Douglas, Speech at Chicago (July 9, 1858), in *Political Debates*, supra note 17, at 13–15.

own internal affairs and domestic institutions."[26] If Lincoln wanted to submit the validity of *Dred Scott* to the political process, Douglas wanted to submit to political process *all* questions concerning the fate of slavery. But he rejected the notion that Congress was the proper agent for resolving those questions: "I deny the right of Congress to force a slaveholding State upon an unwilling people. I deny their right to force a Free State upon an unwilling people. I deny their right to force a good thing upon a people who are unwilling to receive it. The great principle is the right of every community to judge and decide for itself whether a thing is right or wrong, whether it would be good or evil for them to adopt it."[27] If Lincoln abhorred a house divided, Douglas reveled in localist diversity and democratic self-determination.[28]

Douglas's solution to the first problem intensified his second problem. On *Dred Scott*, and hence on ameliorating Southern proslavers, he adopted two apparently inconsistent strategies. One was to interpret *Dred Scott* as compatible with popular sovereignty. Quoting an "eminent Southern senator," he argued that "[w]ithout affirmative legislation in its favor, slavery could not exist any longer than a new-born infant could survive under the heat of the sun, on a barren rock, without protection. It would wilt and die for want of support." In other words, an abstract constitutional right was not sufficient to protect slavery. Slavery, in order to survive, much less to flourish, required the affirmative protection of local laws. Such regulations would never be enacted without the approval of the people of the territory or state. Thus slavery's survival was indirectly linked to popular sovereignty.[29]

Although Douglas did not contend that popular sovereignty was any part of the explicit holding in *Dred Scott*, his pragmatic gloss was problematic in two respects. First, the suggestion that a theory of popular sovereignty circumscribed the Court's decision—even if only implicitly—was so inconsistent with the logic of Taney's opinion that it was simply an implausible reading of the decision, as Lincoln repeatedly insisted.[30] Second, it was an interpretation that was unlikely to endear

[26] Id., at 12.

[27] Id., at 16.

[28] Id., at 17. He reiterated these themes in the First Joint Debate, Ottawa (August 21, 1858), Third Joint Debate, Jonesboro (September 15, 1858), and Seventh Joint Debate, Alton (October 15, 1858), in id., at 88–90, 139–140, 254–255, 280.

[29] Douglas, Speech at Springfield (July 17, 1858), in id., at 62–63. For subsequent iterations of the same theme, see also the Third Joint Debate, Jonesboro (September 15, 1858), Fifth Joint Debate, Galesburgh (October 7, 1858), Sixth Joint Debate, Quincy (October 13, 1858), and Seventh Joint Debate, Alton (October 15, 1858), in id., at 163, 209, 243–244, 261, 282.

[30] Lincoln's Speech at Chicago (July 10, 1858); Second Joint Debate at Freeport (August 27, 1858); both in id., at 23–25, 109.

Douglas to Southern proslavers, who, sharing Buchanan's reading of *Dred Scott*, were now insisting on a nationalist theory that guaranteed the right to hold slaves against local majoritarian interference. These Southerners were not inclined, therefore, to take comfort in the notion that their right depended on the beneficence of local laws. (Ironically, making the right contingent on local legislation would have amounted to a sort of nullification with a twist. Exercising the contingency would have nullified not national laws but what Southerners and the Court contended were national constitutional rights.)

Douglas's second strategy, then, was to embrace *Dred Scott* without the gloss of popular sovereignty. But in Illinois, even among Democrats, he had to use care to embrace the decision indirectly, without specifically endorsing its holding and without stating in so many words that he supported slavery. He did so by insisting on respect for the institutional authority of the Supreme Court and by attacking Lincoln for not being sufficiently respectful of the Court. "The right and the province of expounding the Constitution and constructing the law is vested in the judiciary," he explained. And in expounding the Constitution, the judiciary—especially the Supreme Court—had as its institutional function the protection of "our rights, our liberty, and our property." The Court deserves respect, he said, because of its special place among the constituted authorities; therefore, in resisting *Dred Scott*, Lincoln was undermining institutional arrangements through which both law and basic liberties were protected.[31] The weakness of this second strategy was that it ran headlong against Douglas's theory of popular sovereignty, both because of its nationalist implications and because it held out for the Court a strongly countermajoritarian function. In short, it put his theory at war with itself.

If Douglas's position was self-contradictory, the line of battle between him and Lincoln still seemed fairly distinct. Indeed these and other differences persisted throughout the debates. For example, Lincoln sometimes condemned slavery in moral terms.[32] In contrast, Douglas spoke of slavery mainly as a social and economic issue, whose survival depended directly on cultural, climatic, and material conditions. Lincoln charged that Douglas was aiming for a position of moral neutrality toward slavery. Whatever Douglas's moral commitments, he indeed preferred to resolve questions about slavery through local majorities and not by resorting to substantive national principles. A second difference

[31] Douglas, Speech at Chicago (July 9, 1858), in id., at 18. See also Speech at Bloomington (July 16, 1858), Third Joint Debate, Jonesboro (July 15, 1858), Fifth Joint Debate, Galesburgh (October 7, 1858), Sixth Joint Debate, Quincy (October 13, 1858), Seventh Joint Debate, Alton (October 15, 1858), in id., at 43, 162, 225–227, 241–243, 259, 282.

[32] Lincoln, in id., at 28; 212, 214–215; 233–235; 272, 273, 275–276.

between the two was that Lincoln located the founding of the nation at 1776. Douglas, on the other hand, was a man of the Constitution.[33] He was interested less in the Revolution as the decisive moment for the nation's founding than in the Constitution as a constitutive act whose principal effect was to allocate institutional authority.

IV

One might think that such disparities would prefigure fundamentally different understandings of the Constitution and its treatment of slavery. But as the speeches and debates unfolded, the differences between Lincoln and Douglas became both less distinct and less significant. One reason for the confluence of positions was that Lincoln, shrewd politician that he was, rarely allowed himself to be trapped by the implications of principle.

For example, having seized slavery as a moral issue, he largely adopted Douglas's stance when it came time to deliver an institutional means for making good on his own moral principle. In fact Lincoln advocated two different solutions to the problem of slavery. The more familiar one was that slavery should expand no farther than the states where it then existed in 1858.[34] What made this position compatible with the Constitution, he argued, was that the Constitution's framers "found" slavery here at the time of the founding, recognized their inability to exterminate it, compromised over it as best they could, and took comfort in the belief that it would ultimately become extinct.[35] By adopting this solution Lincoln effectively ceded much of his moral ground, at least where slavery then existed, for it made slavery's abolition dependent largely on cultural, climatic, and material conditions. A natural, gradual abolition, if it did occur, might take one hundred years or more, he said, but he was prepared to accept that contingency.[36]

Lincoln did not consistently oppose the westward expansion of slavery, however. In fact in his second, less familiar solution, he endorsed popular sovereignty (actually state sovereignty) as an institutional device for resolving questions over the extension of slavery. However, for

[33] Walter F. Murphy claims that the Declaration of Independence is a kind of constitution or is part of the Constitution. See his "*Slaughter-House*," supra note 8, at 17 et seq. Without pursuing the problems presented by treating the Declaration as a constitution, I wish to distinguish the two for now.

[34] Lincoln, in *Political Debates*, supra note 17, at 27–28, 92–93, 146–147, 187–188, 233, 249, 273.

[35] Id., at 265, 270.

[36] Id., at 94, 188–189.

popular sovereignty to work properly (and this is what made Lincoln's theory basically one of state sovereignty), it must be subject to two conditions. A territory or its people, he argued, could permit slavery only as early as its petition for admission as a state and only if slavery had been prohibited before statehood.[37] These conditions preserved some distance between him and Douglas, who argued that the people of a territory had authority to permit or bar slavery at any time after the territory was formally established, but one well might wonder about the significance of that distance.

Lincoln's position apparently arose from a fear—which cut against his contention that slavery would eventually die a natural death—that once slavery gained a foothold in a territory, rooting it out would be nearly impossible. Although the experience of the northeastern states testified against such a notion, some similar fear probably motivated antislavers to support Lincoln's position. The motivation was especially strong when the fear linked up with a concomitant hope: When the people of a territory had a chance to ratify a state constitution without having to figure out what to do with a sizable population of slaves (or, for that matter, free blacks), they would reject a regime that included slavery. This hope was animated by several beliefs, including an assumption that free labor represented the wave of the future and a racist aversion to opening up the western territories to blacks. But whatever the motivation, Lincoln's popular sovereignty was, as a practical matter, quite similar to Douglas's. If one takes into account Douglas's assumptions about the constraints that climate and the material conditions of a territory posed for the success of slavery, Lincoln's and Douglas's positions were almost identical.

The same kind of fusion occurred over the implications of the character of the founding. Lincoln's adoption of 1776 as the founding moment permitted him two important rhetorical moves. One would turn out to be crucial, the other largely empty. First, he used the revolutionary founding to argue that the nation existed before the Constitution and consequently that Union was logically prior to the Constitution.[38] Second, placing the founding in 1776 gave him a constitutive text, the Declaration of Independence, that was distinct from the Constitution. That distinction was important for a man who was trying to coax support from abolitionists and antislavers, for whom the second paragraph of the Declaration served as symbolic codification of universal princi-

[37] Id., at 70–71, 95, 109, 143, 249, 272–273.

[38] He later pressed this point forcefully and systematically in his "Address at Cooper Institute, New York City" (February 27, 1860), in *Collected Works*, supra note 14, vol. 3, at 522.

ples of individual human liberty.[39] It was also important because a great many abolitionists were still inclined to view the Constitution as a tool of proslavers. Hence Lincoln's position on the founding was a subtle way for him to secure support from slavery's opponents, some of whom still regarded Lincoln with suspicion,[40] without committing himself outright to abolitionism.

Embracing the Declaration also gave Lincoln a vehicle for challenging Taney's plurality on one issue in *Dred Scott*: that blacks were constitutionally barred from citizenship. Thus at times Lincoln argued that all people, even blacks, were included in the principles of the Declaration.[41] Douglas, perhaps thinking that Lincoln could be damaged by association with racial equality implicit in his interpretation of the Declaration of Independence and in the possibility of citizenship for blacks, pressed the issue through a racist attack on the notion of black citizenship.

> [T]his government of ours is founded on the white basis. It was made by the white man, for the benefit of the white man, to be administered by white men, in such manner as they shall determine. It is also true that a negro, an Indian, or any other man of inferior race to a white man should be permitted to enjoy, and humanity requires that he should have, all the rights, privileges, and immunities which he is capable of exercising consistent with the safety of society. . . . [W]hat are these rights and these privileges? . . . [E]ach State must decide for itself the nature and extent of these rights. Illinois has decided for herself. We have decided that the negro shall not be a slave, and we have at the same time decided that he shall not vote, or serve on juries, or enjoy political privileges.[42]

Douglas said that Lincoln's proposal for "negro equality" would threaten "the blood" and "the government" with "mixture [and] amalgamation with inferior races."[43]

What Douglas did not anticipate was that his charge that Lincoln was a radical egalitarian on matters of race simply would not stick. For one thing, Lincoln would not sit still to be tarred with the brush of egalitar-

[39] The notion that slavery was fundamentally incompatible with the Declaration of Independence did not originate with abolitionists. Evidence indicates that many in the eighteenth century, even some founders, also held to the idea. See, e.g., Bernard Bailyn, "General Introduction: The Transforming Radicalism of the American Revolution," in *Pamphlets of the American Revolution: 1750–1776*, vol. 1 (Bailyn, ed., 1965), at 140–150. It would be a mistake, however, to argue that the Declaration had some kind of "intrinsic" meaning that rendered it incompatible with slavery.

[40] Donald, supra note 13, at 19.

[41] See, e.g., Lincoln, in *Political Debates*, supra note 17, at 9, 32–33, 79.

[42] Douglas, in id., at 19.

[43] Id., at 20. Douglas repeated these and similar arguments throughout the debates. See id., at 65–66, 88–89, 118–119, 140–141, 182, 185–186, 208–209, 262, 280.

ianism or universal citizenship. For another, to the extent that Republicans were prepared to embrace a policy categorically excluding slavery from the western territories (which, again, was a plausible but incomplete reading of Lincoln's positions), racism was an even stronger weapon for Republicans than for Democrats. Thus, even in his early speeches, which were among his most expansive on the implications of the Declaration of Independence,[44] Lincoln emphasized that his aim was to open up the territories for settlement by "free white laborers, who want the land to bring up their families upon."[45]

His philosophical assumption was the supremacy of the white race. His policy was racial separation. "I protest, now and forever, against that counterfeit logic which presumes that because I did not want a negro woman for a slave, I do necessarily want her for a wife. My understanding is that I need not have her for either, but, as God made us separate, we can leave one another alone, and do one another much good thereby. . . . [I]f we do not let [negroes] into the Territories, they won't mix there."[46] Throughout the debates Lincoln consistently pressed themes of racial supremacy and separation while trying to hold onto the symbolic value of the Declaration.[47]

Ultimately Lincoln disavowed even "the social and political equality of the white and black races," including the rights to vote, serve on juries, hold office, or of course marry whites. He argued that regulation of racial relations was a local, not a national, matter. Nor was it an issue of special constitutional concern. He confessed "very frankly that I am not in favor of negro citizenship." Finally, he conceded that his opposition to *Dred Scott* was not because the decision ostensibly prohibited Negro citizenship but solely because of its tendency to nationalize slavery.[48] The similarities between Lincoln's and Douglas's positions on these issues are striking.

Certainly liberalizing sentiments were evident in Lincoln's positions on slavery and racial relations. All was not supremacy and separation. Nevertheless his primary use of the principles of the Declaration of Independence aimed not at racial equality or even the abolition of slavery but rather at the primacy of Union. As late as 1862, one month before he issued the Emancipation Proclamation, he repeated in a prominent letter that his chief aim was "to save the Union. . . . If I could save the

[44] Possible exceptions to this point were the Fifth Joint Debate at Galesburgh and the Sixth Joint Debate at Quincy. See id., at 211–212, 220, 228–230, 251.

[45] Id., at 31.

[46] Id.

[47] See id., at 79, 96, 164, 211–212, 251, 263–264.

[48] Id., at 164, 187, 263–264. Lincoln reemphasized these themes in a speech in Columbus, Ohio, almost a year after the end of the debates. Id., at 283 et seq.

Union without freeing *any* slave I would do it, and if I could save it by freeing *all* the slaves I would do it; and if I could save it by freeing some and leaving others alone I would also do that. What I do about slavery, and the colored race, I do because I believe it helps to save the Union."[49] The Emancipation Proclamation adopted the third strategy, "liberating" slaves only in the seceded states while keeping in bondage slaves of the border states that had remained in the Union.[50]

Even Douglas would have agreed with Lincoln's sentiment that preservation of Union was of paramount concern.[51] Why, then, the persistent perception that Lincoln and Douglas represented such polar positions in the debate over slavery? Apart from what has already been said, one reason is that both men demonstrated a hearty willingness to mischaracterize the positions of the other. Douglas, on the one hand, was fond of representing Lincoln as a radical abolitionist who wanted, by legislation or constitutional amendment, to impose a "despotism," by which Douglas apparently meant the imposition of uniform laws and institutions (including the abolition of slavery) throughout the nation. He accused Lincoln of promoting equal citizenship for blacks, advocating the elimination of the states' authority to prohibit the migration of blacks, and inciting mob rule at the local level through his opposition to *Dred Scott*.[52] None of this, of course, was accurate.

Lincoln, on the other hand, falsely accused Douglas of promoting a "tyranny," of wanting to nationalize slavery, in fact of being part of a conspiracy with Buchanan and Taney to procure and promote the Supreme Court's decision in *Dred Scott*. He offered the contradictory positions that Douglas supported a constitutional right to hold slaves in the territories regardless of local preferences or state constitutions and that Douglas favored acquiring new states and territories without any regard for the issue of slavery. He said that Douglas wanted to expand

[49] Lincoln, Letter to Horace Greeley (August 22, 1862), in *Collected Works*, supra note 14, vol. 5, at 388–389. The letter was published three days later in the New York *Tribune*, of which Greeley was the editor.

[50] Emancipation Proclamation (September 22, 1862), in id., at 433 et seq. The strategy confirms that the primary motivation for issuing the Proclamation was—as Lincoln and others of his administration openly admitted—to punish and weaken the states "in rebellion" in order to resecure the Union. James M. McPherson, *Battle Cry of Freedom: The Civil War Era* (1988), at 502–504, 510; Garry Wills, supra note 8, at 135–142.

[51] Douglas, in *Political Debates*, supra note 17, at 127, 280. Douglas might have disputed the constitutionality of the Emancipation Proclamation, however. Even Lincoln seemed to have doubts about its constitutionality. Randall, *Lincoln the Liberal Statesman*, supra note 7, at 29, including note 4.

[52] *Political Debates*, supra note 17, at 16–17, 20, 38, 41, 43, 46, 47–49, 50, 57, 88, 90, 103–105, 120–127, 133–135, 139–140, 225–226.

slavery into the territories, preserve slavery in the country forever, and foreclose debate everywhere about slavery or its appropriateness.[53]

Such mischaracterizations are standard fare for politicians, and they should not surprise us even in the best of political debates. Politics, after all, like legal trials, is partly concerned with the manipulation of prejudice. If unsurprising, though, the mischaracterizations deserve consideration for reasons other than that they tended to manufacture differences in order to disguise similarities. For the question also arises, why were two prominent Northern politicians inclined to use these misrepresentations when and how they did? Certainly the mischaracterizations pointed to slavery's growing importance in diverse quarters as a divisive issue of national, even constitutional, significance. More important, they revealed crucial cleavages in one geographical region of the polity, for they showed which prejudices—and consequently which misunderstandings and mistrust—could be manipulated for potential political gain. At least they revealed two perceptive politicians' views of where such cleavages lay.

The point, then, is less whether Lincoln and Douglas misunderstood or mistrusted each other than whether there were sufficient levels of misunderstanding and mistrust among their constituents for each to exploit. The answer seems to be that such levels indeed existed, even in a Northern state where slavery had never been legal.

It is noteworthy, therefore, that Douglas did not represent predominant Southern views on the constitutional status of slavery. Nor, of course, did Lincoln. These points may be obvious, but what follows from them is that the significance of the debates lay less in the territory over which Lincoln and Douglas fought than in the ground they shared, and upon that ground fewer and fewer Southerners were inclined to stand. The South was emerging as a constitutional world of its own, one in which Lincoln was anathema and one to which Douglas, try as he might, could not speak coherently.

Harry Jaffa quotes—apparently in approval—the traditional view of Douglas as a "northern man with southern principles."[54] There had been a time when this characterization was accurate. But by 1858 that time had passed. In crucial respects, the most important constitutional "opposites" of 1858 were not Douglas and Lincoln but Douglas and the South, or at least the Deep South. Even if we take seriously the chiaroscuro of Lincoln as an antislaver (although on no account an abolitionist) and Douglas as a proponent of popular sovereignty (with no

[53] Lincoln, in id., at 10, 24, 77, 97–98, 112, 114, 154, 172, 218–219, 220–221, 234, 248, 274–275.

[54] Jaffa, supra note 12, at 20.

substantive position on slavery), the political imperatives that drove each to his position were more common than not. And to the extent that they were similar, they again were quite different from the imperatives that impelled many Southerners to embrace *Dred Scott*'s national protection of slavery and to stop speaking of popular sovereignty or states' rights, at least with regard to the protection or extension of slavery.[55]

Such differentiation suggested the perfection of a constitutional division of the country along geographical lines. That division prefigured the political division that would make itself manifest in the presidential election of 1860. As the Democratic Party tried unsuccessfully to nominate a candidate for president and to resolve the party's constitutional position on slavery, it split into two parties—one Southern, one Northern. The Southern Democrats, consisting of a large number of secessionists, nominated John C. Breckinridge, Buchanan's vice president. The Northern Democrats nominated Douglas. The Republicans nominated Lincoln, largely on the force of his performance in the debates of 1858, despite the fact that Douglas had held his seat. Remnants of the Whig Party and the Know Nothings nominated John Bell under the quixotic banner of the Constitutional Union Party. Although Lincoln won less than 40 percent of the popular vote, that plurality gained him a majority of electoral votes. He won without even being on the ballot in ten Southern states. Douglas, who had the second highest total of popular votes, won only in Missouri and part of New Jersey.[56]

Within weeks of the election, an extraordinary number of Southerners, though probably still not a majority, again began to speak of states' rights and self-determination, whose champion Douglas had been for so long. But even in so doing, they were turning Douglas's theory on its head. The inversion was not so much that the new Southern version was subordinate to an ostensible substantive constitutional right to maintain slavery, a right Douglas did not sanction.[57] For by the

[55] For a detailed account of the nationalization of the Southern constitutional position on slavery, see Arthur Bestor, "State Sovereignty and Slavery: A Reinterpretation of Proslavery Constitutional Doctrine, 1846–1860," 54 *J. Ill. St. Hist. Soc.* 117 (1961), at 172 et seq. See also Fehrenbacher, supra note 3, at 474–475, 517–523.

[56] McPherson, supra note 48, at 221–233. McPherson calls Lincoln's election the "Revolution of 1860" in that it marked the end of "the domination of the Slaveholders." Id., at 233, quoting Francis Adams. The fragility and peculiar circumstances of Lincoln's victory, not to mention Lincoln's commitment not to disturb slavery, made Adams's obituary premature. Slavery's abolition during Lincoln's tenure owed less to the ostensible death of "slave power" or to Lincoln's moral commitments than to military and geopolitical considerations. Calling Lincoln's election a revolution permits McPherson to characterize the secessionist movement as a "counterrevolution," a notion that chapter 7 will dispute in greater detail.

[57] Wells, supra note 22, at 21. Douglas had an opportunity to take the nomination of

close of 1860, as the fate of the Corwin Amendment would soon illuminate, slavery was beginning to dissipate as a constitutional issue of overt rhetorical concern to Southerners. Perhaps more important, Southerners were using states' rights not in the service of a localism that might hold together the diverse parts of the present nation, but instead to create a new nation by dividing the old one in two.

V

For many Southerners the election of a "Black Republican" as president made Calhoun seem a prophet. They worried that the North had gained virtual control of the national political apparatus. Thus they feared that the stability and permanence of their society and institutions were threatened and that "constitutional" government had been transformed into "a great national consolidated democracy" in which the national government was the sole judge of its own authority. The fear, in sum, was that constitutional limitations had broken down. Some Southerners, wanting "the Union as it was," which in their view was a creature of a compact among sovereign states, argued that by electing Lincoln the North had breached the compact.[58]

In several respects these Southerners misunderstood or exaggerated the extent of differences both between the North and the South and between the South and Lincoln. Even conceding serious regional differences, there were substantial similarities across and (enormous diversity within) North and South, even on the question of slavery and the nature of American constitutional union. Moreover, some of Calhoun's fears of Northern political and economic domination remained largely unsubstantiated even up to the eve of the crisis over secession. Granted, Northern economic productivity vastly exceeded the South's by almost every standard of measurement.[59] It was also true that Northern lenders, industrialists, and shippers probably benefited more financially from Southern agriculture than Southern planters did. But despite their differences, the two economies remained mutually dependent throughout the first sixty years of the nineteenth century. Politically, Southerners in Congress had repeatedly blocked efforts to enact what they perceived to

---

the old Democratic Party by embracing the Southern position on slavery, which included recognition of a national right to own slaves and endorsement of a national slave code. He refused. Fehrenbacher, supra note 3, at 524–535.

[58] McPherson, supra note 50, at 239.

[59] See Richard N. Current, "God and the Strongest Battalions," in *Why the North Won the Civil War* (Donald, ed., 1960), at 15.

be injurious national legislation — such as bills providing for homesteads in the territories, a Pacific railroad, and land grants for agricultural and mechanical colleges — even if they had not been able to get their way entirely on questions of tariffs, the annexation of Cuba, or the enactment of a federal code protecting slavery in the territories.[60]

Southerners also misunderstood Lincoln and the probable political consequences of his election, both for the preservation of Southern institutions and for the nature of the Union. As we have seen, although Lincoln had sometimes maintained that slavery was immoral, that it should not be extended into the territories, and that it would eventually die a natural death, he had never proposed that slavery be abolished in states where it then existed. Nor had he espoused the potent national political authority that Calhoun feared.

But regardless of whether Lincoln himself represented a substantial threat to the Union as it stood, Southerners may have been understandably insecure as they tried to envision their future within the United States. Essentially that nation's future lay westward in the territories. Under virtually all congressional plans for designating territories as slave or free, the potential size of slave territories was always much smaller than that of territories where capitalism and wage labor were to be practiced to the exclusion of slavery.[61] One could reasonably expect that such an arrangement would both reinforce the North's advantage in population — to the extent that sectional differences were defined by the presence or absence of slavery, "North" included the old and new Northwest — and eventually translate into the admission of a greater number of free states than slave states. Consequently Northern interests could gain effective control of both houses of Congress, and, as Lincoln's election had demonstrated, they could also gain control of the presidency. Although five Southerners and at least one Northerner with Southern sympathies constituted a majority on the Supreme Court, Northern control of the Congress and the presidency might soon generate a new antislavery majority on the Court.[62] And what if, notwithstanding *Dred Scott*, the Constitution were amended to abolish slavery?

When Southerners began again to speak of secession, many Northerners miscalculated the threat, for they underestimated the intensity,

[60] McPherson, supra note 50, at 193–195.

[61] This disparity was especially true after the admission of California in 1850 and Oregon in 1859 as free states. Moreover, it was probably true notwithstanding the Supreme Court's pronouncements in *Dred Scott*.

[62] Justice Daniel, a Virginian, died in 1860, near the end of Buchanan's term. Buchanan would eventually nominate a successor but not until February 1861, well after Lincoln had been elected. The Senate rejected Buchanan's nominee, paving the way for Lincoln to appoint a new justice as soon as he took office. Warren, supra note 4, at 358–365.

popularity, and sincerity of secessionist sentiment in the South. Even after South Carolina seceded on December 20, 1860, followed in rapid succession by Mississippi, Florida, Alabama, Georgia, Louisiana, and Texas during the first month of 1861, some in the North argued that the states of the Deep South were bluffing and that some concession would keep them in the Union and prevent states of the Upper South from seceding. But what sort of concession might might be appropriate and feasible?[63]

On December 18, 1860, the Senate directed its Special Committee of Thirteen to investigate and report on the "agitated and distracted condition of the country, and the grievances between the slaveholding and non-slaveholding States." Although the Committee was "not . . . able to agree upon any general plan of adjustment,"[64] the House's Select Committee of Thirty-Three, investigating the country's "perilous condition," recommended the adoption of three measures designed to mitigate the danger of overt hostility and to preserve, or reestablish, Union.

The first proposal was to admit New Mexico as a state, either slave or free as determined under its constitution, which would be adopted by territorial convention and ratified by popular referendum.[65] The second was a bill designed to strengthen and expedite the enforcement of the existing federal Fugitive Slave Act and to limit further the operation of personal liberty laws.[66] The third was to amend the Constitution.[67] On March 2, 1861, absent the Senators and members of Congress from the seven states of the Deep South that had seceded, an overwhelmingly Northern Congress approved a substitute resolution proposing the adoption of what would become known as the Corwin Amendment:

[63] McPherson, supra note 50, at 235, 229–231, 255–257.

[64] "Report of the Committee of Thirteen" (December 31, 1860), Rep. No. 288, *Index to the Reports of the Committees of the Senate of the United States for the Second Session of the Thirty-Sixth Congress.*

[65] "Report on the Disturbed Condition of the Country" (January 14, 1861), Rep. No. 31, *Reports of the Committees of the House of Representatives, Made During the Second Session of the Thirty-Sixth Congress, 1860–1861*, vol. 1. Although slavery was then permitted in the territory of New Mexico, most people seem to have assumed that the institution would never flourish there and that the new state would eventually become a free state even if its constitution on admission to the union permitted slavery. The House defeated the proposal. McPherson, supra note 50, at 256.

[66] "Report," supra note 65.

[67] Id. As originally proposed, the amendment read as follows: "Article XII [*sic*]. No amendment of this Constitution having for its object any interference within the States with the relation between their citizens and those described in section second of the first article of the Constitution as 'all other persons,' shall originate with any State that does not recognize that relation within its own limits, or shall be valid without the assent of every one of the States composing the Union."

> *Resolved by the Senate and House of Representatives of the United States of America in Congress assembled*, That the following article be proposed to the Legislatures of the several States as an amendment to the Constitution of the United States, which, when ratified by three-fourths of said Legislatures, shall be valid, to all intents and purposes, as part of the said Constitution, viz.:
>
> *"Article Thirteen.*
>
> No amendment shall be made to the Constitution which will authorize or give to Congress the power to abolish or interfere, within any State, with the domestic institutions thereof, including that of persons held to labor or service by the laws of said State."[68]

The aims were obviously to forestall further secessions and to bring back seceded states by supplying explicit security on the question of slavery.

In his First Inaugural Address, President Lincoln went out of his way to acknowledge the amendment, which, as he accurately put it, required "that the federal government, shall never interfere with the domestic institutions of the states, including that of persons held to service." He indicated that he supported this policy. Specifically he said that he did not object to making it explicit that the individual states had control over their domestic institutions, exclusive of federal interference; that he did not object to such a provision's being made irrevocable; and that such a provision was probably unnecessary inasmuch as it was already then "implied constitutional law."[69]

[68] U.S. Statutes at Large, vol. 12, 1859–1863, 251 (Sawyer, ed., 1863). As soon as Congress adopted the proposed amendment, President Buchanan signed it. *Journal of the House of Representatives of the United States: Being the Second Session of the Thirty-Sixth Congress* (March 2, 1861), at 486; *Journal of the Senate of the United States* (March 2, 1861), at 396–397). Lincoln did not sign the amendment, as I indicated in "The 'Original' Thirteenth Amendment and the Limits to Formal Constitutional Change," in *Responding to Imperfection: The Theory and Practice of Constitutional Amendment* (Levinson, ed., 1995), at 215, 219. For an explanation of why the president's approval was unnecessary, see Herman V. Ames, *The Proposed Amendments to the Constitution of the United States during the First Century of Its History* (1896; repr. 1970), at 196, 295–296; *Hollingsworth v. Virginia*, 3 U.S. (Dall.) 378 (1798).

[69] Lincoln, "First Inaugural Address," supra note 20, at 262, 270. (Lincoln may have understood the amendment to protect slavery only where it then existed, but neither the amendment's plain language nor Lincoln's speech suggests such a limitation.) His inauguration as president was not his first occasion for espousing the view that slavery was constitutionally protected. In 1837, as a member of the Illinois General Assembly, he had opposed a resolution that "the right of property in slaves, is sacred to the slave-holding states by the Federal Constitution." Instead he proposed a substitute: "The Congress of the United States has no power, under the constitution, to interfere with the institution of slavery in the different states." David Herbert Donald, *Lincoln* (1995), at 63–64.

Three states ratified the amendment—Ohio, Maryland, and Illinois—all of which would find themselves on the Northern side in the Civil War. Herman Ames insisted that "[o]ther Northern States would have undoubtedly ratified it, if it had promised to stay secession."[70] But Southerners had ceased seeking parchment guarantees for slavery in the existing constitutional order, and hence the amendment failed to achieve its purposes. The outbreak of military conflict and the secession of four more states in the Upper South merely sealed a division that had already occurred.

[70] Ames, supra note 68, at 196–197.

CHAPTER SIX

Constitutional Autonomy, Discourse, and Failure

I

The division of the polity was a *constitutional* division in two respects. First, it had to do with the very character, structure, and survival of the political order. Second, it arose in response to disputes over the values, institutions, and ways of life that the Constitution permitted, required, or prohibited. In other words, it was precipitated by arguments over what the Constitution was and what it meant. The first observation does not add much to our understanding of the Constitution or constitutionalism. The second, if true, is more significant, because it presumes that constitutions matter. It presumes, in fact, that constitutions can be quite powerful, for they can alter the world of politics in fundamental ways, even to the point of destroying certain aspects of that world. Alteration and destruction are simply—sometimes unavoidably—aspects of constitutional politics.

Chapter 1 claimed that if a constitution is to succeed in making a political world, it must be interpretable. But interpretation alone is an arid endeavor. In a constitutional polity, the aim of constitutional interpretation is to make one or another interpretation real in the world. To achieve that aim, one must be able to talk publicly about the constitution and what it means. Thus, if it is to succeed in making a world, the constitution must be capable of generating a discourse that is distinct from other ways of talking about and making the world. We might call it a "partially autonomous" discourse.

Mark Tushnet uses a synonymous phrase—"relative autonomy"—in connection with law. By "law," Tushnet refers to the work of lawyers and judges. Law has relative autonomy, he says, because it is distinct from the "political and economic structures of capitalism." It is partially independent of the interests or ideology of the dominant class(es) of capitalist society.[1]

Whatever the merits of Tushnet's view of *legal* discourse, nineteenth-century *constitutional* discourse in the United States was autonomous in ways other than the one he suggests. First, and most obvious, the Con-

[1] Mark Tushnet, "A Marxist Analysis of American Law," 1 *Marxist Perspectives* 96 (1978).

stitution originally embodied two forms of economic organization—capitalism and plantation agriculture—that were distinctive, even if they were not always at odds with each other. At a minimum they envisioned different, perhaps competing, forms of property. They implied divergent forms of social organization. They also embedded in the constitutional order an internal division that may have inherently rendered the Constitution partially autonomous from capitalism (narrowly conceived).

Second, *constitutional* discourse—at least in the United States and perhaps generally as well—is not entirely equivalent to *legal* discourse (i.e., the talk of lawyers and judges). As chapters 2, 3, and 5 demonstrate, nineteenth-century constitutional discourse was much larger than what lawyers and judges might say. What these people said about issues like sovereignty, states' rights, slavery, or citizenship was deeply significant, both in principle and consequence, but it was only a fraction of the constitutional discourse on those questions. Even in our own time, notwithstanding some people's tendency to equate constitution with law and law with the pronouncements of judges, constitutional discourse is distinguishable from law, strictly construed, and from what judges say. (In fact a constitution is prior to law in that it makes certain forms of law possible.)

We have seen some of the ways in which constitutional discourse and interpretation contributed to the breakdown of the American constitutional order. But how might we make sense of that contribution, not simply empirically but as a theoretical matter related to the proper functions of a constitution? I wish to pursue that question here in greater depth.

Section II argues that written constitutions have both integrative and disintegrative properties and that those properties are "natural" functions of the roles of interpretation and discourse in constitutional orders. Section III speaks to the "realist" challenge that interpretation or discourse is too weak to cause a political order to fail. That section considers how two prototypal realists, Hobbes and Thucydides, addressed the power of language to dissolve a political order. Section IV addresses in greater detail the extent to which constitutional failure in the United States in the nineteenth century resulted from a breakdown of constitutional discourse. I argue in that section that the breakdown of the political order was a function of two phenomena: (1) a failure of constitutional discourse, that is, a failure of the constituent parts of the order to understand one another or to generate authoritative meanings, and (2) a failure of will.

A skeptic might argue, however, that any indication that the breakdown of the American order in 1860–61 was even remotely a consequence of constitutional discourse is illusory. That individual might further claim that something else was "really" at stake in the failure of the order. Sections V and VI try to meet these claims by addressing two prominent explanations for what was indeed behind constitutional argument: the pursuit of morality and the pursuit of interest. These sections argue—and this is the third and most important basis for the autonomy of constitutional discourse—that the Constitution was partially *autonomous* from both morality and interest because it was *connected* to both. That autonomy—distinguishing constitutional discourse from questions of either morality or interest—permitted the Constitution not only to participate in making a new political order but eventually to precipitate a breakdown of that order. To invoke the typology of chapter 1, fidelity to the norms and practices of *constitutionalism* and *the Constitution* produced a failure of *constitutional discourse* and, in turn, the *constitutional order.*

II

That a constitution might help destroy its own "creation" seems counterintuitive. It seems so in part because we are accustomed to thinking of constitutions as integrative devices, as vehicles for establishing and maintaining an ordered and more coherent political world. For some, the alternative to a constitutional world is no world at all. To borrow from physics, constitutions supply a gravitational force that keeps the polity's constituent elements from flying off into the void, into the dark, chaotic, unprincipled, and unworldly outer space of a politics of pure will.[2]

One way a constitution might serve as an instrument for imposing order is by providing a means for people in a political society to talk to one another. Some might call it a language, others a grammar. For now those subtle distinctions are not as important as the recognition that a constitutional text might supply a means by which "a people" linguistically establish and maintain a politics. Under this view, a constitution might draw people of diverse aims, backgrounds, and characteristics within a single gravitational sphere.

Whatever the means for imposing order, under a strong version of the "ordering view," a constitution "succeeds" as long as it *maintains* order or *sustains* conversation, as long as it can hold the center. If the discussion thus far tells us anything, however, it tells us that constitutions do

[2] See H.L.A. Hart, "American Jurisprudence Through English Eyes: The Nightmare and the Noble Dream," 11 *Ga. L. Rev.* 969 (1977); William F. Harris II, "Bonding Word and Polity: The Logic of American Constitutionalism," 76 *Am. Pol. Sci. Rev.* 34 (1982).

not always succeed according to such criteria, for by 1860 the American constitutional order was on the verge of breaking down. In fact, if we once again borrow from physics, we might say that through interpretation, constitutions can simultaneously exert two forces on or within the constituted world: one gravitational, pulling to the center, holding things together; the other centrifugal, permitting the world, or some of its elements, to fly off. In its most extreme forms this centrifugal tendency might produce a breakdown of constitutional discourse, which in turn might precipitate the collapse of constitutional order, although it need not do so in all cases. Still, in many ways, the impending failure of the American order did not look like a gravitational failure, at least not the kind in which constituent parts are thrown off hither and yon. Granted, there was evidence of the disintegration of a constitutional center that might have held the polity together. But as frantic as the country's politics became, it rarely resembled the dissolution to randomness, darkness, or chaos suggested by H.L.A. Hart's nightmare.

Instead, the order's looming failure was almost like a "genetic" mitosis. It had an organic character, one that might seem incongruous, especially in the American case, given the Constitution's decidedly artificial nature and architectonic function. These "unnatural" characteristics are understandable, for if a constitution were designed merely to mimic nature, human or otherwise, or to ratify natural tendencies, it is far from clear why anyone would feel the need to use it at all.

Thus, although "organic" seems to describe the impending breakdown, its aptness might largely grow out of the seemingly natural character of certain exogenous considerations rather than something distinctly "constitutional." For example, the plausibility of the organic metaphor might be explained by the fact that the failure was quite gradual (having evolved over roughly seventy years), that it occurred along geographical lines, or that it appeared to be largely dichotomous (which might suggest less a dissolution to chaos than a reordering resembling the mitotic division of an organism). But the order's imminent collapse was "organic" in a deeper sense, deeper because it was partly interpretive and because of the centrality of interpretation in the constitutional polity. To press the biological metaphor, interpretation can be the impetus for the creation of new constitutional forms. That act of creation can be a wondrous or awful thing, as the series of cases culminating in *Dred Scott* testifies.

The breakdown of discourse, then, might well threaten the stability, perhaps also the viability, of a constitutional regime at particular times. But whether it is a function of centrifugal tendencies or some process of morphogenesis, such a breakdown is not necessarily an abnormality to be rectified, for it may be an integral part of the interpretive component of constitutional politics. Thus the dissolution of a particular regime or order need not signify a constitutional failure from the standpoint of constitutionalism. Indeed it may well signify that constitution and interpretation are functioning properly. Constitutions carry the seeds of their own destruction or the destruction of the order they represent. In a real (and not just philosophical) sense, what binds dissolves.

If true, those claims reinforce the aptness of a strategy that treats constitutions not as sacred texts but as experiments that can fail. That a particular experiment might fail does not mean that the larger enterprise of which it is a part is also a failure. Why this is so is a function of the nature of interpretation, for part of what binds a constitutional polity is argumentation grounded in its constitution. Such argumentation clearly requires some sort of understanding of what the constitution means, which in turn presupposes interpretation. But we have already seen that interpretation can generate or reflect multiplicities of understandings. When those understandings, those interpretations, produce or derive from worldviews that are fundamentally incompatible with one another, the breakdown of an order can occur—not always, perhaps rarely, but sometimes. *When* it occurs depends in part on how widely shared the different worldviews are, how deeply felt, and how closely they implicate categories of constitutional interpretation or the commitment to maintaining a particular constituted polity.

III

Perhaps, though, the realists who trace their pedigree to Thomas Hobbes are right. It may be implausible that a political order will fail through interpretation, through an inability to regenerate or maintain itself by reference to its constitution. The possibility of such a failure seems to grant too much power to constitutional discourse, which, involving merely words, after all, is arguably quite weak. But even in Hobbesian terms, the proposition that language matters may not be so far-fetched. Although a proponent of absolute sovereignty and a progenitor of *realpolitik*, Hobbes was impelled to defend his position in a work notable for at least two features. First, it was astonishingly wordy. Second, it took as part of its strategy the demolition and reconstruction of the very language people used to talk about politics in seventeenth-century England.[3] Given his additional claim in *Behemoth* that belief

[3] Thomas Hobbes, *Leviathan* (1651) (Macpherson, ed., 1968), especially at 85–222; Don Herzog, *Happy Slaves: A Critique of Consent Theory* (1989), at 73, 82–109.

plays a central role in the maintenance of a political order,[4] it appears he was quite respectful, even fearful, of the power of certain forms of language in politics. Language was fearsome for Hobbes not simply because of its power to persuade but, perhaps more important, because it was integral to the formation and maintenance of beliefs and the ways in which people viewed the world. It was not weaker but stronger and more insidious for its grounding in culture and society.

Hobbes's solution was to have people talk as little as possible (one of *Leviathan*'s aims was to take people's language away from them) or to leave talking to the experts (i.e., the sovereign and the scientists). Of course that solution met with frustration in seventeenth-century England. But even had the solution been plausible for a polity of monarchs or technocrats or for a polity built mainly on accident and force instead of on reflection and choice, it would have been more problematic in a polity partaking of some attributes of democracy, whose lifeblood is language, whose aristocrats are orators, and whose structure of authority includes "a people" who make decisions by talking.

As Thucydides, another realist, saw, however, democracy's lifeblood was also one of its greatest dangers, for language threatened the longevity and stability of fourth-century (B.C.E.) Athenian democracy in two ways. First, political rhetoric could paint a powerfully appealing self-portrait that was patently at odds with society's everyday life. Compare, for example, the world of prosperity, happiness, and peace evoked in Pericles's funeral oration with the adjoining descriptions of the suffering and misery that Athenians actually faced and the war they eventually waged.[5] The genius of Pericles was that he could convince people they were flourishing and virtuous despite a wealth of contrary evidence. Language's power to evoke an image of the world depended fundamentally on its power to exploit illusion. It could unify through sleight-of-hand; its effectiveness was only enhanced by the plausible human impulse to ward off political, social, or military disaster by telling happy stories. The danger of such a power was that happy stories could not forever forestall the unpleasant intrusion of certain social, political, and economic realities.

Second, however, language could have the opposite effect. Instead of papering over differences, it could exacerbate them. Instead of forestalling disintegration, it could hasten it. It could threaten unity and stability by magnifying cleavages. For example, as Athens was increasingly stressed by its commitment to the Peloponnesian War, by the absence of

[4] Thomas Hobbes, *Behemoth: The History of the Causes of the Civil Wars of England* (1682) (Molesworth, ed., 1840, 1969).

[5] Thucydides, *The Peloponnesian War* (Wick, ed., 1982), at 106–126.

a unified leadership, by incipient revolutions both at home and among its allies, and by repercussions of the plague, Athenian "society became divided into camps" and was distinguished by quarreling, extremism, and lack of trust. As a result, words began fundamentally to change their value. They "had to change their ordinary meanings and to take those which were now given to them." With the ensuing disintegration of social and international relations, words became virtually useless, persuasion impossible, promises unreliable, and, with "the hopelessness of a permanent state of things," force became its own justification.[6]

Notwithstanding the substantial merits of Thucydides's first account of the corrosive power of language, his second account assumes too much. First, he was too suspicious of the danger that multiplicities of meaning posed for the polity. Perhaps his suspicion arose out of nostalgia for a time when a few men like Pericles could hold the center in politics by controlling the content of the language people used to talk about politics.[7] Such multiplicities are unavoidable in the normal operation of a linguistic politics, although not all verbal disagreements lead to the breakdown of an order. Second, Thucydides seems to have assumed that language is radically malleable, having little autonomy or resilience against manipulation, and that especially in times of stress, language is captive to considerations of perceived interest. Third, as chapter 7 considers at length, even when discourse breaks down, constitutionalism sometimes permits regimes to dissolve themselves without allowing force to become its own justification. Movement to a world outside an established order need not imply movement to a Hobbesian world of force and violence.

IV

By early 1861 constitutional order in the United States had clearly broken down. In some respects, moreover, an essential element in that breakdown was the maintenance of a system of slave labor in much of the Southern part of the country.[8] Further, as I have already suggested, the crisis of 1860–61 was basically constitutional in character not simply because of its consequence—that it involved a collapse of the basic structure and implicated some of the fundamental values of the country—but also because it followed from conflicting accounts of what the

[6] Id., at 199–201.

[7] This is in contrast with many constitutions that authorize a language but do not consistently prescribe meanings.

[8] But see Anne Norton, *Alternative Americas: A Reading of Antebellum Political Culture* (1986).

Constitution meant. In short, the breakdown was a function of constitutional *discourse*, of meaning, of the polity's ability to regenerate or maintain itself by reference to the Constitution. Quite literally, people talked their way out of Union.

In general, the breakdown of discourse can take one of two forms; it can be "objective," pertaining to *authority*, or "subjective," pertaining to *understanding*. With respect to the former, discursive failure might appear as political society's inability to generate common authoritative meanings; that is, authoritative interpretations—those partaking of legitimacy because of their compatibility with certain types of expectations—become difficult, perhaps impossible. Those expectations may be either procedural or substantive and may be derived either internally (from within the constitutional text) or externally (from sources other than the text). With respect to the latter form, discursive failure might appear simply as the inability of constitutional interpreters to understand one another in their supposedly common polity.

Both forms of breakdown were evident over the question of slavery in the nineteenth-century United States, and both were bred by distrust. Lincoln and Douglas had capitalized on such distrust in their debates, but the debates were only discrete examples of a much wider and deeper phenomenon. Indeed distrust, fueled by alienation, had for decades informed the strategies of both Southerners and abolitionists in interpreting and resolving questions of attachment to the Constitution. *Dred Scott* was the watershed, for it intensified tendencies already present in the polity, lending credence to Northern fears of Southern designs on a national empire for slavery and of conspiracies within national political institutions to promote such an empire. The fervor of Northern reaction to *Dred Scott* convinced many Southerners that these were people on whom the South could no longer rely as political partners. After 1859 the extent to which Northerners viewed John Brown as a martyr only confirmed this sense. When it was revealed that a group of abolitionists in New England had actually financed and abetted some of Brown's activities, Southern separatism reached its highest point since the nullification crisis of thirty years before.

The prevalence of mistrust helped provoke a crisis of authority. Not surprisingly, the best evidence of a breakdown of interpretive authority was *Dred Scott* itself, which not only helped polarize the country but also weakened the institutional authority of the Supreme Court. Simply, a significant proportion of the Northern population viewed the decision as unacceptable and illegitimate.

But we have seen that courts are not the only institutions authorized to interpret the Constitution. In fact the operation of "normal" political processes can also embody a kind of interpretation, as can popular responses to the outcomes of those processes. The reaction of the Deep

South to Lincoln's election as president certainly signified a flagging faith in the authority of constituted processes and in the capacity of political institutions to protect Southern interests. If, from the standpoint of political process, Lincoln's election became what the Constitution "meant," many in the South were unwilling to accept such a meaning.

Similarly misunderstandings—or, more accurately, incommensurabilities—were acutely apparent. With regard to the status of slavery in the territories, Douglas had laid his hands on one such incommensurability by simultaneously grabbing hold of the tails of two tigers, pulling in opposite directions: popular sovereignty and *Dred Scott*'s constitutional right to hold slaves. He could hold onto both only at great risk, and when threatened with being devoured, he consistently let *Dred Scott* loose and held onto popular sovereignty. There may have been some place in the world where both principles could conceivably have been espoused, but not in Illinois or the Deep South or New England or anywhere else outside the border states. If the two positions were not inherently incompatible, they were increasingly *becoming* so in the United States because of the meanings with which the polity was imbuing them. Before *Dred Scott*, the differences among members of mainstream political institutions were largely disagreements about versions of popular or state sovereignty. After *Dred Scott*, the differences and the discursive strategies for approaching them became both simpler and more complex.

It was as if the Supreme Court and radical Southerners were attempting to seize the agenda of the constitutionalist wing of the abolitionist movement. In doing so, Southern proslavers had latched onto another incommensurability: nationalist versus localist solutions to the constitutional problems slavery posed. Before *Dred Scott*, few sober Southern politicians in the national political arena, except in their most expansive moments, would have defended a *national* right to own slaves. After *Dred Scott*, few dared reject it. But Southerners' persistent fears about their place in the Union continued to beg for localist solutions. Having abandoned localism for the illusion of a quick fix on the question of slavery, however, the South had compromised its capacity to regain the turf in a principled way on other questions of constitutional import. Although reclaiming localist constitutionalism would not have been theoretically impossible, it would have been exceedingly difficult in light of both the political pressures of the day and the rapidity with which forces for separation were gathering in the Deep South.

The South's dilemma, then, was this: Most national politicians from other regions who were proponents of policies sympathetic to the South were impelled by their own political circumstances to adopt localist constitutional positions with which Southerners were increasingly unprepared to live. Because these positions were localist, they were largely silent on the constitutional status of slavery. On the other hand, the South despised many of those politicians who were willing to ratify a nationalist constitutionalism on slavery, both because they tended to be unsympathetic to policies favoring the South and because they adopted national constitutional solutions to the problem of slavery, solutions such as abolition and nonextension that were fundamentally opposed to the emerging Southern position.

Such were two of the most salient incommensurabilities at work by 1860. On the surface they resembled the sorts of differences that frequently exist in almost all political societies, especially those of some complexity. What made them so potent was that they pertained to persistent problems of national political import. Indeed they went to the heart of regional and national political identities; moreover, they implicated cultural, economic, and moral cleavages that had aggregated along geographical lines.

Such considerations made dealing with these conflicts stressful, but did not necessarily make political life impossible. The crucial question, therefore, was whether the differences were ones with which people were prepared to live—a question largely of will, not merely interpretation. Southerners—though probably not a majority even by early 1861—were becoming inclined to answer no. But they did so mainly on the basis of a crucial misunderstanding or intentional mischaracterization. Having rejected Douglas's constitutional position, they swallowed whole his account of Lincoln as an abolitionist, egalitarian, nationalist, "Black Republican." Secessionist or not, they saw in Lincoln the leader of a national democracy now completely beyond their control or even influence. They saw him as inflexible and unsympathetic to "Southern interests." The distance between Lincoln and the South was wide enough without such misperceptions. With them, the gulf was enormous. If there were rational ways to test the validity of such perceptions, few people at the time were prepared to employ them. That unwillingness is important because it demonstrates that constitutional politics does not operate solely on the basis of objective considerations. It operates substantially, perhaps primarily, on the basis of a combination of perception and will. But the pertinence of considerations of perception posed a challenge to the possibility of government by constitution.

V

Even if the argument is correct that language is sufficiently powerful to bring down a political order, one might still doubt that in the American case it was actually the Constitution or constitutional discourse that was breaking down the order. Skepticism about the Constitution's contribution to the failure of the order might arise partly from Thucydides's observation of the capacity of language to perpetrate illusion. Or it might stem from the connection between constitutional interpretation on the one hand and perception and will on the other. For if a constitution can be responsible for the failure of an order, it must be able to constrain politics, which means it must be capable of producing results other than those people might want in a particular circumstance. The skepticism might also arise from some combination of the two; that is, people might use constitutional language, blinded to what is really going on by the spell of illusion it casts. What is really going on, of course, has been the subject of intense debate since Thucydides's time.

Using a modified version of Thucydides's mirror we might give two accounts of American constitutional failure that not only are congruent with the two ways in which language facilitated the collapse of Athenian politics but also illuminate two potential explanations for the American order's failure. I shall take up the first account here, the second below in Section VI. The first is connected less directly to the notion that constitutional discourse is an illusion than to the less radical claim that what is indeed at stake in games of constitutional language is morality.[9] According to this account, much of the political and constitutional rhetoric of the mid-nineteenth century was a lie, both morally and phenomenologically (assuming the two are distinguishable for political purposes). That rhetoric invoked such values as equality and individual liberty (traceable in part to the second paragraph of the Declaration of Independence, if not always to the Constitution itself) and the transformative character of the national founding. Elitism and the institutions that propped up slavery "disproved" the rhetoric of equality and liberty, while the persistence of localist worldviews and economic and cultural divisions undermined the rhetoric of nationhood and unity.

With regard to the American case, this view assumes three points: First, constitutional debates over slavery were essentially part of a process by which some in the country were mightily straining to do the right thing; second, the content of the categories of liberty and equality and the meaning of the founding were objectively definable apart from their institutional manifestations; and third, arising from the first two points, the values the account identifies and the content it gives them are consistent with what we now tend to embrace as proper political

[9] See, e.g., Michael S. Moore, "The Interpretive Turn in Modern Theory: A Turn for the Worse?" 41 *Stanford L. Rev.* 871 (1989), at 955–957. Cf. Joseph Raz, "Morality as Interpretation," 101 *Ethics* 392 (1991).

values. The third point does not substantively speak to the connection between constitution and morality in the nineteenth century, but it does indicate one possible reason that we find the moral explanation so attractive, if not historically compelled. That said, this section now focuses on the implications of the first two assumptions.

No one can sensibly doubt that constitutional interpretation is importantly a moral enterprise. At the very least, it directly impinges on significant moral questions. Moreover, morality often motivates people to interpret a text as they do. Certainly American constitutional interpretation as it pertained to questions of slavery was bound up with morality in these ways, just as child labor, pornography, and abortion have been connected to morality in the twentieth century.

It would be impossible, for example, to understand the development of antislavery constitutionalism or Frederick Douglass's use of textually attentive interpretive principles to transform his theory of constitutional meaning without appreciating the deep connection between morality and constitutional interpretation. Similarly, though perhaps more controversially, Southerners who adopted a constitutional strategy for defending their way of life considered that way of life to be not only defensible but also positively sanctioned by established moral authority such as the Bible. From a psychological standpoint, it would have been difficult to separate the impulses that motivated the moral choices or assumptions of proslavers or antislavers from the choices they made about or the understandings they derived from constitutional interpretation. In interpreting the Constitution on the question of slavery, both sides saw themselves as engaged in an activity with unquestionably moral consequences.

Constitutional interpretation and moral inquiry were not coextensive, however. The Garrisonians held distinct assumptions about the immorality of slavery and read the Constitution with those assumptions in plain view. They had every moral incentive to read the Constitution as being fundamentally opposed to slavery, but they did not. That they did not do so was partly explainable by moral impulses, which manifested themselves in the Garrisonians' plausible acknowledgment of the impracticality of securing at the time an institutionally authoritative adjudication in the polity that slavery was unconstitutional. But the sense the Garrisonians made of what the Constitution meant with regard to slavery was not dictated by those impulses.

The point, again, is not that constitutional interpretation is not a moral enterprise. In many respects its aim and consequence have to do with practical questions about what people "ought" to do or are permitted to do. Those questions are often moral in flavor. But it would be a mistake to assume that constitutional interpretation is "essentially" about generating readings of the Constitution that always lead us to a morally correct result. Even if it were desirable for constitutional interpretation to presuppose such a purpose, it is doubtful that interpretation could consistently achieve it.

In the first place, constitutional interpretation is often a vehicle for more (or less) than simply doing the right thing. It is also a vehicle for the promotion of perceived interest, which may have precious little relation to what we take to be the morally correct result in any given case.[10] Moreover, whatever moral content constitutional interpretation has is universally mitigated by pragmatic considerations of what modes of action are possible and at what cost.[11]

Further, interpretation takes place within a system of social relations, values, and structures of political authority. Often its aim—not simply for base or self-interested reasons but because it is part of how constitutions function—is to reinforce that system or structure, which usually has a useful logic and even a moral justification apart from the correctness of the result in a particular case or from the particular commands of a constitutional provision. Hence, as H.L.A. Hart recognized, some types of explicit moral evaluation are appropriate as critiques of or justifications for the system or structure as a whole.[12] That is so, again, not because interpretation is devoid of moral impulses or consequences but because the logic of the order and imperatives of maintaining it mitigate the range and force, for example, of explicitly moral claims one can make from within the system through interpretation. These considerations make Garrisonian interpretations, which informed their secessionist impulses, understandable.

But to return to the second assumption of Thucydides's first model of political breakdown, whether morality informs or motivates interpretation or serves as a ground for critically evaluating an order, it is not useful to think of morality in this context as transcendental. To illustrate this point, we might focus on the libertarian values of the second paragraph of the Declaration of Independence.

Thomas Jefferson, the principal draftsman of the Declaration (the Continental Congress was its formal author), was by many indications morally opposed to slavery. He expressed dissatisfaction with the institution of slavery and with the reticence of his contemporaries to con-

[10] The power of interest may help to explain how moral relativism often flourishes in capitalist economic systems.

[11] I take this to be a noncontroversial point with which even Aquinas agreed. Thomas Aquinas, *Summa Theologica* I:II, Questions 90 and 97.

[12] This is partly what is at stake in Hart's distinction between secondary rules of recognition and primary rules of obligation. H.L.A. Hart, *The Concept of Law* (1961), at 97–120. See also his *Law, Liberty, and Morality* (1963), at 1–24.

front the problems slavery posed for American society. In his autobiography he noted that even before the American Revolution he had sponsored and pressed for the adoption of legislation in Virginia that would have abolished the slave trade and emancipated the slaves in the state.[13]

After the Revolution, he repeatedly expressed opposition to slavery and sympathy for slaves. His opposition was grounded partly in recognition of the deplorable conditions under which slaves suffered[14] and partly out of objection to what slavery did, not to the slaves but to the country. Slavery, he said, was "an unhappy influence on the manners of our people," engendering "a perpetual exercise of the most barbarous passions, the most unremitting despotism," which each succeeding generation learned to imitate.[15] He sometimes objected to slavery in terms almost religious.[16]

It also appears that he viewed slavery as incompatible with the principles of the Declaration, which he perceived to have driven the Revolution. His original draft of the Declaration contained a clause criticizing the slave trade. Congress deleted the clause, not only "in complaisance to South Carolina and Georgia, who had never attempted to restrain the importation of slaves, and who on the contrary still wished to continue it," but also because of the reluctance of "[o]ur northern brethren who had long been making money from the slave trade."[17] Even without the specific clause criticizing the slave trade, he indicated in later pronouncements that the Declaration's more abstract commitments were inconsistent with slavery.

> What a stupendous, what an incomprehensible machine is man! who can endure toil, famine, stripes, imprisonment & death itself in vindication of his own liberty, and next moment be deaf to all these motives whose power supported him thro' his trial, and inflict on his fellow man a bondage, one hour of which is fraught with more misery than ages of that which he rose in rebellion to oppose.[18]

[13] Thomas Jefferson, *Autobiography* (1821), in *Thomas Jefferson: Writings* (Peterson, ed., 1984), at 5, 34, 44.

[14] Jefferson, "Answers and Observations for Demeunier's Article on the United States in the *Encyclopedia Methodique*" (1786); "Letter to Jared Sparks" (February 4, 1824); "Letter to James Heaton" (May 20, 1826); all in *Writings*, supra note 13, at 592, 1484, 1516.

[15] Jefferson, *Notes on the State of Virginia* (1787), in *Writings*, supra note 13, at 288.

[16] Jefferson, "Answers and Observations," supra note 14, at 592; *Notes*, supra note 15, at 289. In the latter work, he said, "I tremble for my country when I reflect that God is just: that his injustice cannot sleep forever: that considering numbers, nature and natural means only, a revolution of the wheel of fortune, an exchange of situation, is among all possible events: that it may become possible by supernatural interference!"

[17] Jefferson, *Autobiography*, supra note 13, at 18, 22.

[18] Jefferson, "Answers and Observations," supra note 14, at 592.

A year later he argued that maintaining slavery both "trampl[ed] on the rights" of slaves and turned government despotic. Always implicit in such arguments were notions of how slavery affected the political identity of the slave and of what that identity in turn implied for the country in which slaves found themselves:

> For if a slave can have a country in this world, it must be any other in preference to that in which he is born to live and labor for another: in which he must lock up the faculties of his nature, contribute as far as depends on his individual endeavors to the evanishment of the human race, or entail his own miserable condition on the endless generations proceeding from him.[19]

And when Congress in 1820 adopted the Missouri Compromise, Jefferson was almost anguished:

> I regret that I am now to die in the belief, that the useless sacrifice of themselves by the generation of 1776, to acquire self-government and happiness to their country, is to be thrown away by the unwise and unworthy passions of their sons, and that my own consolation is to be, that I live not to weep over it.[20]

But even Jefferson, who was probably far more libertarian than most white Americans of his day on the question of slavery, never came to terms with what he saw as the logic of the principles of the Declaration. For example, he continued to hold slaves until his death. Further, he eventually softened his public pronouncements against slavery and limited his efforts to secure the adoption of public policy that would have substantially curtailed the institution.[21] Much of his discussion of slavery—including his expression of fears of miscegenation,[22] his contention that blacks were shiftless and lazy, and his proposals combining the gradual emancipation of slaves with the deportation and colonization of freed blacks[23]—was imbued with racist assumptions, as Lincoln's would be decades later.

One is tempted to attribute such shadings in Jefferson's thought and behavior to the tension between rhetoric and the inertial power of practice. Or, at the level of society, the tension might be one between dis-

[19] Jefferson, *Notes*, supra note 15, at 288.

[20] Jefferson, "Letter to John Holmes" (April 22, 1820), in *Writings*, supra note 13, at 1434.

[21] Jefferson, "Answers and Observations," supra note 14, at 592; *Autobiography*, supra note 13, at 44; "Letter to James Heaton," supra note 14, at 1516.

[22] Jefferson, "Letter to Edward Coles" (August 25, 1814), in *Writings*, supra note 13, at 1345.

[23] Jefferson, "Letter to Jared Sparks," supra note 14, at 1484–1487.

course and institutions. In fact both Don Fehrenbacher and Winthrop Jordan argue that the Declaration of Independence was clearly incompatible with the institution of slavery. Fehrenbacher argues, for example, that with the infusion of rhetoric from the European Enlightenment into the American revolutionary vocabulary, there was a tension, even an incompatibility, between the revolutionary tradition (especially as embodied in the notions of natural rights, liberty, and equality) and slavery. That there was an incompatibility is reinforced by the fact that much of colonial rhetoric vilified the conditions of slavery and servitude under which the Colonies were ostensibly being held by the Crown.[24] Jordan claims more emphatically that the rhetoric which drove the American Revolution clearly required, as a matter of principle, the abolition of slavery and that the primary question by the end of the Revolution was "not *if*, but *when* and *how*" slavery would and should be abolished. He further states that the failure to abolish slavery at the end of the eighteenth century was a missed opportunity.[25]

In fact, however, the Declaration's incompatibility with slavery, even at the time of the Revolution, was much less apparent than Fehrenbacher or Jordan allows. True, a simple reading of the Declaration's second paragraph—"that all men are created equal, that they are endowed by their Creator with certain unalienable rights"—suggests that slavery, for men at least, was problematic. But finessing the pull of the text would have been easy enough, for example, merely by reading "all men" to exclude blacks or perhaps to include only whites of western European descent. Such a reading would not have been implausible at any time between the Revolution and the Civil War. Or one might read the second paragraph in the context of the overall purpose of the Declaration, which was primarily to secure collective rights of self-determination. As David Brion Davis has pointed out, slavery was an important part of the American system that was to be self-determined.[26]

Thus, if there were a "missed" opportunity to abolish slavery, it was missed in part because many people could plausibly read the Declaration's principles as neither presenting nor logically requiring such an opportunity in the first place.[27] As I suggested in chapter 1, the reasons

[24] Don E. Fehrenbacher, *The Dred Scott Case: Its Significance in American Law and Politics* (1978), at 16–17.

[25] Winthrop Jordan, *White over Black: American Attitudes Toward the Negro, 1550–1812* (1968), at 342, 374.

[26] David Brion Davis, *The Problem of Slavery in the Age of Revolution: 1770–1823* (1975), at 256.

[27] John Chester Miller argues that "in the context of events of 1775–1776," the Declaration "denies inferentially" to blacks (or at least to slaves) the very rights that whites were claiming against the Crown. Miller, *The Wolf by the Ears: Thomas Jefferson and Slavery* (1977).

for that result have to do with the operation of language in social contexts. For even if it were true that language is "free in the world," that it can have a life and force apparently all its own, it also seems true that language's ability to describe or constrain the world depends in part on its recognizability. It depends, that is, on the recognizability of language as such and of its referential content. Meanings are neither immanent in words themselves nor objectively imposed by some transcendental source. Their boundaries are generated by or become comprehensible within the contexts of particular cultures at given times in history.

This circumstantial grounding of meaning manifests itself in at least two related ways. First, the symbols embodied in language are typically recognizable, at least in part, through historical or conventionally established usage. The categories of the American Revolution had roots extending at least as far back as seventeenth-century England. For example, such notions as natural law, human equality, popular sovereignty, limited government, natural rights, and the right of revolution all found symbolic and practical expression in the English Civil War, Parliament's Nineteen Propositions, the writings of Henry Parker,[28] the army debates,[29] John Lilburne's and William Walwyn's tracts,[30] and John Locke's *Second Treatise*.[31] Although the categories were established in usage in the colonies by the eighteenth century, the content of these categories was not the same for Britons of the seventeenth century as for Americans of the eighteenth.[32] Like white Americans later, however, Locke could defend slavery at the same time that he proclaimed natural rights.[33]

Second, current meanings are informed both by concrete experience and by historical understandings. Notwithstanding Jefferson's opinions concerning the logical implications of the principles of the Declaration of Independence, the rhetoric of the Revolution, at least as understood by the revolutionary leaders and probably most citizens, did not necessarily imply the immediate or eventual abolition of slavery. The tenuous link between the principles of the Revolution and abolition is underscored by Congress's refusal in the Declaration to criticize the slave trade.

[28] Henry Parker, "Observations upon Some of His Majesties Late Answers and Expressions" (1642), in *Revolutionary Prose of the English Civil War* (Erskine-Hill et al., eds, 1983), at 35 et seq.

[29] "Extracts from the Army Debates, October 1647," in id., at 70 et seq.

[30] John Lilburne, "Englands New Chains Discovered" (1649); William Walwyn, "The Bloody Project" (August 1648), in id., at 101 et seq., 89–90, 100, 103 et seq.

[31] John Locke, *Second Treatise of Government* (1690) (Macpherson, ed., 1980).

[32] An extensive analysis of the nature of the differences in the content of the categories is beyond the scope of this study. For one well-documented argument concerning the transformation of the meaning of the categories, see Garry Wills, *Inventing America: Jefferson's Declaration of Independence* (1978).

[33] Locke, supra note 31, at Section 85. Cf. id., at chapter 4.

Hence the line between rhetoric and practice or between discourse and institutions is not easily drawn where individuals are concerned. The distinction is even more difficult to make when the object of analysis is a society. The difficulty exists even when the language seems to have a plain, and plainly moral, content. Thus, whether moral discourse intersects with or is clearly distinguishable from constitutional discourse, it shares with the latter at least one characteristic: it is conventional, at least as it acts in the constitutional world. Even if divine intercession or cosmic moral rationality were still widely considered plausible today, as each was in Jefferson's day, even if some transcendental source for morality in fact exists, the moral sensibilities that make their way into constitutional interpretation are most usefully understood as functions of human experience. For in order for morality, transcendental or otherwise, to play an effective role in the construction or evaluation of ostensibly authoritative constitutional meanings, it must first make itself either manifest or covertly effective throughout some significant, though not necessarily majoritarian, portion of the population. Once it becomes so manifest or effective, regardless of its initial source, it is ultimately conventional in application.

What follows from such an understanding of morality in the constitutional world is that proslavery thought was "moral" (or more to the point, "moralist") in this respect. Clearly it was not "moral" from the perspective of our present understandings of what is right or good. But it was "moralist" in that it was part of a discourse concerned with questions of what people ought to (or may) do.

One is tempted to dismiss proslavers' claims about the morality of slavery as pretextual disguises for the promotion of material interests. Moral claims, like constitutional ones after all, can serve to rationalize interests. But there is little evidence that the proponents of slavery saw their moral and religious claims as mere rationalizations. In fact there is every indication that they sincerely believed that slavery was sanctioned by God or by the natural order of things. Thus, if such claims were pretexts, most of their proponents do not seem to have been aware of it.

Of course proslavers could have been deluded about the role moral justifications played in the rationalization of their order. In fact, given the complexity of human motivation in the construction of rationalities, some such delusion was probably at work. But proslavers' moral claims, like those of antislavers and others, were strands of webs of beliefs and practices which helped to hold together the world. As long as self-conscious reflection and choice can play a role in the creation of human environments, it seems likely that moral claims had some power apart from their connection or congruence with material interests. We should not be sanguine, however, about the ability of moral reflection within the constitutional context to deliver us from evil, for human beings are often incapable of discerning "true" morality from "false" (whether "true" and "false" are transcendental categories or hinge on their compatibility with "internal" standards).

But it would be a mistake to dismiss cavalierly the moralist character of proslavery thought simply out of abhorrence at its content. To do so would be to misunderstand why an institution we find patently repugnant could persist for so long in "our" constitutional order, for we cannot begin to comprehend the place of slavery in the order by resorting to easy moralizing. Accepting the proslavers' moral claims, on the other hand, enables one to appreciate that the connection between morality and interpretation can have consequences both desirable and despicable, that the introduction of a strongly moralist component into constitutional interpretation or law is not a panacea or a safeguard against practices that may eventually be considered outrageous, and that we today may suffer from blindnesses (akin to those of proslavers) parading under labels of morality.

Few people expressed the theoretical complexity of the relation between morality and the Constitution more poignantly or incisively than Frederick Douglass, who, in his early constitutional thought, argued for maintaining some distinction between morality and constitutional interpretation. For reasons of both morality and self-interest, he was intensely opposed to slavery. Yet he was also initially convinced that the Constitution was a proslavery pact. Nevertheless Douglass defended the idea of constitutional government, which he conceived as government by written constitution. He may well have overestimated the extent to which written constitutions could produce discrete and predictable results over time, as his own eventual conversion to antislavery constitutionalism attested. Still, he did not misunderstand that written constitutions could help to establish real if imprecise limits on government. They could do so by virtue of their being visible, public, and interpretable.

In short, Douglass agreed with Madison on the difference between a constitution and a law: A constitution is "established by the people, and unalterable by government," whereas a law is "established by the government and alterable by the government."[34] Douglass also understood that some separation of moral sensibilities from the activity of constitutional interpretation was essential to maintaining a degree of autonomy for the Constitution. Autonomy was crucial, both theoretically and practically, because from it followed the very possibility of principled limits to governmental power, which in turn made sensible the notion of empowering government through a constitution. Something about the

[34] James Madison, *The Federalist*, No. 53 (1788).

idea of maintaining a politics through written constitution was sufficiently valuable that Douglass was not prepared to sacrifice it to morality, even to moral convictions he believed were fundamental to civilized society and intrinsic to his own personal identity. Without some boundary between morality and Constitution, interpretation would truly become a pretext for the mere imposition of will, which could make the Constitution the property of the very government it was designed in part to create and regulate.

It was Douglass's and the Garrisonians' ability to interpret, their capacity to see the Constitution as having limits or meaning independent of their will, that allowed them to exercise their moral judgment to reject the object of interpretation and the order it represented.[35] On such terms, of course, the "success" of constitutional interpretation, as a vehicle for maintaining limits in the polity, could have easily led to the failure and not just the rejection of the order. That their interpretations did not do so was partly because neither antislavery constitutionalism nor the Garrisonian rejection of the Constitution was ever a serious contender as authoritative constitutional theory. That neither Douglass's nor the Garrisonians' interpretations led to the failure of the order was also partly because Southerners eventually co-opted the strategy of rejecting the order, not explicitly for moral reasons but for reasons they saw as "internal" to the Constitution itself.

VI

If we expect to rely on interpreters' good faith to maintain for the Constitution some practical autonomy from moral discourse, we are resting our expectations on a thin reed. Even had Douglass been correct that the principled maintenance of the constitutional enterprise demands that constitutional interpretation distinguish itself to some extent (or on some level) from moral concerns, the enforcement of that "separation" would be impossible without another impulse in interpretation, that of the pursuit of interest. As it competes with moral concerns, interest not only may be disguised in constitutional discourse but may permit the maintenance of constitutional autonomy without having to rely exclusively on conscientious interpreters.

The force of interest is evident in Thucydides's second account of how language participated in Athenian political failure. As modified to meet the American case, the second account goes something like this:

[35] That Douglass eventually moved toward an antislavery constitutionalism does not undermine the power of his insights in this regard.

Economic, cultural, ideological, and political change, bred in part by and in turn generating the country's increasingly continental face, produced changes in the nature and distribution of (real and/or perceived) interests and consequently in the objects of people's political affections.[36] These changes altered people's commitments to and/or interpretations of the Constitution. Consequently the working assumptions, institutional arrangements, and social practices that helped form the lens through which people read the Constitution became so disparate, diffuse, or incompatible concerning such fundamentally constitutive matters that constitutional discourse "broke down." The heart of this account is that economics, that is, considerations of material interest, were largely responsible for creating the identities and the various visions of the polity that drove constitutional discourse. It was these factors that precipitated constitutional failure.

This second account trades more directly on the idea that language is simply a cloak or an illusion.[37] Since Thucydides, that idea has found expression in Marx and among some of the radical proponents of Legal Realism, some adherents of the Critical Legal Studies movement, most members of the Law and Economics movement, some twentieth-century political scientists, and others. For the most part these critiques have been more directly concerned with jurisprudence than with constitutional theory, or with law writ small than with law writ large.

Even had Madison been correct that enacting laws and making constitutions are distinct enterprises, the difference between law and constitution partially collapses when we try to come to terms with the ways language and interpretation function in a constitutional polity. Granted, differences in the levels of abstraction of law and constitution are possible. Constitutions are presumably constitutive on theoretical levels or in structural ways that law, being more attentive to the particularities of daily existence, is not. Further, interpretation of laws may be characterized by greater tendencies toward predictability and the reduction of ambiguity than is constitutional interpretation. Even so, both law and constitution are manifested in language, participate in structuring social and political relations, and are grounded in theoretical assumptions concerning the appropriateness or desirability of forms of social and

[36] Of course people's affections are often distributed ambivalently and ambiguously across an array of objects. Thus determining the relative hierarchy of objects of affections, especially when two or more of them conflict, is a difficult matter even for "the people" themselves. For example, many (maybe most) Americans were quite conflicted over the objects of their political affections right up to the outbreak of hostilities in 1861. David M. Potter, *The Impending Crisis: 1848–1861* (1976), at 448 et seq.

[37] If such commerce is not required by logic, it is consistent with the experience of recent developments in legal theory.

political organization and of certain types of individual and collective behavior. Thus critiques of law are roughly applicable to the problem of generating meanings from a constitution.

The gist of the critiques equating law with interest is grounded, explicitly or implicitly, in Marx's description of law as a "juridical illusion, which reduces law to mere will."[38] This notion of illusion made its way into legal philosophy in several forms. Jerome Frank, for example, pointed out the unavoidable role of fictions in law. He also claimed that "the law as we have it is uncertain, indefinite, subject to incalculable changes" and that the vision of law as being "approximately stationary and certain is irrational and should be classed as an illusion or myth."[39] For Frank and other Legal Realists, the power of law resides not merely in an authoritative documentary record or in a rationalized legal method but in juridical will, in what a judge or some other authorized legal interpreter *will do* in a given circumstance.[40] So viewed, law is politics carried out by other means, just as politics may be war carried out by other means.[41]

Expanding on these themes, members of the Critical Legal Studies movement have suggested that law does not, perhaps cannot, constrain because the categories that constitute it contain or represent fundamentally irresolvable inconsistencies. This irreconcilability derives not only from the fact that the categories themselves are inconsistent, both internally and with one another, but also because they embody deeper contradictions among competing aspirations for and visions of society.[42] According to these critics, two points follow. First, the choice from among competing categories will always be a function of will, not of principle. Second, and following from the first, law ends up reflecting not "a coherent, richly developed normative theory" but the "many conflicts of interest and vision that lawmaking involves, fought out by countless

[38] Karl Marx, "The German Ideology: Part I" (1846), in *The Marx-Engels Reader* (Tucker, ed., 1978), at 188.

[39] Jerome Frank, *Law and the Modern Mind* (1930; Peter Smith ed., 1970), at 5, 13, 349.

[40] See Karl Llewellyn, *The Bramble Bush* (7th printing, 1981), at 3. Of course Llewellyn's formulation comports with Oliver Wendell Holmes's pronouncement that "prophecies of what the courts will do in fact, and nothing more pretentious, are what I mean by the law." Holmes, "The Path of the Law," 10 *Harv. L. Rev.* 457, 461 (1897).

[41] This is a reversal of Clausewitz's famous dictum that "war is not merely an act of policy but a true political instrument, a continuation of political intercourse, carried on with other means. What remains peculiar to war is simply the peculiar nature of its means." Carl von Clausewitz, *On War* (Howard and Parat, eds., 1984), at 87.

[42] Duncan Kennedy, "Form and Substance in Private Law Adjudication," 89 *Harv. L. Rev.* 1685 (1976).

minds and wills working at cross-purposes."[43] Thus legal categories merely replicate "all of the significant ideological controversies of the political culture."[44] As one legal historian argues, "Legal history is only social history, political history, educational history, urban history, and labor history in a fashionable, mystical, and somewhat impenetrable and awesome disguise."[45]

Marx's assertion that law and constitutions are illusions—combined with Realists' claims of radical indeterminacy and some critics' contention that law is simply a disguised form of political, social, and ideological warfare—constitutes a profound indictment of the power of constitutions to constrain politics independent from what anyone might want. According to these claims, a constitution has precious little autonomy from human will, for the application of a constitution to the affairs of the world cannot be separated from the will(s) of the person(s) employing it. Such a view does not logically entail the further contention that what is really at stake in constitutional interpretation is material interest.[46] Political battles, after all, can still be ideological. But it does suggest that constitutional battles are essentially battles of power. Even when ideological in character, they closely implicate the conditions and resources by which power is maintained. Quite often those conditions and resources are material.

In short, according to such notions, law is an instrument for waging war over the conditions for establishing, maintaining, or (re)distributing power. Robert A. Dahl, for example, has argued that constitutional discourse has been a device for legitimating governmental decisions and hence for reinforcing the prevailing values of ruling elites.[47] Other instrumentalist theories, from both the Left and the Right, view law and the Constitution as reinforcing certain economic institutions and rela-

[43] Roberto Unger, "The Critical Legal Studies Movement," 96 *Harv. L. Rev.* 561, 571 (1983). Compare Unger's account of law as a theoretical enterprise that is bound tightly to a robust notion of internal consistency to Robert W. Gordon, "New Developments in Legal Theory," in *The Politics of Law* (Kairys, ed., 1982), at 290; Oliver Wendell Holmes, *The Common Law* (1881) (Howe, ed., 1963), at 5: "The life of the law has not been logic: it has been experience."

[44] Andrew Altman, "Legal Realism, Critical Legal Studies, and Dworkin," 15 *Phil. & Pub. Aff.* 205 (1986), at 229.

[45] Wythe Holt, "Now and Then: The Uncertain State of Nineteenth-Century American Legal History," 7 *Ind. L. Rev.* 615 (1974).

[46] For the materialist account of constitutional meaning, see Charles A. Beard, *An Economic Interpretation of the Constitution of the United States* (1935).

[47] Robert Dahl, "Decision-Making in a Democracy: The Supreme Court as a National Policy-Maker" (1957), in *The Borzoi Reader in American Politics* (Keynes and Adamany, eds., 1971); and Dahl, *A Preface to Democratic Theory* (1956), at 105–112.

tionships.[48] Neither Dahl's theory of prevailing values nor the economic instrumentalist theories reject outright the possibility that language can constrain political decision. Nevertheless, implicit in them all is a belief in the manipulability, perhaps corruptibility, of language.

These theories are a serious challenge to chapter 1's account of constitutional law as an autonomous "enterprise" — "an undertaking that by its structure and substance establishes its own ground rules."[49] The challenge, however, is more apparent than real, for one may accept many of the critics' observations without ratifying the conclusion that constitutional government is a sham, that a constitution is nothing more than a pretext for the imposition of a will to power. It may be such a pretext, but the important question is whether it is nothing more.

On one level the critics are amply correct. Despite its tangibility, a constitution is in many respects an illusion or disguise. It "embodies" abstractions. Certainty in the interpretation of a constitution is often patently chimerical. A constitution is an illusion in the same sense that any language or body of linguistic categories is an illusion. It is a social construction, a fiction, something other than what it purports to be. It is fictional in that it is representational in character. (The representational quality of a constitution is even more problematic than conventional uses of language, since constitutions usually lack material referents and often lack a clearly defined conceptual referent.) At times the fiction takes on mythic qualities.[50] As we have seen, the Preamble to the Constitution supplied textual support for its own myth: The people, employing the written word, created a new polity. Whether one takes them

[48] See, e.g., Richard Posner, *The Economic Analysis of Law* (1972); Posner, *The Economics of Justice* (1981); Willard Hurst, *The Legitimacy of the Business Corporation in the Law of the United States, 1780–1970* (1970); Morton J. Horwitz, *The Transformation of American Law: 1780–1860* (1977), at 1–30. It makes sense to distinguish these instrumentalist theories from the functionalist theories of certain Legal Realists. The Realists had argued that since law (applied by the judge as the mouth of the law) both affects and effects social and economic policy, judges should self-consciously attend to the policy implications of their decisions when engaging in legal interpretation and constructing judicial opinions. See Holmes, "The Path of the Law," supra note 40; George D. Braden, "The Search for Objectivity in Constitutional Law," 57 *Yale L. J.* 571, 594 (1948).

[49] Stanley Brubaker, "Taking Dworkin Seriously," 47 *Rev. of Pol.* 45, 48 (1985). The notion of "enterprise," as I have employed it, is a revision of Dworkin's. Ronald Dworkin, *Taking Rights Seriously* (1978), at 105, 284–290.

[50] Jerome Frank, citing Tourtoulon, classified a fiction as "an untrue assertion which one enunciates without being his own dupe or wishing to dupe others" and a myth as an untrue assertion that amounts to "self-deception." Frank, supra note 39, at 340–341. Frank's classification seems mistaken on two fronts. First, myth is a subset or type of fiction, not a class unto itself. Second, myths need not imply self-deception. They *may* deceive, as fictions generally may, but they need not do so, at least not in the manner Frank seems to intend.

to be the people of a nation or of states, that myth is a fiction, having only a limited empirical base, that tries both to connect a political society's past with its present and to supply some ground for the legitimacy of the order.

But as we have also seen, some myths, some fictions, are useful and can be made "true" after the fact. To the extent that a society is willing to suspend disbelief in their (un)reality and that they do valuable work for the society, myths and other fictions can be indispensable. Unquestionably, like any cognitive framework, myths can illuminate certain aspects of reality while masking others. They can also limit one's vision of the possible. Acknowledging the ways in which myths constrain does not deny that myths (or constitutions) do valuable work. For insofar as they comport with society's experience and with its visions of itself as a society, insofar as a people is prepared to identify with them, they can structure and constrain institutions and action in effective, useful ways.

For example, we may assume that a constitution's function is substantially instrumental, even pretextual, that people use it to achieve ends other than those "inside" the text itself. We should not be surprised, then, when Lynd tells us that the Constitution was largely a pact between Southern planters and Northern capitalists.[51] Nor should we be surprised that both classes tried to use it to their advantage. But why would they (or anyone) have been inclined to resort to the Constitution? One claim is that it merely serves as a rationalization or cloak for achieving aims that enhance their material positions or their beliefs and prejudices. Another, weaker claim is that it happens to be one way the established regime justified its coming into being and its maintaining a virtual monopoly on the exercise of coercive power.

But the question persists: Why the need or inclination to rationalize by using a constitution? One answer may well be that it is an effective disguise, but it may also be that it helps to promote a kind of legitimacy. A constitution, however, can serve as a means for achieving legitimacy only if something about its content or pedigree or the way it is applied in and by the polity makes it appear legitimate, or, more weakly, renders it an appropriate instrument for achieving ostensibly legitimate results. Depending on the character of the regime, those results will be tested in part by people other than the favored classes and by standards other than the interests of those classes. In the nineteenth-century United States, which had some democratic characteristics, the relevant broader constituency consisted generally of citizens (who were almost always white, landed men over the age of twenty-one).

[51] Staughton Lynd, *Class Conflict, Slavery, and the United States Constitution* (1967), at 3–21, 135–152.

So unless everyone in the polity was deluded except for planters and capitalists, something about the Constitution rendered it distinctive and transformed it into a power partially independent of other modes of power for resolving disputes and organizing society. That distinctiveness frequently persisted even when favored classes controlled the formal institutional means of interpretation.

A working constitution, then, is a kind of trick people play on themselves.[52] That truth, of course, relies on people's belief in the possibility of such trickery. If people believe the constitution works, it can (but need not) work. Some minimal belief in the utility of constitution-as-instrument is presupposed by the notion of constitution-as-enterprise. But nothing like the thickly textured, quasi-religious devotionals that regularly appear in American constitutional literature is required.[53] One can sustain the constitutional enterprise even if motivated by narrow self-interest and even if perfectly aware of the pretextual uses to which a constitution can be put. It is a trick, after all, not necessarily a cruel hoax.

Consequently, that a constitution and constitutional discourse can often end up reflecting and reinforcing social and economic institutions and prevailing values in the culture might be explained in ways apart from the argument that constitutions do not constrain. If constitutions work at all, institutional arrangements, human relationships, and cultural values are in part constitutional constructs. It is not a sign of a constitution's failure—in fact, depending on the account of the source of the constitution's authority, it may be a sign of its success—that the constructive (or constitutive) process is a mutual one. Simply put, as a constitution shapes institutions and relationships, institutions and relationships in turn shape the constitution. Given the character of interpretation, it should not be surprising that a constitution is interpreted in part by reference to background institutions, values, and relationships or that competing aspirations for, visions of, and interests in society are reflected in the constitutional text and make their way into its construction. Moreover, given the mutually constructive relationship between constitution and culture and given the diversity of institutions, values, and relationships that exist even in a fairly homogeneous society, it also should come as no surprise that a constitution reflects such diversity, even tensions, at times even contradictions.

None of these characteristics is avoidable. In fact, even if they were, it is questionable whether it would be desirable to avoid them, especially

[52] See Harris, supra note 2, at 36.

[53] One can see the "minimalist" approach to constitutional faith in countries like Ireland, Japan, Germany, and Italy.

in a polity that is in some ways accountable to people outside government. For much of what we now think of as liberty or freedom—individual or cultural autonomy and the ability to maintain some sense of human difference within the context of recognizable communities—depends on the viability of some device for social structuring whose structuring capacity can effectively mediate human relations at the same time that its ambiguity can permit enough play in the structure to allow for diversity.

It may be just such a quality that permits constitutions to traverse the difficult terrain between the authority of majoritarianism and the accommodation of individuals and groups. Perhaps, too, such a quality contributes to a constitution's autonomy, if not from interest entirely, at least sometimes from the interests of dominant classes. It may also permit, for better and worse, constitutional change, for it supplies some room—though sometimes only a nutshell—for non-dominant others to generate distinctive accounts of the constitution's meaning and thus claim the constitution as their own.

It is ironic, or maybe simply perverse, that such constructive and desirable capacities could exist in an instrument that at one time helped maintain a system of racial slavery. But the same possibility for innovation that could produce the judicial doctrines that led to *Dred Scott* were also responsible for the philosophies of antislavery constitutionalists like the later Frederick Douglass. The constitutional thought of Calhoun in the South could rest comfortably in local resistance to the capture of fugitive slaves in the North. The nationalist constitutionalism of John Marshall, congenial to capitalism and opposed to slavery, could find a home in *Dred Scott* and *Ableman*. The movements for both nullification and secession in the South derived from ostensible fidelity to the national Constitution. Each movement had counterparts in the North. All, North and South, stemmed from an abhorrence to aspects of the same Constitution (or constitutional order).

Indeed, perhaps such ambivalences are necessary for maintaining a constitution, not simply because a constitution that is to "endure for the ages" must be expressed in general terms but because a constitution that can sustain itself at any given time must be able to generate more than one meaning, apparently sometimes even opposite meanings. As stated in chapter 1, if a constitution is to generate among citizens even minimal levels of attachment or the possibility of reflection and even rejection, it must be capable of permitting people to see or read themselves into or out of it.[54] Thus ambivalence, which may derive from ambiguity, is essential to the life of a constitutional order. Ambivalence

[54] See also Sotirios A. Barber, *On What the Constitution Means* (1984).

and ambiguity, after all, were partly responsible for holding the country together before the Supreme Court attempted in *Dred Scott* to resolve finally and authoritatively the problem of slavery. Their function suggests that people who want the security of constitutional union may have to settle for a degree of uncertainty. But by the winter of 1861, especially in the South, uncertainty was increasingly intolerable.

CHAPTER SEVEN

No Exit? Secession and Constitutionalism

I

Cass Sunstein has proclaimed that "no serious scholar or politician now argues that a right to secede exists under American constitutional law."[1] The comprehensiveness of Sunstein's claim might seem extraordinary but for the fact that it is so close to being accurate. Very few American scholars are willing to concede that secession is constitutionally permissible, at least in the United States, even though many of us have cheered secessionist movements abroad.

Three factors begin to explain the American aversion to a constitutional theory justifying secession. First, the most prominent—and to date most nearly successful—example of secession from the United States was associated with the perpetuation of slavery, which almost all now agree was an evil of staggering proportion. Second, secession is seen as disloyalty to country, or worse as treason, which Americans might condone elsewhere but not in the United States. Third, secessionism in the 1860s led to the most destructive war in the history of the country—destructive, that is, *to* the United States—which has led many to equate secession with civil war. And war, most agree, is usually undesirable.

But standing astride all three factors is the figure of Abraham Lincoln, who even today casts a long shadow across the American constitutional stage. In fact, with respect to secession, he casts shadows in two directions. With respect to the first, consider Sunstein's position, which is essentially a version of Lincoln's theory of perpetuity. We know secession is unconstitutional, says Sunstein, for two reasons. First, we have judicial precedent on point, specifically the Supreme Court's pronouncement in *Texas v. White*,[2] which held that "[t]he Constitution, in all its provisions, looks to an indestructible Union, composed of indestructible States." Second, and more important, Sunstein says that secession is barred by principles of constitutionalism. Thus "whether or not secession might be justified as a matter of politics or morality, constitutions ought not to include a right to secede," and "courts should not find

[1] Cass Sunstein, "Constitutionalism and Secession," 58 *U. Chi. L. Rev.* 633 (1991).

[2] *Texas v. White*, 74 U.S. (7 Wall.) 700 (1869).

such a right to be implicit in constitutions." In the American case, Sunstein says, this position arises out of the "spirit of the original document, one that encourages the development of constitutional provisions that prevent the defeat of the basic enterprise."[3]

An extended response to Sunstein's position awaits; I might offer, however, two brief observations about his basic claims. First, *Texas v. White* was an attempt to reconcile Lincoln's theory of Union with the Radical Congress's policy of Reconstruction. But because the two were irreconcilable, the opinion is fundamentally incoherent and—putting aside questions about the bindingness of judicial precedent—of little value. Second, even if Sunstein is correct that secession defeats the enterprise in at least one respect, even if it marks the failure of a constitution or of a constitutional order, it need not signify a failure from the standpoint of the principles of constitutionalism. Indeed, *perpetuity* may be incompatible with the principles of constitutionalism.

But the argument from perpetuity was not Lincoln's only position. In our own time, Akhil Amar has staked out ground that falls within Lincoln's second shadow. Amar's constitutional strategy is strongly textual but ultimately rests on a nationalist theory of the Constitution. He borrows a prop from John Marshall to support Lincoln's insistence that "the People" of the Constitution were the people of the nation as a whole. Consequently secession could not be accomplished simply on the motion of the seceding states but had to rest on a decision of the nation as a whole.[4] For reasons described more fully below, although Amar's claim is constitutionally defensible, it may be a twentieth-century imposition on nineteenth-century constitutional thought.

My own position is basically this: First, secession—the separation of a geographically coherent unit from what had previously been a "whole"—is sometimes a plausible strategy for an alienated minority and a plausible national solution to problems of social, economic, and political stress. Second, notwithstanding secession's plausibility, Abraham Lincoln rejected its constitutionality. Most strongly (with Sunstein), he claimed that secession was simply incompatible with the notion of perpetuity, which he said every constitutional polity must presuppose. More weakly (with Amar), he sometimes suggested that secession was permissible only if the entire nation approved. Third, Lincoln was wrong on both counts. His strong claim was wrong as a matter of principle. His weak claim was inaccurate with regard to the Southern secession from the United States in the nineteenth century.

[3] Sunstein, supra note 1, at 633, 644 (including his note 7).

[4] Akhil Amar, "Of Sovereignty and Federalism," 96 *Yale L. J.* 1425 (1987), at 1455–1462.

Textually secession might lay claim to the Tenth Amendment as a residual or "reserved" constitutional power. At first blush, the connection between secession and that provision might seem peculiar, as conventional applications of reserved powers pertain to the ongoing life of a polity, not to the polity's division or demise. On reflection, however, the connection does no apparent violence to the text of the Tenth Amendment, which, like most crucial components of the Constitution, is notoriously vague.

But regardless of whether one can find authority for secession in the Tenth Amendment, I argue that secession need not rest on any particular textual provision. In fact I suspect that in moments of secession the gravitational pull of textual claims will ordinarily be quite weak. Nor need secession's authority rely on the contingencies of history. But the absence of text or history does not imply that secession is justified solely by considerations of necessity or *realpolitik*. Nor, at the other extreme, does the legitimacy of secession levitate in a transcendental cloud of moral philosophy.

Instead, there are *constitutional* justifications for (and limits) to secession. Those justifications and limits derive from accounts that constitutional regimes supply about their own origins; that is, the most powerful arguments for secession derive from the character of the founding of the regime from which secession is sought. This position is "originalist" in the weak sense that it relies on accounts of the founding to generate justifications for dissolution, but not in the stronger sense that locates particular interpretations of the constitutional text at the time of the founding. My argument trades on the tendency of constitutional regimes to rationalize themselves and to justify their existence by referring to the manner in which they were created. The ostensible manner of entering into constitutional union also becomes the means for leaving. In this way, constitutional theory must presuppose a theory of secession.

In the lore of the United States, not to mention the Preamble and Tenth Amendment to the Constitution, the authors of constitutional text are "the people." But much depends on how the people are configured for constitutional purposes.[5] From the beginning there were at least two accounts of who the people were (and on whose behalf they acted in creating the new constitutional order). Both were visible in the dispute between Federalists and Antifederalists over ratification of the Constitution. Ratification did not end the dispute but merely transplanted it and revised the concrete issues over which it would be con-

[5] For an insightful discussion of the competing configurations, see Wayne D. Moore, *Constitutional Rights and Powers of the People: A Theory of Constitutional Politics* (1996), especially at chapter 1 and the conclusion.

ducted. With respect to secession, the foundational myths presupposed by the federalist and antifederalist accounts of constitutional authority pointed in different directions. But under either account, I argue, secession is permissible. At stake in the difference between the two accounts is simply the institutional method by which secession may be authorized.

Constitutional forms of justification necessarily exclude other modes of justification. Recent literature on secession has presented three such modes that are distinguishable from the one I employ in this essay. The first is geopolitical, or what Akhil Amar calls "geostrategic."[6] Geopolitical argument gives primacy to considerations of national defense (paying attention to both military and geographic concerns) and the strategic balance of power within the nation. No one can doubt that such considerations are of *constitutional* significance in the Aristotelian sense of the word. Nor can one deny that the founders of the American constitutional order were exquisitely sensitive to their role in sustaining security from without and stability within. Considerations of geopolitics also bear directly on strategic calculations of both the conservators of a regime and would-be secessionists.[7] But those considerations do not speak directly to the *principles* that must undergird the authority and maintenance of a constitutional enterprise as I have described it.

The second mode is moral. It justifies and critically evaluates acts of secession by resorting to principles of moral philosophy or to moral standards that transcend the Constitution or the logic of a particular constitutional order. Allen Buchanan supplies a perceptive and wide-ranging example of a moralist mode that grounds arguments for secession in liberal political theory.[8] Clearly any constitutional argument for secession is, in some fashion, moral in character. Nevertheless I resist the inclination to rely on transcendental moral arguments. First (and most weakly), the moral justifications cut more than one way in the American case. Second, such arguments are often insufficiently tied to constitutional language, the logic of the order, or the basic principles of constitutionalism to permit them to qualify as "constitutional" arguments. Third, I suspect that thickly textured moral arguments tend to

[6] Akhil Amar, "Some New World Lessons for the Old World," 58 *U. Chi. L. Rev.* 483 (1991), at 486.

[7] Amar seems to treat Lincoln's observations in his First Inaugural Address as dispositive of the geopolitical feasibility of the secession of the Southern states. Id., at 490–491. Although such a conclusion is sustainable only by supplying substantially more evidence and argument than Amar or Lincoln provides, it is beyond my purpose here to address the issue in greater detail.

[8] Allen Buchanan, *Secession: The Morality of Political Divorce from Fort Sumter to Lithuania and Quebec* (1991).

pale in times of social, economic, or political crisis, which are precisely the times when we typically find secessionist movements.

The third mode is fundamentally economic. James Buchanan offers what he calls a "constitutional" theory—that the right to secede was originally implied in the Constitution of the United States as a hedge against excessive taxation, incursions on free trade, and restrictions on the movement of capital.[9] But apart from his general, largely unsupported invocation of original intent, his ultimate justification for secession is a form of theory whose rationality is exclusively economic, and a narrow version of economic rationality at that.[10] Consequently it leaves precious little room for politics or, as McIlwain called it, "gubernaculum."[11] Thus Buchanan's is not an autonomously *constitutional* theory.

II

When South Carolinians fired on Union troops at Fort Sumter, they did more than simply short-circuit adoption of the Corwin Amendment. They aborted an experiment in whether principles of constitutionalism might be employed not merely to build a nation but also to dismantle it. Could Union be *dissolved* through reflection and choice instead of through accident and force? Provoking Lincoln to resist disunion with force had not been an end in itself for secessionists in South Carolina, although elements of misguided militancy, anachronistic heroism, and romanticized visions of war certainly played parts in their calculations. Rather the primary goal had been to prevent Northern efforts at appeasement, of which the Corwin Amendment was part, from derailing the engine of secession by dividing the South.[12]

Questions about the Corwin Amendment's substantive constitutionality or morality aside,[13] one of the Amendment's purposes (if not its justification) had been to stave off secessionist sentiment in the Upper South. If the nation could delay the secession of the states of the Upper South by mollifying them on the constitutional status of slavery, then it might ultimately thwart secessionism there. Over time, the Deep South

[9] James M. Buchanan, "Europe's Constitutional Opportunity," in *Europe's Constitutional Future* (Mather, ed., 1990), at 4–7.

[10] Id., at 7–9. See also James M. Buchanan and Roger L. Faith, "Secession and the Limits of Taxation: Toward a Theory of Internal Exit," 77 *Am. Econ. Rev.* 1023 (1987).

[11] Charles H. McIlwain, *Constitutionalism: Ancient and Modern* (1947), at 67–92.

[12] James M. McPherson, *Battle Cry of Freedom: The Civil War Era* (1988), at 273.

[13] Although I do not address these questions here, see my "The 'Original' Thirteenth Amendment and the Limits to Formal Constitutional Change," in *Responding to Imperfection: The Theory and Practice of Constitutional Amendment* (Levinson, ed., 1995).

might be coaxed back into the Union after it realized how economically tenuous and politically isolated it would be and that the nation was not intent on the abolition of slavery. The firebrands in South Carolina feared that this strategy of appeasement might work.[14] They worried that if they did not strike while the iron was hot, they might forever lose the moment. Seizing the moment, however, and ensuring the participation of their sister states in the Upper South required, they thought, inciting Lincoln into attacking Southern soil. They banked on the proposition that an assault against one state in the region would solidify opposition to Union and induce the sister states to defend their kindred land. The secessionists invested wisely. Such was the strength of Southern political identity that when Lincoln tried to resupply Fort Sumter, the states of the Upper South, which were hardly committed to secession, rose to the aid of South Carolina and the other seceded states.

Other fears also drove the secessionists. Some, in the tradition of Calhoun, distrusted the strength of mere parchment guarantees. They were persistently apprehensive about the South's constitutional status within the Union and hence about its capacity to preserve a way of life. Slavery, of course, had not completely fallen away as an issue dividing the two regions, for concerns about preserving a Southern way of life clearly continued to implicate slavery.[15] But the failure of the Corwin Amendment to assuage Southern insecurity intimated that slavery was not the sole issue dividing the nation. In the "Southern mind" the central issue had become self-determination and the primary goal the institutionalization of Southern political identity. Indeed some argued that these had been the genuine issues at stake in debates over slavery all along. On the other side, the willingness of many Northerners to embrace explicit constitutional protection for slavery indicated that they were not prepared to sacrifice Union on the altar of freedom. But they *were* prepared to sacrifice slaves on the altar of Union.

III

When a group of people finds that it no longer wants to belong to a particular polity, that its members insufficiently sense the "mystic chords of memory" that bind a nation both institutionally and culturally, the group has several options. It may persevere within the system, hoping for (or despairing of) a change in the political character of the nation through a change either in constituency or of ethos. But the most

[14] McPherson, supra note 12, at 255–257, 273.

[15] Ordinances of secession in five of eleven states mentioned slavery as a reason for Southern insecurity and secession.

radical Southerners believed that the South had already suffered too long as an oppressed minority, and they were beginning to find converts among moderates as well.[16]

If the disaffected group is small in number or widely dispersed geographically, its members might consider simply leaving. In his critique of tacit consent as a justification for political regimes, David Hume recognized some of the profound practical impediments to expatriation—the cost of traveling and resettlement and the difficulty of learning a new language and manners—which are especially burdensome for people who often have the most reason to leave.[17] Hume did not mention the deterrents to procuring employment that provides a decent wage (including the difficulty of securing permission even to enter another country and to work there) or the risks of statelessness in a world where citizenship has been described as "the right to have rights."[18] There are also the psychic costs of uprooting self and family from one's home, which is especially traumatic for people who have a strong sense of place, as did many in the South. For some Southerners expatriation would have been a rejection not only of nation but also their country, their home.

If the group is especially large, is convinced of its moral or technological superiority, or believes its mission divinely sanctioned, it might opt for revolution. Revolution might take on more than one meaning in this context. It might take the form of a *radical alteration* in the government's structure or purposes, most radically by dismantling entirely the nation's government and erecting a new one in place of the old. Alternatively or even additionally, it might imply the willingness of opponents of the existing regime to use *systematic violence* to achieve their aims. John Brown's attempt to seize the U.S. military garrison at Harper's Ferry was revolutionary in both senses.

Certainly secession can be revolutionary in either sense. In the end, however, the South's attempt to secede was revolutionary only in the second sense, not in the first. For one thing, most secessionists, despite fanciful pretensions at a national slave empire before 1860, were content to let be the national government and the rest of the nation. They were content, that is, simply to leave. For another, the Southern aim, at least in several respects, was hardly a radical alteration of existing relations, even within the seceding states. Instead the aim was to preserve

[16] Jesse T. Carpenter, *The South as a Conscious Minority, 1789–1861* (1930), especially at 181–184, 190–194.

[17] David Hume, "Of the Original Contract," Essay 12 (1748), in *Social Contract: Essays by Locke, Hume, and Rousseau* (Barker, ed., 1948), at 155–156.

[18] Chief Justice Warren's plurality opinion in *Trop v. Dulles*, 356 U.S. 86 (1958), at 101–103.

what many saw as the extant order, and hence it was conservative in many respects.

By 1860 there was some authority for considering such a move revolutionary, even had it been conducted peacefully. Kenneth Stampp argues that the conceptual foundations for the constitutional illegitimacy of secession were laid between 1830 and 1833—not surprisingly, in response to the crisis over nullification. Daniel Webster, he notes, considered secession an act of treason. Edward Livingston, senator from Louisiana, said it was "extralegal," as the states had transferred their "attributes of sovereignty . . . to the General Government . . .; the States have abandoned and can never reclaim them." Under the Constitution, he argued, the national government was "sovereign and supreme." Secession was revolution.[19]

John Quincy Adams derived from a theory of consent the notion that consent could not be withdrawn. He traced the origin of Union to the Declaration of Independence. That "primitive social compact of union, freedom and independence" committed all the "States whose people were parties to it" to membership in the Union forever. Adams's doctrine would have covered the infidelity of South Carolina in the early 1830s; however, it would not have reached Alabama, Mississippi, Louisiana, Texas, Arkansas, Florida, or Tennessee, as none of them had been a "party" to the Declaration of Independence.[20]

In his *Commentaries*, published in 1833, Joseph Story joined Livingston in explicitly linking arguments against secession to a theory of the Constitution. He argued that the Constitution had been intended to serve "as a permanent form of government, as a fundamental law, as a supreme rule, which no State was at liberty to disregard, suspend, or annul." It was "designed for perpetuity." In his later years James Madison agreed. Secession, he said, was never permissible merely as an act of political will, but was justified only for "intolerable oppression" under accepted theories of revolution.[21]

In the context of the crisis over nullification, the most important argument against secession was President Andrew Jackson's. He pressed a nationalist theory of the historical origin and theoretical foundation of the Union that even his sometimes enemy John Marshall would have embraced. Union, Jackson said, antedated the existence of the states. Departing from Adams's theory that the Declaration of Independence was binding on the states because they consented through their prede-

[19] Kenneth Stampp, "The Concept of a Perpetual Union," 65 *J. Am. Hist.* 5 (1978), at 28–29.

[20] Id.

[21] Id., at 30–31.

cessors, the colonies, Jackson argued that the Declaration was binding on the states precisely because they were *not* present (in fact or by proxy) when the Declaration created the Union. Because the Union *historically* predated the states, he said, it was *theoretically* preeminent as well. Thus the Constitution did not alter the relative primacy of Union and states. It reinforced the primacy of Union by establishing the nation as supreme. National supremacy was a function of the manner in which the Constitution was ratified: by the people. The Constitution was not simply a treaty or compact among the states. It was a national charter creating a national government that bound the people directly because it owed its existence to them. Secession, then, at least in the case of the United States, would "not break a league, but destroy[ ] the unity of a nation."[22]

Adams, Story, Madison, and Jackson were inclined to conflate secession with nullification. This identification was partly a function of an American historical phenomenon: talk of secession had almost invariably accompanied talk of nullification. From a psychological standpoint the two were undoubtedly motivated by the same interests or impulses. For example, in debates during the crisis over nullification, some Southern radicals, though not Calhoun, had sometimes argued that nullification and secession were kindred theories. Indeed some modern scholars have suggested that secession is a logical extension of the doctrine of nullification.[23]

In fact the two theories are often different sides of the same coin. Logically, or perhaps simply pragmatically, they are almost mutually exclusive in that each tends to ameliorate the impulse that generates the necessity of the other. Under almost all conceivable circumstances, nullification would have provided sufficient security for local self-determination that the need for an exit from the Union would have been practically nil. Especially in Calhoun's hands, nullification was an attempt to reconstruct the notion of a national majority so as to render secession unnecessary and to defuse it as an explosive constitutional issue.

IV

Just as a discontent or alienated minority has certain options, a nation trying to hold itself together has two general strategies short of permit-

[22] Andrew Jackson, "Proclamation by Andrew Jackson, President" (December 10, 1832), in *A Compilation of the Messages and Papers of the Presidents, 1789–1897* (Richardson, ed., 1896), vol. 2, at 640–656.

[23] Arthur Bestor, "State Sovereignty and Slavery: A Reinterpretation of Proslavery Constitutional Doctrine," 54 *J. Ill. St. Hist. Soc.* 117 (1961), at 119; Stampp, supra note 17.

ting secession (or, of course, dissolution altogether): (1) It might permit some sort of nullification or local control on matters of constitutional import; or (2) it might employ the coercive power of the nation to preserve Union. Both solutions seek long-term cohesion. The first achieves cohesion in exchange for a short-term sacrifice of national supremacy in the national application of constitutional standards. The second achieves cohesion by putting at risk one of the basic tenets of constitutionalism: choice. Both risk further disintegration over time, but the second may well remove evidence of that disintegration from sight. In the United States in 1861 the most extreme version of the first solution, nullification, had been rejected so often for so long that it was widely considered politically untenable, as illustrated by Chief Justice Taney's rejection of Wisconsin's claims in *Ableman.* The more moderate version, embodied in principles of localist Antifederalism, had been rendered inaccessible, at least with respect to the status of slavery in the nation and the territories, by the increasing tendency of both sides of the debate to seek out national solutions, especially after *Dred Scott.* Lincoln opted for a pragmatic combination of the two solutions, muting his nationalist rhetoric on the question of slavery, while emphatically asserting the supremacy of national authority.

But nationalism is a double-edged sword, for secession is ironically most plausible as a constitutional strategy in the context of a strongly nationalist constitutionalism. That irony may begin to explain why some Southern radicals were inclined to resort to secession in 1860–61. *Dred Scott* stood partly for the proposition that the only logical or practical solution to the cleavages that slavery was cutting was a national one. Certainly Taney's rhetoric was strongly nationalist, and his reasoning threatened to obliterate geographical limits to the institution of slavery within the nation. Such nationalism might have satisfied Southerners, even the most committed firebrands, as long as *Dred Scott* was law.[24]

But when Abraham Lincoln was elected president in 1860—having argued two years earlier that "a house divided against itself cannot stand" at the same time that he opposed the extension of the Supreme Court's decision in *Dred Scott* as precedent binding the Court or the polity—the substantive content (or consequence) of nationalist constitutionalism seemed ready to turn on its head. Some Southerners perceived Lincoln as committed to the adoption and enforcement of a national

[24] Ironically Madison and Livingston had argued almost thirty years earlier that states were obliged to respect decisions of the United States Supreme Court, while the Southern nullifiers were attacking the Court. By 1860 the South was fully committed to upholding *Dred Scott*, while Northern abolitionists were talking of flouting the decision.

antislavery policy. His election, they erroneously believed, demonstrated that a majority in the nation was now committed to the same thing.[25]

Fear, necessity, and hope can motivate radically different interpretations of the same text or event. Many Southerners, and certainly most secessionists in the South, were disposed to read Lincoln's positions on nationalism and abolition through the lens of fear rather than hope. They also chose to read him in this way, but with more justification, when he spoke on secession. In his First Inaugural Address, the same speech in which he pledged support for a constitutional amendment explicitly protecting slavery, he said that "in contemplation of universal law, and of the Constitution, the Union of these States is perpetual."[26] He cited no specific tenet of universal law but did offer three other reasons, one concerning the logic underlying the creation of nations, one concerning the history of Union and the definition of "perfection," and one grounded in specific presidential obligations under the Constitution. Four months later, in his Message to Congress in Special Session, he would add two more arguments of substance, one from a theory of democracy and one implicating the right of self-preservation.[27]

First, said Lincoln, every nation ever created presupposed perpetuity. "It is safe to assert that no government proper, ever had a provision in its organic law for its own termination. Perpetuity is implied, if not expressed, in the fundamental law of all national governments." In other words, the proposition of perpetuity went without saying. Because the Constitution did not speak explicitly to the legality of secession, perhaps even if it had, the nationalist presumption prohibited secession, according to Lincoln. At one point in his First Inaugural, Lincoln subtly suggested that there might be a constitutional mode for accomplishing secession but only by "all the parties who made it." He

[25] This belief was not necessarily inconsistent with the fear that appeasement by the nation on the question of slavery would derail secession. For example, secessionists might have worried that the motives for appeasement were weak, insincere, or short-lived or that parchment guarantees would henceforth be so weak that as soon as the movement for secession was stopped, pressures on Southern institutions would revive.

[26] Abraham Lincoln, "First Inaugural Address—Final Text," in *The Collected Works of Abraham Lincoln* (Basler, ed., 1953), vol. 4, at 264.

[27] Lincoln, "Message to Congress in Special Session" (July 4, 1861), in *Collected Works*, supra note 26, at 421. Actually Lincoln offered two other claims in this message. The first was an invocation of the slippery slope: If one state can secede, then all might secede; where will it end, and who will pay the bills? Id., at 436. The second raised the improbable specter of the destruction of republican government: The national government is obliged to guarantee to the states a republican form of government; if, however, the states secede, they might adopt nonrepublican institutions at some time in the future; therefore the nation is obliged to prevent the possibility. Id., at 440. Because these claims are exceedingly weak, I shall not respond to them here.

derived this mode from his assumption that procedures for the Constitution's own ratification required unanimity. But he did not say who the parties were or how their will might be represented. Nor did he indicate the slightest willingness to engage the mode as a practical possibility.[28]

Second, "[t]he Union is much older than the Constitution." In his First Inaugural Address Lincoln traced the origin of Union unbroken from the Articles of Association of 1774, through the Declaration of Independence and Articles of Confederation, to the Constitution, whose Preamble stated its object to be "to form a more perfect Union." "But if destruction of the Union, by one, or by a part only, of the States, be lawfully possible, the Union is *less* perfect than before the Constitution, having lost the vital element of perpetuity."[29]

Third, he insisted that the Constitution did not confer on the president the authority "to fix terms for the separation of the States." Moreover, it imposed on him an oath to "preserve, protect and defend," as he put it, "the government" of the nation. Consistent with his reading of the oath, he would defend the government against the dissolution that secession threatened.[30]

Fourth, the United States, he said, was engaged in "an experiment" in "popular government." Popular government is democratic government. Democratic government requires that a majority govern and that the minority acquiesce in majoritarian decisions. The only permissible response to policies with which a minority disagrees is to try to change policy at the next election. "[T]here can be no successful appeal, except for ballots themselves."[31]

Fifth, and following from the fourth, is an oft-quoted series of questions, which I can frame no better than Lincoln:

> [T]his issue embraces more than the fate of these United States. It presents to the whole family of man, the question, whether a constitutional republic, or a democracy—a government of the people, by the same people—can, or cannot, maintain its territorial integrity, against its own domestic foes. It presents the question, whether discontented individuals, too few in numbers to control administration, . . . can . . . break up their Government, and thus practically put an end to free government upon the earth. It forces us to ask: "Is there, in all republics, this inherent and fatal weakness?" "Must a government, of necessity, be too *strong* for the liberties of its own people, or too *weak* to maintain its own existence?"[32]

[28] Lincoln, "First Inaugural Address," supra note 26, at 264–265.

[29] Id.

[30] Id., at 270, 271.

[31] Lincoln, "Message to Congress," supra note 27, at 439.

[32] Id., at 426.

Although at the time of his inauguration he foreswore "bloodshed or violence . . . unless it be forced upon the national authority," there was no question that Lincoln considered secession illegal, "that no State, upon its mere motion, can lawfully get out of the Union,—that *resolves* and *ordinances* to that effect are legally void." More than simply illegal, though, secession was on his terms a "dissolution," an act of revolution "against the authority of the United States." "I therefore consider that, in view of the Constitution and the laws, the Union is unbroken."[33] He would continue to hold that view throughout the Civil War.

His principal claim, moreover, was not simply that the Union was unbroken in this case. It was that Union could not be broken in *any* case, at least not constitutionally. The weaker version of Lincoln's position might have left room for a constitutionally justified theory of secession. But when he implied that there might be a constitutional way out of the Union, his vehicle—the consent of "all the parties"—was more stringent than a fair reading of Article VII might allow. Even if his reading of Article VII were supportable, Lincoln's public position consistently undermined and finally rejected the notion that secession might be constitutional. His ultimate position—the one he held to most firmly and the one he relied on in prosecuting the war—was that Union was perpetual.

V

For more than a century Lincoln's doctrine, reinforced by Union military victory and the Supreme Court's confused benediction after the war, has made national perpetuity and the illegitimacy of secession appear to be brute constitutional facts. The emphatic character of the military solution, the ascent of the myth that the forces of Union had all along fought the Civil War to free the slaves, and the martyrdom of Father Abraham tended to obscure the constitutional weakness of Lincoln's claims. I shall address his claims seriatim in this section. Beginning here and continuing in the next two sections, I shall explain why the logic of constitutionalism requires a theory of secession.

First, constitutionalism and (ironically) written constitutions themselves attest to the notion that some things go without saying. One function of constitutional theory is to articulate and justify those unsaid things. Lincoln was correct, then, that the creation of a nation, whether by written constitution or not, might presuppose one or more principles

[33] Lincoln, "First Inaugural Address," supra note 26, at 265–267. At one point in his final draft he inserted the word *revolutionary* in place of *treasonable*, which he had used in his first draft. Cf. id., at 253, with id., at 265.

that are fundamental to the enterprise of state building or constitution making. But for reasons more fully set out below, he was wrong in assuming that perpetuity is logically necessary or phenomenologically universal in the creation of nations generally or in the formation of American Union.[34] Even his weaker claim, that the dissolution of Union requires the consent of "all the parties," is a dubious account of what Article VII requires, and it begs for a description of who must consent to secession and how they may do so. Further, his assumption that secession was equivalent to dissolution was at best only partially accurate, for nonviolent or "constitutionalist" secession accomplishes merely the withdrawal of a geographic part of the nation and leaves the old national government intact over the rest.

Second, Lincoln's account of the unbroken pedigree of national Union was historically and theoretically suspect. As Stampp points out, apart from the question of whether the states or the Union was older, the Constitution itself undermined the notion that the Union's existence was unbroken from 1774 (or 1776). The very process and product of the Philadelphia Convention were illegal from the standpoint of both the Articles of Confederation and the Convention's charter granted by Congress under the Articles. Moreover, the procedures for ratifying the proposed Constitution did not require that all the states consent to the new plan of government before it became effective. Under Article VII the Constitution was "valid" after only nine states had ratified it, although only among the states that had ratified it. Non-unanimous ratification would have effectively operated as a secession of the larger part from the smaller, for it would have meant that at least two "national" governments (and hence two unions) existed—one under the aegis of the Constitution, the other under the Articles of Confederation—controlling two separate territories where once there had been one. Alternatively, if the Constitution's non-unanimous ratification operated to dissolve the Confederation, as a secession or revolution would under Lincoln's theory, then as many as five governments (and arguably five unions) could have existed where once there was one. Each of the four nonratifying states, bound neither to the Constitution nor to the Articles, could have exercised its own sovereign authority.

As Stampp and others have noted, the Constitution's self-described purpose of forming "a more perfect Union" does little to reinforce continuity of Union if one emphasizes the word *form*.[35] Besides, the idea

[34] Compare the Basic Law of the Federal Republic of Germany, which explicitly provided for its own death upon reunification but did not die, with the Articles of Confederation of the United States, which proclaimed a "perpetual" union but did die.

[35] See Stampp, supra note 19, at 8–9. Stampp notes that some of the Constitution's framers, attempting to avoid responsibility for dissolving the Union, argued that the

that perpetuity is a necessary adjunct to perfection would seem silly except that so many intelligent people have cited it. Why might perfection not permit the *abandonment* of old, imperfect forms of association in favor of new and better ones? At the very least, the congruence of perfection and perpetuity needs more than simple assertion to support it.

Third, although Lincoln's contention that he was bound by his oath to protect the national government was probably deeply felt, it was nonetheless incompatible with the text and theory of the Constitution. The oath set out in Article II, Section 1, requires that the president "preserve, protect and defend the *Constitution*," not the national government [emphasis added]. Lincoln would shortly convert his conflation of the national government and the Constitution into a hierarchy in which the former was superior to the latter. For example, in justifying his suspending the writ of habeas corpus, he suggested that the preservation of government was the end of constitutionalism, the Constitution itself only a means; thus the Constitution could be suspended in the interest of the latter. This hierarchy, of course, ran counter to the constitutionalist notion—originating in James Madison's *Federalist*, No. 53, and reframed by Frederick Douglass—that the Constitution and its processes and values were distinct from government, in part because they were designed to serve as standards against which to measure the actions of government.[36] The Constitution may well be an instrument or means, but not in the way Lincoln suggested.

Fourth, Lincoln's argument from democracy assumed too much in two ways. On the one hand, it assumed that the Constitution had institutionalized a radical form of democratic politics in which the majority ruled and minorities must submit. If Lincoln were correct in this regard, then Calhoun's fears of a "national consolidated democracy" were justified. In fact, however, notwithstanding the polity's pretensions to de-

---

Union had already been "destroyed by the failure of certain states to respect their obligations under the Articles of Confederation."

[36] Lincoln, "Message to Congress," supra note 27, at 429–430; Frederick Douglass, "Comments on Gerrit Smith's Address" (March 30, 1849), in *The Life and Writings of Frederick Douglass* (Foner, ed., 1950), vol. 1, at 374–379. Lincoln's nationalist hierarchy has been repeated by others over the years. See, e.g., Herbert D. Croly, *The Promise of American Life* (1909), at 75, 77. Croly's superior devotion to nation stems partly from what he considers the intrinsic value of Union, partly from his contention that devotion to Union was also devotion to another good—democracy. Both notions, for different reasons, are problematic. See also Nevins's claim that whatever else the Civil War might have accomplished, it was justified because it saved the Union. Willard L. King and Allan Nevins, "The Constitution and Declaration of Independence as Issues in the Lincoln-Douglas Debates," 52 *J. Ill. St. Hist. Soc.* 7 (1959). But see David Donald, "Died of Democracy," in *Why the North Won the Civil War* 79 (Donald, ed., 1960).

mocracy and the South's constant carping about its status in the Union, the Constitution supplied a large number of institutional constraints on majoritarianism. Whatever else it did, the Constitution did not institute radical democracy. In fact it could not have done so and still be true to either of its prevailing foundational myths.

On the other hand, Lincoln's democratic theory, standing alone, cannot account for a deeply alienated, potentially permanent minority. It is one thing for a democracy to say that the majority's will must govern in most circumstances. It is quite another for it to insist that on a range of issues going to the heart of a people's constitutive political identities, the people must nonetheless submit. At that point democracy takes on an authoritarian, totalizing character that may be incompatible with constitutionalism's principle of limits and that radically undermines the conditions under which constitutional attachment can occur. Constitutional politics rests on authority but is not authoritarian in the sense Lincoln suggested.

Fifth, then, Lincoln's argument from self-preservation touches one of the deepest, most vexing problems of constitutionalism: Must constitutional government be too weak to preserve itself? I cannot provide a comprehensive answer to such a difficult question in this context, but I shall venture two observations that cut against the answer Lincoln proposed. First, in almost every iteration of the question, Lincoln presupposed that the issue was fundamentally one involving a challenge to national authority *by violent means*. It may be that the firebrands of South Carolina dug their own graves on this issue by provoking Lincoln to resist force with force. But had the South Carolinians resisted resorting to violence, they would not have triggered Lincoln's argument from self-preservation, at least not in the form he offered it.

The other observation about self-preservation is this: Violence aside, the answer to Lincoln's question is yes. Plainly government may coerce obedience when it acts authoritatively and when those on whom it acts are citizens or denizens (in the case of aliens, slaves, or other noncitizens) of the polity. But when the people presume to act, not as mere citizens but as constitutional sovereign, then government must respect and submit to those people, even to the point of its own dissolution. Otherwise, at least according to the foundational myths that have underwritten the Constitution of the United States, constitution making itself is a theoretical and practical impossibility. There are times when government must permit its authority to be destroyed. Perpetuity is at odds with these notions.

But in the United States the profound success of perpetual union has effectively buried part of the American constitutional tradition. Throughout the first half of the nineteenth century, secession was a recurrent theme of constitutional arguments, especially in New England. Unhappy over Jefferson's election as president in 1800 and incensed over his purchase of Louisiana from the French three years later (arguing that the nation would soon be overrun with what they termed *negro boroughs*), northeastern members of the Federalist Party began to talk of disunion as early as 1803. Their talk intensified after the adoption of the Embargo of 1807, which they considered a threat to Northern capital.[37]

The War of 1812 provoked an especially strong reaction in New England. Some states refused the United States the use of their militias and discouraged capitalists from lending money to the nation to support the war effort. In December 1814, atop a wave of secessionist sentiment, delegates from Massachusetts, Connecticut, Rhode Island, two counties in New Hampshire, and one county in Vermont met in what became known as the Hartford Convention. One month later they produced a "Report" detailing the conditions under which they would remain in the Union. These conditions included the adoption of seven constitutional amendments which, ironically for the Federalists, would have excluded slaves from computations for the apportionment of representation, required a supermajority for the admission of new states, and radically reduced national governmental authority. The Convention's Report concluded with a thinly veiled threat to reconvene and proceed with secession if the proposed amendments were not adopted and the war not ended.[38]

Between 1819 and 1821 the admission of Missouri provoked another crisis of faith, both in the North and South.[39] So did the Mexican War, which invigorated debates over the disposition of the Western territories. These debates in turn provoked threats of secession by the South. When it appeared in 1850 that California would be admitted as a free state, a group of Southern radicals, some bent on disunion, called a convention of Southern states for June 1850, though unionist sentiment held sway.

But the most persistent talk of secession, both before and after the Mexican War, came from Garrisonian abolitionists. As early as 1837 Wendell Phillips had anticipated Lincoln's "house divided" speech, warning that the North as well as the South was corrupted by slavery, that the two systems could not coexist, that unless slavery were eradicated "there must grow up a mighty slaveholding State to overshadow

[37] William M. Wiecek, *The Sources of Antislavery Constitutionalism in America, 1760–1848* (1977), at 107–108; Stampp, supra note 19, at 23–25.

[38] "Report of the Hartford Convention" (1815), in *American History Leaflets, Colonial and Constitutional* (Hart and Channing, eds., 1906), no. 35, at 1–2, 25–27.

[39] Stampp, supra note 19, at 25–26.

and mildew our free institutions." Disunion must follow from Southern supremacy.[40]

Secession was a natural corollary to Garrisonian non-resistance. But though Garrison had repudiated the Constitution in the earliest days of *The Liberator* as "the most bloody and heaven-daring arrangement ever made for the continuance and protection of a system of the most atrocious villainy ever exhibited on earth," disunion did not become an official tenet of Garrisonianism until 1843. Then the Massachusetts Anti-Slavery Society adopted a resolution, championed by Garrison himself, "[t]hat the compact which exists between the North and the South is 'a covenant with death, and an agreement with hell'—involving both parties in atrocious criminality; and should be immediately annulled." At its annual meeting the following year, the American Anti-Slavery Society ratified resolutions encouraging abolitionists "to withdraw from this compact . . . and by a moral and peaceful revolution to effect its overthrow." The Society said the constitutional order was so corrupted by slavery that the only way for the North to avoid culpability was to secede. "NO UNION WITH SLAVEHOLDERS!" became the Garrisonian battle cry. As the Mexican War wound down, Garrison intensified his disunionist position in the most impassioned terms.[41]

Garrisonian incitement to secession continued throughout the 1850s. Garrison's public burning of the Constitution in 1854 was symbolic incitement to separation. In 1857 he proposed a National Disunion Convention.[42] Between 1857 and 1858 even more talk of disunion erupted among Garrisonians as well as other Northerners outside that camp.[43]

Henry David Thoreau had his own peculiarly individualistic brand of secession. Drawing on transcendentalist moral philosophy rooted in Protestant Christianity, he raised the ultimate question of civic duty: What should be an individual citizen's obligation toward a government that participated in, perpetuated, and promoted the expansion of slav-

[40] Wendell Phillips, "The Right of Petition," Speech at Quarterly Meeting of the Massachusetts Anti-Slavery Society (March 28, 1837), in *Speeches, Lectures and Letters* (1891), at 4–5.

[41] Walter M. Merrill, *Against Wind and Tide: A Biography of William Lloyd Garrison* (1963), at 204–214. See also Truman Nelson, ed., *Documents of Upheaval: Selections from William Lloyd Garrison's "The Liberator," 1831–1865* (1966), at 202–207. See also Robert M. Cover, *Justice Accused: Antislavery and the Judicial Process* (1975), at 170; Louis Filler, *The Crusade Against Slavery, 1830–1860* (1960), at 178; David M. Potter, *The Impending Crisis, 1848–1861* (1976), at 48.

[42] See Filler, supra note 41, at 205–206, 216.

[43] Id., at 258–259, 303. Filler's claim that by 1857 disunion was a "popular Northern view" is overstated, but it rightly emphasizes that secessionism was not simply a Southern phenomenon.

ery? Thoreau supplied an answer in his essay "Resistance to Government" (later renamed "Civil Disobedience"). The citizen's allegiance to government followed from his moral duty as a human being.

> It is not a man's duty, as a matter of course, to devote himself to the eradication of any, even the most enormous wrong; he may still properly have other concerns to engage him; but it is his duty, at least, to wash his hands of it, and, if he gives it no thought longer, not to give it practically his support. If I devote myself to other pursuits and contemplations, I must first see, at least, that I do not pursue them sitting upon another man's shoulders. I must get off him first, that he may pursue his contemplations too.[44]

Here he parted company with Garrison. For according to Thoreau, the Garrisonian claim that *Northern states* should dissolve the Union effectively sidestepped one's own *individual* moral responsibility not to perpetuate slavery. "Why do they [the Garrisonians] not dissolve it themselves,—the union between themselves and the state . . .? Do they not stand in the same relation to the state that the state does to the Union?" Abolitionists, he said, should not wait for a majority in Massachusetts to secede from the Union. "[A]ny man more right than his neighbors constitutes a majority of one already."[45]

Nor did antislavery secessionism stop at mere talk. The City of Lawrence, Kansas, declared itself independent from the state in 1857. In addition, at least four localities attempted to secede from the South after the start of the Civil War, although they were motivated more by devotion to Union than by opposition to slavery. With the help of Union troops, the region we now call West Virginia seceded from Virginia in 1861.[46] In 1861 a unionist meeting in eastern Tennessee called for the secession of that region from the State of Tennessee. The call came to naught.[47] In 1862 citizens in Winston County, Alabama, met to consider declaring the county the "Free State of Winston" but never formally ratified the proposal.[48] There is also a legend that Jones County, Mississippi, seceded from the Confederacy in 1863, declaring itself the "Republic of Jones." In truth, since the beginning of Southern secession, the people of Jones County had displayed a mixture of union-

[44] Henry David Thoreau, "Civil Disobedience" (1849), in *Walden and Other Writings by Henry David Thoreau* (Howarth, ed., 1981), at 642.

[45] Id., at 643, 645, 651.

[46] McPherson, supra note 12, at 297–299.

[47] Eric Foner, *Reconstruction: America's Unfinished Revolution, 1863–1877* (1988), at 13.

[48] Samuel A. Rumore, "Building Alabama's Courthouses: Winston County," *The Alabama Lawyer* (November 1989), at 320.

ist sentiment and populist opposition to virtually all forms of political authority. After the war began, the county became home to anti-Confederate guerrillas. But although Jones County did not formally secede, had it done so, it would have concretely demonstrated a philosophical heritage of sustained lineage.[49]

VI

Political regimes form, they fall apart. Nations are born, they die or break apart. The sun also rises. The very fact of birth or of founding would seem to rebut any pretense of eternal existence. Why should we hold, then, that a Union, born as recently as 1774 or 1776 or 1789, is perpetual? Never mind the arrogance or presumptuousness of the belief. What of its compatibility with what we see in the world? Of course, to say that unions formed must die is not to say they should or must do so at any given time. But even if Lincoln had principled or pragmatic reasons for preserving the nation in 1861, one might wonder whether they justified the sacrifice of 620,000 human lives. (Of course Lincoln's choices should not blind us to the responsibility of Southern folly for the debacle that ensued.)

Empirical and pragmatic considerations aside, consent theory also might argue against perpetuity. If people can consent to form a nation, they might just as well, if consent is to be true to itself, consent to get out. Such an account seems both principled and nicely commonsensical. Still, like nationalism (indeed like every philosophical category), consent is a double-edged sword. It can bind as well as free. Moral theorists might argue, for example, that consent implies a promise and that some promises are ever binding, like a marriage unto death. After all, in regimes authorized by consent, people enter freely by choice; therefore, perhaps, they should be bound *by virtue of* that choice. Or, to make a somewhat weaker argument, if people have benefited from their voluntary association with others, their receipt of benefits estops them from withdrawing.[50] Or others, having a stake in the benefits of interdependent association, might expect and deserve a continuation of the society that supplies those benefits. Or people might be entitled to a continuation of society if, having foregone certain benefits that went to people who now want to secede, they are denied an opportunity to reap the

[49] Richard Aubrey McLemore, ed., *A History of Mississippi* (1973), vol. 1, at 518–525; Rudy H. Leverett, *Legend of the Free State of Jones* (1984).

[50] See Plato's *Crito*, in *Four Texts on Socrates* (West and West, eds., 1984), at 99–114. The arguments Socrates offered in the *Crito*, however, may not have been his genuine position on the question of political allegiance and obligation.

benefits in the future; in short, to permit secession gives advantages to those who, for reasons of accident, ability, or greed, reap benefits most quickly.

Even were it possible to derive from the act of consent a moral theory of perpetually binding authority, the arguments for perpetuity from consent must account for several peculiarities in the American system (perhaps in any large, diverse political or social system). First, times change. Circumstances arise that could not have been foreseen at the time of consent. For a committed moralist, mere change, even if unforeseen, might not abrogate what he or she perceives to be the moral character of the promise. But some changes, occurring by leaps or in increments, can ultimately be so drastic that later circumstances may bear little resemblance to those that originally gave rise to consent. It would be a harsh moralist, indeed, who would demand that people bind themselves to promises regardless of circumstance. Besides, there are promises and there are promises. Thus, even if one might want to argue that some types of promises, like vows of marriage, are morally binding forever, the creation of a state (even by consent) is an altogether different sort of enterprise, implying an ambiguity, complexity, uncertainty, and set of purposes that distinguish it from marriage and hence from the moral constraints of the marriage vow.[51]

Second, it would be difficult to underestimate (perhaps to estimate at all) the extent to which the American people actually consented to Union under the Articles of Association, Declaration of Independence, Articles of Confederation, or even the Constitution.

Third, by the time of secession in 1860–61, the people who formed the original Union, or consented to forming it, were not the same as those ostensibly bound to it. As Hume observed, subjects (or citizens) who were not part of the formation of a compact hardly ever consent in any strong sense of the word to its perpetuation. Continuing to reap the benefits of union might imply some form of consent, but as already noted, the force of the implication, given the strength of inertia, is weak. One might argue that the framers of the Constitution anticipated this problem and remedied it by providing devices for popular participation in government through regular elections and by institutionalizing a process by which the basic rules of the game might be amended. As beneficial as these innovations were, however, the impediments to participation and to amending the Constitution were substantial during the

[51] Compare "covenantal" constitutional theories, which argue that it is the essential character of constitutions that they represent a transformative bond akin to a covenant of marriage or to the relationship between Yahweh and the Jewish people. See Daniel J. Elazar and John Kincaid, eds., *Covenant, Polity, and Constitutionalism* (1980). I claim, however, that even a covenantal constitutionalism cannot preclude secession.

period of the founding and continue to be so today. Moreover, the weak and episodic forms of participation that we see today, while possibly promoting stability,[52] do not firmly or manifestly establish a continuing ratification of or consent to the regime of the Constitution.

Finally, one should not minimize the profound sense of estrangement and alienation that an apparently permanent minority can feel toward what it views as dominant forces in the society. That sense can be particularly keen in a majoritarian system of politics. It might be ameliorated by the systematic enforcement of certain rights; but, as the history of the United States has shown, such rights are often weak weapons against an oblivious or aroused majority. Although estrangement and alienation in themselves do not necessarily provide a moral justification for breaking whatever bonds consent might form, they certainly can supply an incentive for separation. And they might provide pragmatic grounds for the whole to let the part go, for there are times when the felt (or real) community of interest necessary and sufficient to sustain a polity by consent ceases to exist.

Perhaps the most we can say of consent is that it does not seem to solve the problem. It is likely, moreover, that moral theory is not the place to look for solutions. After all, I suspect that analytic moral rules, which frequently are not powerful forces in "normal" times, are profoundly weak in times of political breakdown. Even when morality plays a role in human decision, its influence may be more often exercised through intimations, through the recognition of generalized sensibilities of what is right or wrong, than through the rigorous application of analytical distinctions. Whatever the merits of moral theory, a more plausible solution to the problem of dissolving ties of political obligation may come from looking in a different place.

VII

Political regimes—even constitutional ones, including our own—arise to some degree from illegality. (That is not to say that they must arise from coercion or violence, although almost all do to some extent.) Their illegality is one characteristic that distinguishes them from their predecessors. Were they legal, they would continue to seem part of the existing regime. But as Robert Cover noticed, if the way of founding a new regime resides in illegality (from the standpoint of an existing regime), in acts incoherent or incompatible with the logic of the old regime, it

[52] See Robert Dahl, *Who Governs? Democracy and Power in an American City* (1961), at 305–325.

supplies a potential way out of the new regime as well.[53] The illegality for getting in becomes the legality for getting out. That illegality has this capacity lies partly in its authority as precedent.

Precedent has no intrinsic bindingness. As either a process or a set of substantive outcomes, it has no intrinsic moral value, although it may make claims on morality because of its congruence with (or its eventual acceptance as part of) people's felt sense of what is right. To the extent that people rely on that congruence or acceptance to justify the regime, the mode of founding becomes a measure of that regime's legitimacy. But the founding need not simply be a brute fact of the matter; it might become an event that begs for an explanation by any regime that tries to justify itself. This potential is one reason for the appearance and power of mythical stories of political foundings. The founding, or its story, becomes a means for self-justification. It becomes a part of the logic (or phenomenologic) of the new regime that estops it from denying the constitutional authority of the mode by which it was founded and by which it justifies itself.

In the American context, the need to justify the new constitutional regime fueled debates throughout the antebellum period over the authority of the Constitution, the status of states in relation to the nation, and the role of the people both as authorizers and as participants. The debates were important and persistent, not as academic exercises in the creation of myth and not merely because the character of the American myth was such that the content of the debates revealed (and disguised) what was at stake in justifying the creation and maintenance of the constituted order; they were important because the chosen myth was perceived to bind the order itself even when the issue was the very survival of the order. More simply, myth helped describe a logic for getting out.

To argue, though, that a myth of the order's creation supplied a logic for getting out only begins the inquiry, for we have seen from the beginning that at least two such accounts competed for primacy. They differed from each other over two fundamental questions: Who was the creator, and how was the creation accomplished?

VIII

By our present lights, the story that might have seemed most "mythically" plausible was the familiar federalist account of the founding, which was refined by John Marshall and extended by Lincoln. Marshall

[53] Robert M. Cover, "Foreword: *Nomos* and Narrative," 97 *Harv. L. Rev.* 4 (1983), at 15–16. Although Cover refers to secession as "revolutionary" (id., at 23–24), secession sometimes also derives from the same "jurisgenerative" properties or impulses he associates with (extra-institutional) acts of interpretation.

held that the Constitution was a document of special significance, both national and covenantal. Although he conceded that states had attributes of sovereignty, the Constitution authorized the nation to supersede the authority of states within certain domains of action. Consequently the Constitution required a special mode of ratification—ratification by the people of the whole nation. Making a nation was an act of sovereignty superior (but not entirely oblivious) to the sovereignty of the people of a state.

Lincoln expanded and intensified the nationalist dimension and covenantal implication of Marshall's federalism in two ways. First, he pushed the creation of the nation backward, past the ratification of the Constitution to the adoption of the Declaration of Independence, perhaps further. This expansion permitted him to make a second, crucial move concerning the sovereignty of states. This move resembled Andrew Jackson's claim in the crisis over nullification. Put briefly, in the beginning in North America there were no states, only dependent colonies. At a critical moment in history, there arose from those colonies a unitary people—a Union—who threw off their bonds of dependence through a Declaration of Independence and forged new collective bonds of independence in the Revolution. The states did not exist until after the formation of Union. The Constitution later reinforced the preexisting bonds of Union, and states continued to exercise authority *under* the Constitution, which was basically an instrument of national union.

As Lincoln expressed it: "The Union is older than any of the States; and in fact it created them as States." Thus "[o]ur States have neither more, nor less power, than that reserved to them, in the Union, by the Constitution—no one of them having been a State *out* of the Union." "Tested by this, no one of our States, except Texas, ever was a sovereignty. And even Texas gave up the character on coming into the Union."[54]

The logical implication of either version of the federalist myth was that secession could not be accomplished by a mere state, for secession was not a matter of simple separation. Instead it was a dissolution of the bonds of nationhood that could not be accomplished authoritatively except by the national people as a whole.[55] But how might the will of the national people be expressed? The institutional possibilities were numerous: the vote of at least a majority of the people in every state,[56] the approval of a majority of the people or of the delegates to conventions in nine-thirteenths of the states,[57] the vote of a majority in conventions or in legislatures of three-fourths of the states,[58] the vote of major-

[54] Lincoln, "Message to Congress," supra note 27, at 433–435.

[55] *Cohens v. Virginia*, 19 U.S. (6 Wheat.) 264 (1821), at 413–414.

[56] This was consistent with Lincoln's conclusion that Article VII required unanimity.

[57] This mode would have been consistent with the text of Article VII.

[58] This would have been consistent with part of the procedure of Article V.

ities in both houses of Congress,[59] or, most simply, the vote of a majority of people in the nation regardless of residence.[60]

As an added protection against precipitous action, one might convert majoritarian decisions in any of the preceding modes into super-majoritarian decisions. Or some combination of modes might also have been conceivable. For example, if the *admission* of states to the Union required concurrent ratification of the national legislature and of some representative body of the states to be admitted, perhaps the *withdrawal* of states required a similar expression of concurrent majorities (or super-majorities). Under the most stringent version of concurrent majorities, a majority in Congress would have had to combine with a representative majority in *all* the states, since all were conceivably affected by any state's withdrawal.

Some version of the federalist myth might well be intuitively appealing to many of us today. But we should remember this about the manner in which myth binds: Myths rely for their authority (and therefore their power) on the extent to which they comport with perceived reality, which in turn relies partly on the reality that people want to see or believe in. For a variety of reasons, much of the country during the period preceding the Civil War was either unprepared to believe in the federalist myth of the popular founding or unwilling to commit to many of its nationalist implications.

Despite the nationalist dimensions of one strand of proslavery constitutional doctrine after *Dred Scott*, many Southerners and others sympathetic to slavery would have been suspicious of extending nationalist constitutionalism to other arenas. Some of those people may have suspected that a national power strong enough to protect slavery would have also been strong enough to destroy it. For other proslavers, quite happy to indulge in nationalism where slavery was concerned, the impulse for a weak central government persisted for reasons including an inherited Jeffersonian constitutional tradition, a continuing antagonism to Northern capital and its consistent demand for the assistance of a strong national government, and an intensifying regional identity. The growth of Southern identity cut two ways, depending on the context. From within the constitutional Union, it historically supported a distinctly localist constitutionalism, consistent with a tradition traceable to men like Calhoun; but from an external perspective—external to the Constitution, though internal to the Southern region—it became the foundation for "Southern nationalism."

Abolitionists and other opponents of slavery also were wary of the

[59] Hortensius (1814), in Stampp, supra note 19, at 24.

[60] No one suggested this as a method for authorizing secession, and it would have had little foundation in the text or logic of the Constitution.

implications of nationalism, but for different reasons. First, Marshall's antiseptic myth of the popular founding was largely incompatible with the Garrisonians' pessimistic account of the Constitution as "a covenant with death." Second, and related to the first, lawyers, judges, and even members of Congress who helped enact fugitive slave laws had converted—antislavery constitutionalists would have said "perverted"—nationalism into a tool of "the slave interest." Third, and a consequence of the first two points, opponents of slavery had their own localist constitutional tradition. They wanted a vehicle for mitigating the harsh effects of Taney's nationalist constitutionalism on the issue of slavery, when they did not want a way out of the Union entirely.

Others, who were neither proponents nor opponents of slavery, might also have understandably resisted the myth of the popular founding and its implications. As if to emphasize the point, people regularly treated the term used to denominate the nation—the United States—as if it were plural rather than singular.[61] Hence, "We the People of the United States" were not necessarily the people of a single Union or nascent nation. They were the people of *states*, then united, but perhaps not always so. Finally, some, including Lincoln, referred to the United States as a "confederacy."[62] Secessionism aside, the United States was not yet a nation, as late as 1861.[63]

These considerations lent force to the antifederalist account that the founding was an act of sovereign states, or, if popular, an act of the *people* of those states. If the Union had been continuous over time, so this story went, it was not the Union that Lincoln invoked as a device for preventing secession. It was more akin to a Swiss-style confederation of states. Further, if states (or the people of states) could get into the Union, they could get out as well. But how?

IX

There were two possible constitutional ways out, both riding atop the antifederalist account of the constitutional founding. The first and most directly constitutional mode of egress was for a convention in each state to adopt an ordinance of secession, just as state conventions over the

[61] Granted, such usage could simply be a holdover from British practice, or it could be explained in other ways. It is possible, after all, for language to explain too much. But the use of the plural is certainly suggestive. See James M. McPherson, *Abraham Lincoln and the Second American Revolution* (1991), at viii.

[62] Lincoln, "Reply to the Illinois Delegation" (March 5, 1861), in *Collected Works*, supra note 26, vol. 4, at 275.

[63] McPherson, supra note 61, at viii.

years had ratified the Constitution as a condition of the admission of states to the Union. South Carolina had employed a convention for proposing its Ordinance of Nullification thirty years earlier, as it had in an abortive attempt to secede in 1852. The state activated the device once more to adopt on December 20, 1860, its Ordinance of Secession "dissolv[ing] the Union between the State of South Carolina and other States united with her under the compact entitled 'The Constitution of the United States of America.'"

As this self-description made clear, South Carolina's version of the origins of constitutional Union dismissed any notion that the Constitution was a covenant of a national people. The Constitution was instead a compact, resembling a treaty, among the states and could be rescinded for cause on the motion of one of the states. This account imported distinctions—which Madison had invoked to different effect decades before—between a compact or contract on the one hand (which could be dissolved on the motion of one party in the event of a breach by another) and a national constitution or covenant on the other (which, presumably, could not so easily be dissolved).[64]

In rapid succession during the first two months of 1861, Mississippi, Florida, Alabama, Georgia, Louisiana, and Texas followed South Carolina's lead. Conventions in each state adopted ordinances of secession dissolving ties between the state and the Union. Eventually, after hostilities erupted, Arkansas, North Carolina, and Virginia followed suit, partly out of loyalty to the region. Most of the ordinances included provisions specifically rescinding or repealing prior ratifications of the Constitution (as amended) and declarations that the state "resumed" the exercise of what Virginia called "all the rights of sovereignity [*sic*] which belong and appertain to a free and independent State." Some absolved their citizens and public officials of responsibility to abide by their oaths or allegiances to the Constitution of the United States. In an apparent but notoriously vague reference to constitutional rights to own slaves, Mississippi, Louisiana, and Arkansas cautiously recited that rights acquired and vested under the United States Constitution would continue in force despite the repeal of the Constitution within the states' territories. The ordinances of Texas and Virginia were ratified by popular votes. In the case of Texas, the referendum was an attempt to cure a defect in the selection of the convention. In Virginia's case, it was an expression of the location of sovereign authority.

Within a few days after adopting its ordinance, South Carolina's convention approved a Declaration of Causes justifying the state's secession

[64] Albert Bushnell Hart and Edward Channing, eds., *American History Leaflets*, no. 12, "Ordinances of Secession and Other Documents, 1860–1861" (1912), at 3.

from the Union. The Declaration provided a list of abuses that were unified by twin themes. First, the states of the North had violated the "compact between the States," thus justifying its rescission. Almost every example of the breach of the compact pertained to slavery. Second, the national government, which was now in the hands of a political party beholden solely to Northern states, had "become[ ] destructive of the ends for which it was instituted," thus justifying its "abolition" within the territory of South Carolina and its replacement with a government compatible with principles of self-government. So the two fundamental pillars of Southern insecurity were joined: self-government (the struggle for which, on the national level, had been virtually lost in the 1830s with the demise of nullification as a plausible constitutional theory) and the protection of slavery (a battle Southerners thought would be lost on the heels of Lincoln's election). Had it been ratified, the proposed Corwin Amendment might have partially assuaged fears concerning the latter; however, it would not have addressed worries about the loss of self-government, unless slavery had been the sole constitutive characteristic of Southern political identity.

Four of the nine other states that resorted to conventions as vehicles for seceding also offered reasons for their separation. But unlike South Carolina's Declaration, these other states' reasons were brief, underdeveloped, and sometimes little more than afterthoughts. Two of the four, Louisiana and Arkansas, did not directly mention threats to slavery as a justification for secession. Self-government and solidarity with the rest of the region were the most prominent themes, even of the two states, Texas and Alabama, that did cite threats to "property" or to "domestic institutions."

The five other states that seceded by convention did not give any reasons for their action. Perhaps some matters, including slavery, simply no longer needed to be said. But why would that have been so? The answer may lie in part in the character of the device by which secession was accomplished. South Carolina's ambivalent approach to secession—first adopting an ordinance that listed no reasons and then a declaration listing causes—indicated the confusion some felt over the character of the act. The form of the Declaration of Causes, even some of its language, reflected that of the Declaration of Independence, ostensibly an act of *revolution*. Without exception, however, the ordinances of secession appeared in the form of *legal* enactments. They were ratified by the same constitutional, now legal, process defined in the basic law.

Perhaps the "real" impulse for secession was the protection of slavery. Or perhaps it was nothing more than a selfish and petty preoccupation with national political processes: If we cannot nullify your laws, we shall nullify your Constitution. It was the strategy of one who was either dissatisfied with substantive outcomes, which in the Southern case would have been unwarranted, or unwilling to continue to play by basic rules that were systematically perceived as a disadvantage, which was the source of Calhoun's distress all along. Even so, it was part of a search for a "constitutional" way out of the Constitution. Some might argue that if that were the character of the act, constitutional *reasons* were required. But it may be the peculiar characteristic of secession as a constitutional device that it needs no substantive justification. It is sanctioned constitutionally if it is compatible with the process by which the Constitution was ratified. If it is the constitutionally defined sovereign act of a sovereign, it is justified by that fact. No further warrant is needed.[65]

X

The second way out relied on a different version of the founding. It combined Lincoln's claim that Union antedated the Constitution with an antifederalist account of the character of that Union. In February 1861 the legislature of Tennessee submitted a proposition to the state's citizens that would have authorized calling a convention to decide whether Tennessee should secede from the Union. The proposition lost by a vote of 69,675 (55 percent) to 57,798 (45 percent), a fairly substantial margin. The Unionists had held the day. But after South Carolinians fired on federal troops at Fort Sumter in April, Lincoln called up a militia of seventy-five thousand troops and declared his commitment to use force to suppress the "combinations" of the states of the Deep South. In Tennessee, unionist moderation succumbed to regional solidarity. In special session in May 1861, Tennessee's legislature ratified a "league" with the Confederacy—whose Congress had approved a new constitution on March 11 and submitted it to the seceded states for their ratification—and adopted a "Declaration of Independence" by which it "dissolv[ed] the Federal relations between the State of Tennessee and the United States of America."[66]

The legislature adopted its Declaration rather than an ordinance of secession out of a quixotic desire to avoid being drawn into debates over "the abstract doctrine of secession." Instead it chose simply to

[65] See Exodus 3:13–14: Then Moses said to God, "If I come to the people of Israel and say to them, 'The God of your fathers has sent me to you,' and they ask me, 'What is his name?' What shall I say to them?" God said to Moses, "I AM WHO I AM." And he said, "Say this to the people of Israel, 'I AM has sent me to you.'"

[66] Hart and Channing, supra note 64, at 1–2, 16, 19; Ralph A. Wooster, *The Secession Conventions of the South* (1962), at 179–180.

assert its "right as a free and independent people to alter, reform, or abolish our form of Government in such manner as we think proper." The notion clearly drew part of its force from its association with Thomas Jefferson's Declaration of Independence eighty-five years before. If that association made it seem that Tennessee's Declaration, like South Carolina's Declaration of Causes, was revolutionary instead of constitutional, that appearance rested partly on assumptions about the character of the American Revolution itself. It is tempting to imbibe the myth that the Revolution was part of a new creation, that its aims and principles were universalist innovations made possible because the political world was being reinvented on the North American continent.

In important (perhaps crucial) ways, however, the American Revolution was not so radical at all. For Locke's principles for justifying revolution, which were an unmistakable part of Jefferson's Declaration of Independence, were actually quite conservative. They demanded that acts of revolution would occur not for "every little mismanagement of public affairs" but only after "a long train of abuses."[67] And if Locke's *Second Treatise* was an anticipatory justification for the Glorious Revolution, that event was hardly revolutionary and was "glorious" only in that it efficiently replaced one monarchical house with another without the spilling of blood.

Second, notwithstanding Jefferson's maxim prohibiting revolution for "light and transient causes," it is striking just how insubstantial some of the causes for the Revolution now seem and how conservatively most of the revolutionaries framed their demands. The colonists' claims were primarily about self-government and the proper nature of representation under the British Constitution. They were demands that the colonists be accorded the rights of British subjects.[68] The Revolution was less a revolution than a constitutionally justified secession that could not be accomplished without the assistance of arms. Edmund Burke may have been right: The colonists in separating were being truer to principles of the British Constitution than were the British themselves.[69] In drawing on that aspect of the American Revolution, Tennessee's Declaration of Independence may have been similarly true to principles of the Constitution and of constitutionalism. (Certainly it was no less con-

[67] John Locke, *Second Treatise of Government* (1690) (Macpherson, ed., 1980), at Section 225.

[68] Gordon S. Wood, *The Creation of the American Republic, 1776–1787* (1969), at 3–17.

[69] Edmund Burke, "Speech for Conciliation with the Colonies" (March 22, 1775), in *Burke's Speech on Conciliation with America* (Lamont, ed., 1897), at 19–20. David A. J. Richards argues that the Revolution was basically a dispute over interpretation of the English "constitution." See his *Foundations of American Constitutionalism* (1989).

sistent with principles of constitutionalism than was the Constitution of the United States.)

Nevertheless one aspect of Tennessee's Declaration distinguished it from Jefferson's and emphasized its constitutional character. Like most of the ordinances of secession, Tennessee's Declaration offered no reasons to the world, candid or otherwise. It was not a justification to (or from the perspective of) the outside. It was simply a statement, as if for consumption from the inside. It contained no argument; it opened with a terse pronouncement of the source of its authority ("We, the people of the State of Tennessee"); it "abrogated and annulled" all prior "laws and ordinances by which the State of Tennessee became a member of the Federal Union of the United States of America"; and it "resume[d] all the rights, functions, and powers which . . . were conveyed to the Government of the United States." It did not say so, but it might have traced its constitutional pedigree to the principle textually embodied in the Constitution's Tenth Amendment.[70] It was, or purported to be, an authoritative statement of the political rights of the people and state of Tennessee. As confirmation of its self-stated authority, the citizens of Tennessee ratified it in a popular referendum by a margin of 104,913 (69 percent) to 47,238 (31 percent). Like the ordinances, it required no further justification.[71]

These secessions were "constitutional" not simply because of their method, by which an ostensible sovereign was acting in a manner consistent with constitutional precedent (consistent, that is, with the logic of the existing order). Nor were they constitutional merely because of their subject matter, which pertained to the deconstitution and reconstitution of a people. They were also constitutional in their aims. Many in the South argued that their purpose in seceding was either to recapture or to secure rights that they thought had been lost or were in jeopardy under the Constitution of the United States, just as one aim of the Revolution had been to secure for Americans the rights of British subjects. Secession was their way of recovering what they perceived to be *their* Constitution.

In their ordinances of secession, the conventions of Alabama and Mississippi authorized their states to become part of a new "Federal Union," formed "upon the principles of the Constitution of the United States."[72] Perhaps not surprisingly, the Constitution of the Confederacy

[70] Louisiana's Declaration was explicit on this point.

[71] Hart and Channing, supra note 64; Wooster, supra note 66, at 188.

[72] DeRosa supplies a nice account of the "American" origins of the Confederate Constitution. He argues that the political theory of the secessionists was essentially antifederalist and that "the fundamental constitutional principle that distinguishes the C.S.A. Constitution from the U.S. Constitution is the locus of sovereignty." Marshall L. DeRosa, *The*

was almost identical to the Constitution of the United States, except for a few items that the Confederate framers would not permit to go without saying. First, the sovereign authority for the Confederate Constitution was expressly acknowledged to derive from "the people of the Confederate States, *each State acting in its sovereign and independent character*" [emphasis added].[73] Second, "the institution of negro slavery" was guaranteed constitutional protection without euphemistic evasion.[74] And there was one other, ironic way in which the two constitutions differed. The Confederate Constitution took as its explicit purpose "to form a permanent government."[75]

XI

There would seem no stronger example of the failure of a constitution than that one or more ostensibly constituent parts of the regime that it formed and regulated would separate from the whole by dissolving the political ties that once bound it. Even if carried out peacefully, such a separation clearly evinces a failure of the constitutional order. But the failure of the order is not necessarily a failure of the Constitution or of constitutionalism. On the contrary, secession may well signal the *success* of constitutionalism and of the Constitution itself. One criterion for understanding this proposition is whether, drawing on Alexander Hamilton's maxim in *The Federalist*, No. 1, it permits the *de*constitution of politics through "reflection and choice" rather than through "accident and force."

Such a position may seem perverse, not to mention morally bankrupt, in the context of slavery. That secession in the United States was ultimately used to attempt to support and perpetuate a system of slave labor was not predestined, however. It was historically contingent on a number of factors, including patterns of immigration and settlement, the remarkable success of Northern capitalism, and political and cultural developments both planned and unexpected. At times in the country's history the movement for secession was every bit as strongly and conscientiously pursued in New England as it was in the South.[76] Had New England seceded, forming a slaveless commercial republic, or had

---

Confederate Constitution of 1861: An Inquiry into American Constitutionalism (1991), at 5, 120 et seq. My differences with DeRosa are subtle but significant.

[73] Constitution of the Confederate States of America, Preamble.

[74] Id., Article IV.

[75] Id., Preamble.

[76] Filler, supra note 41, at 303.

the Garrisonians persuaded the North and the West to secede and establish a new republic of free citizens, we might well now view secession as an institution of liberty and righteousness. In American constitutional thought, it might have become a sword against tyranny and oppression, as John Brown certainly intended his foray at Harper's Ferry to be. Besides, in the American case, slavery would have been protected in the South within or without the Union, although many Southerners feared things would be otherwise. Slavery might not have survived in perpetuity, as its proponents imagined in 1860–61. It might have lasted "only" one hundred years, which Lincoln said he was willing to tolerate.[77] But it would have persisted, had secession never been dreamed or attempted.

To return to a theme addressed in chapter 6, we should frankly acknowledge that constitutions can help form us without making us good. Although some constitutions might well help make people better, even good, and perhaps not solely by accident or force, they do not *have* to do so. Similarly, as a constitutional institution, secession might make a people better, but there is no guarantee. Given people's propensity for brutality and destruction, not to mention short-sightedness and miscalculation, the constitutional possibility of secession may be valuable if it makes the disintegration of politics somewhat safer for human beings. Some have argued that one aim of liberalism is to lower the stakes of politics in order to make it safer for human habitation. Secession may serve a similar function in reverse. Instead of lowering the stakes of politics and political and constitutional debate per se, the constitutional possibility of secession might ironically help to raise them. It might do so because it can lower the stakes of political disintegration, so that political orders break apart without disaster. But if the possibility of secession does not raise the stakes of politics, even if it were to debase them, that would not make it any less constitutional.

[77] Lincoln, First Joint Debate (Ottawa) and Fourth Joint Debate (Charleston), in *Political Debates Between Abraham Lincoln and Stephen A. Douglas* (1894), at 94, 188–189. One hundred years roughly corresponds to the period after which most forms of legal racial segregation were abolished and sharecropping declined as a form of economic organization.

CHAPTER EIGHT

Remaking America: Reconstruction and Constitutional Failure

I

Conventional wisdom has it that victory by the forces of Union averted a tragic end to the American constitutional experiment and laid the foundation for successfully remaking the polity. With respect to the latter, there were essentially two questions—one substantive, the other procedural: (1) To what extent, if any, would the fundamental principles of the order be revised after the war? (2) If revision was in the offing, how would it be constitutionally enacted? Congress's answers to both questions were embodied in the Thirteenth, Fourteenth, and Fifteenth Amendments, known collectively as the Reconstruction Amendments.

Under those Amendments the polity altered its fundamental principles in the following respects: First, the Thirteenth Amendment abolished a basic form of property—slavery—without compensating former owners. Second, the Fourteenth Amendment fully articulated a notion of national citizenship, rooted in birthright and not regulated by political institutions of the states or the nation. Third, in the context of the outcome of the Civil War, the Fourteenth Amendment suggested that the nation was indeed superior to the states. Fourth, the Fourteenth Amendment explicitly declared equality to be a constitutional value. Fifth, implicit in the arrangements of the Fourteenth Amendment, national rights would be institutionally enforceable even against the states. Sixth, the Fifteenth Amendment guaranteed all (male) citizens, regardless of "race, color, or previous condition of servitude," the right to vote.

Congress had three procedural options for pursuing these changes: a new constitution, amendments to the existing Constitution, or mere statute. In fact Congress did pursue a number of changes through statute; but a constellation of considerations, including doubts about the adequacy of the constitutional foundation for statutory changes, impelled Congress to alter the *constitutional text*.

Ultimately, of course, Congress chose the second route: alteration by amendment. But was this the proper procedure for accomplishing the changes Congress wanted to enact after the Civil War? Was it constitutionally appropriate? Was a more effective procedure available for revising the polity?

One of the most highly praised works of constitutional theory in the past decade is Bruce Ackerman's *We the People: Foundations*. With regard to the substance of the Reconstruction Amendments, Ackerman challenges what he calls the standard lawyer's view that the Amendments were merely emendations of the original Constitution, not new creations. The constitutional program of the Amendments, says Ackerman, represented a substantial departure from the constitutional principles that held before the Civil War.[1]

This claim is correct. Each of the six principles of the Reconstruction Amendments was, in its own way, new to the polity. Whether any one of them would have marked a substantial departure from existing principles is debatable. Undoubtedly, though, taken together, the Amendments' principles were the core of a fundamentally different political world.[2] They broke with the Antifederalists' world so plainly that little more need be said on the matter. But they also broke with the antebellum Federalists' world, which after all embraced constitutional protection for slavery; said almost nothing about the superiority of national citizenship; acknowledged a huge degree of autonomy, even sovereignty, in states; incorporated equality only obliquely, narrowly, and inexplicitly; refused to enforce most constitutional rights against states; and was happy to deny basic rights of citizenship, including the right to vote, to slaves and free blacks.

With respect to the procedure by which the Amendments became part of the Constitution, Ackerman says that the process of ratification violated basic antebellum assumptions concerning permissible modes of constitutional change. This claim, too, is correct, for the postbellum polity did not adhere to the principles and processes of Article V in adopting the Amendments. But, says Ackerman, that was all right: The Reconstruction process presented to the polity a new procedure for fundamental constitutional change. According to this new method, Congress acted as a kind of national vanguard of the people. It permitted

[1] Bruce Ackerman, *We the People: Foundations* (1991), at 81–83, 88–91.

[2] But see Walter F. Murphy, who argues in "*Slaughter-House*, *Civil Rights*, and Limits on Constitutional Change," 32 *Am. J. Jurisprudence* 1 (1987), that the postwar amendments were actually the *culmination* of the (true) forms and values of the original order; that is, the amendments perfected the original Constitution both in getting the political morality right and in rendering the Constitution more coherent. My opposing position stems from a more skeptical account of what it might mean to get political morality right and from a more pessimistic reading of the prewar Constitution. Consequently my view is closer but not identical to the dissents in *Slaughter-House Cases*, 83 U.S. (16 Wall.) 36 (1873).

"the general citizenry first to understand and then to participate decisively in the resolution of the critical issues of constitutional identity raised in the aftermath of Civil War." Thus national political institutions took responsibility for the fate of the nation; the people realized the rightness of the action; and a new constitutional ethos was borne of the truncated process of constitutional revision.[3]

Without attempting to supply a comprehensive empirical or theoretical account of the character or significance of Reconstruction, I wish to contest two claims that lie at the heart of Ackerman's thesis. First, I contend that the Reconstruction Amendments did not succeed, that in fact they failed to achieve their ostensible purpose of establishing a fundamentally new set of normative and institutional arrangements in the United States. Second, I maintain that formal modes of constitutional revision—modes that adhere to rigorous procedures—are sometimes not only desirable but necessary to establish constitutional authority. There are good reasons in constitutional theory to believe that a *reconstitution*—by a process akin to that of Article VII—was appropriate for remaking the polity after the war. Short of that, *reconstruction* was a second-best alternative that could succeed only by a rigorous adherence to the amending procedures of Article V. But, largely for practical reasons, the polity did not—indeed could not—adhere to processes of either reconstitution or reconstruction.

Stated somewhat differently, it is part of the character of written constitutions, as participants in the establishment and maintenance of political authority, that a polity take formal steps to demark certain forms of substantial political change. The nature of the steps may depend on the fundamentality of the change being pursued.[4] Because the postwar amendments signified substantial changes in the values and institutional relations of the polity, the adoption of those changes required the use of stringent procedures; however, the manner in which the postwar amendments were ratified was inadequate to accomplish the changes signified by the amendments themselves. Because there was no practical way to remake the nation on grounds consistent with the demands of constitutional theory, the revision of the polity was bound for failure unless an alternative ground could be found for firmly establishing constitutional authority.

Indeed there was such an alternative: The catastrophic nature of the Civil War itself might have been sufficient to establish for the postbellum order a new mythic ground that was largely invisible to both federalist and antifederalist myths before the war. For reasons I offer

[3] Ackerman, supra note 1, at 42–47.

[4] See William F. Harris II, *The Interpretable Constitution* (1993), at 191–208.

below, I believe that alternative is problematic in the context of the experience of the United States.

II

There is a sense in which a "constitutional" order—a political order ostensibly governed by a written constitution—is a genuinely new creation. One should not exaggerate the extent that this is so, however, for the appearance of a constitutional regime in the world is in many respects part of an organic (perhaps evolutionary) process of political, social, cultural, and technological change. As Wendell Phillips might have said, a constitution is not made. "It comes out of the past. Its foundations are laid far back."[5]

Nevertheless, the insinuation of a written constitution into the political affairs of human beings does suggest that the political order arising from (or laying claim to) that constitution is in some ways a new thing under the sun, if not a new order for the ages. For one thing, the *substantive values or forms* of politics reflected in the constitution may be radical departures from those of the prior regime. For another, even if the content of the constitution itself is not significantly new, the *procedure* by which the constitution comes into being and claims authority might imply a radical break with the past.

Newness may be intrinsic to the very nature of a constitution. For part of what a constitution does (or might do) is to constitute a people or the political life of a people. At the same time that a constitution is a creation, then, it is, by its very design and purpose, also a creator; that is, it typically aims at the creation of new forms of politics, perhaps even the creation of a new "people."

If this new political life can be carried out effectively by relying on traditional or "normal" forms or values, then there is little need to articulate those forms or values in a constitution. In such a society a constitution is superfluous, apart perhaps from serving as a conservator of forms and values that already are part of the traditions and ethos of the people.[6] Such a traditionalist constitution does little "constituting" of that people.

As we have seen, the authority claimed by a nontraditionalist constitution (or by the political regime claiming such a constitution) is in

[5] Wendell Phillips, "Public Opinion," Speech before the Massachusetts Anti-Slavery Society (January 28, 1852), in *Speeches, Lectures, and Letters* (1894), at 35.

[6] This conservative constitution seems to be the one claimed by Justice Antonin Scalia. See, e.g., his opinion in *Michael H. v. Gerald D.*, 491 U.S. 110 (1989). See also Scalia, "Originalism: The Lesser Evil," 57 *U. Cin. L. Rev.* 849 (1989).

some respects mythic in character. This is so partly because of the irony implied by the constitution's simultaneous functions as creation and creator. Take the Constitution of the United States, for example. The Civil War would seem at least to have destroyed the antifederalist myth that the Constitution was a creature of sovereign states. Instead, as the federalist myth would have it, the Constitution had authority because it derived from the sovereign people of the nation as a whole. They were the ultimate source of political authority in the world. They *created* the Constitution.[7] But, ironically, they were also to be a *creation* of the Constitution, for in important respects they did not exist as "a people" before the Constitution was ratified, notwithstanding Lincoln's claim to the contrary.

Similarly, though perhaps not at the same level of irony, the Constitution simultaneously is law and makes law possible; that is, while the Constitution establishes standards for making and recognizing law, it also claims to be binding law itself.[8]

If this latter conception—that the Constitution both *is* law and is the *foundation* for law—raises a potential irony, it may be resolved by conceiving of different forms of law or of law at different levels of abstraction. Either way, one might imagine that there exists some external, noumenal, or "natural" definition of law applicable to both the Constitution and positive law. Or one might suppose that the internal definition of law—that is, the manner in which the Constitution itself claims to be authoritative—is roughly identical to the authority of law *under* the Constitution. The former irony—that the people might be both creators and creations of the Constitution—is more difficult (though perhaps not impossible) to finesse in such a way, however.

The problem of constitutional authority is not an idle one, for when a constitution appears on the scene, it may not be clear why anyone should bother to pay it any mind at all, much less accept it as binding (higher) law. Although I do not wish to discount unfairly the possible role of natural law as a ground for the authority of a constitution or a constitutional order, I suspect that the internalist account makes more sense in the case of the United States. But as was shown in chapter 7, one possibility that follows from the internalist account is this: Notwithstanding our impulse to impose an aura of legality on the Constitution, one plain characteristic of the Constitution was its *illegality*. It was

[7] See William Rehnquist, "The Notion of a Living Constitution," 54 *Texas L. Rev.* 693 (1976), and John Marshall's opinion for the Supreme Court in *M'Culloch v. Maryland*, 17 U.S. (4 Wheat.) 316 (1819).

[8] The claim is rooted in the language of Article VI of the Constitution and in John Marshall's theory of the nature of the Constitution. See, e.g., *Marbury v. Madison*, 5 U.S. (1 Cranch) 137 (1803).

illegal both from the standpoint of the instructions that Congress issued the constitutional convention (to amend the Articles of Confederation) and from the perspective of the Articles themselves (which purported to be perpetual). If it were illegal in these (and other) ways, however, the illegality was part of what made the Constitution a new thing under the sun. It was also an element that made the Constitution recognizable as a constitution, as an instrument for the establishment (perhaps for the maintenance) of a new political regime. Illegality was part of what made the new regime distinct from the former one.[9]

Thus we inherit two difficulties concerning the authority of the Constitution. The first is the irony of the people as both creators and creations of the Constitution. The second is the fundamental illegality of the constitutional order. As was suggested in chapters 2 and 7, one way to resolve both difficulties is to resort to mythical accounts of the creation and authority of the Constitution. Such accounts permit one to traverse the metaphysic of the people's two bodies without inquiring too deeply into its plausibility or logic. They also permit one to generate from the founding itself new criteria of legality and political authority, criteria that justify the new regime without compelling it to submit to standards that justified or bound the old one.

III

Had the Constitution not been a substantial departure from the Articles of Confederation, it would not have been necessary for the new regime to establish its authority independent from the Articles. The Constitution could have promoted itself as a mere emendation of the Articles. To contend that a constitution is an appropriate vehicle for pursuing fundamental change in the polity, however, is not necessarily to suggest that a new constitution *must* be employed every time a society wishes to fundamentally alter the manner in which it engages in politics. It is possible to envision a society—even a "constitutional" one—that might wish to pursue basic change by means other than the adoption of a new constitution. For example, a society already residing under a constitution might have reasons to pursue such change within the structure of the established order.

Put somewhat differently in light of the experience of the United States, simply because the country employed a constitution to replace the regime in 1789 does not mean that the country was required to adopt a new constitution in the wake of the Civil War. Hence, at the

[9] See Robert Cover, "Foreword: *Nomos* and Narrative," 97 *Harv. L. Rev.* 4 (1983).

end of the Civil War, the United States had a choice: (1) to *reconstitute* the country by adopting a new constitution; or (2) to *reconstruct* the country by amending or simply affirming the old Constitution.

In theory, at least three reasons existed for adopting the strategy of reconstitution. All three rest partly on Alexander Hamilton's observation that the Constitution was an "experiment" in whether it was possible to establish government through "reflection and choice" rather than through "accident and force."

First, the Civil War was the most serious challenge to the constitutional order (if not to the Constitution itself) in the history of the country. It was so serious, in fact, that it provoked extraordinary, indeed extraconstitutional, measures to preserve the Union. When constitutional modes of maintaining order are abandoned in such systematic fashion, it may make constitutional sense to require that constitutional modes be self-consciously reestablished once order is restored.[10]

Second, after Lincoln's death, the Radical Republicans in Congress acted as if they rejected Lincoln's theory and accepted the Southern claim that the Civil War had dissolved the bonds of Union. The Radicals also contended that Northern victory had put the South in the position of a conquered province. Dominion by conquest has an honored place in the pantheon of American values and experience, but its compatibility with basic principles of constitutionalism is doubtful. Notwithstanding questions concerning the constitutional legitimacy of Southern secession or the wisdom of the Southern response to Lincoln's attempt to resupply Fort Sumter, some method of establishing the authority of the postwar regime, other than force or coercion, was constitutionally desirable.

War, of itself, does not have the capacity to establish *constitutional authority*, as opposed to mere *political power*. After all, war by its nature is linked to accident and force, which Hamilton implied are incompatible with the constitutionalist values of reflection and choice. Certainly circumstances exist in which constitutional authority can legitimately be *sustained* by force, but that authority can never be *established* merely by force. Thus, although war may establish some of the conditions for constituting a new political order, it alone cannot supply authority for the victor. The authority of any regime that grows primarily from force and violence rests on a slender reed.

The upshot of the first and second arguments is this: The suspension of constitutional ways or the forcible imposition of constitutional order may well compel a (re)commitment to reflection and choice, not only as elements of normal constitutional process but also as characterizing the

[10] See John Finn, *Constitutions in Crisis: Political Violence and the Rule of Law* (1991).

constituent acts that supply the regime's authority. Those constituent acts, the argument might go, cannot underwrite authority when they are accomplished by force or compulsion.

Third, as already mentioned, the constitutional program of the Radicals in Congress—embodied in the Thirteenth, Fourteenth, and Fifteenth Amendments—proposed a fundamental alteration of the order's basic forms and values. Consequently the Radicals' constitutional program supplanted dominant conventional understandings of the meaning of the original Constitution. In the process, it rendered that Constitution incoherent.[11]

The theoretical nature of this third argument is also an outgrowth of Hamilton's contention that constitutionalism is concerned fundamentally with establishing government by reflection and choice. As noted in chapter 1, a constitutional order can avoid accident and force only when constitutional decision is grounded on constitutional principle. Constitutional principle is possible in turn only if the constitution on which principles rest is coherent. Coherence, then, is indispensable to establishing and sustaining constitutional government. For if the constitution is fundamentally incoherent, then one cannot construct defensible standards for testing the validity of constitutional principle. And if one cannot do that, then constitutional decision is arbitrary and accidental, and the attempt to establish limits to power is quixotic, as force becomes its own justification.

IV

But whatever its wisdom or insight, theory is often weak. So it was after the Civil War, for the impulse to employ the strategy of reconstruction (as opposed to that of reconstitution) was a strong one. In fact, at first blush, the impulse might even have seemed theoretically justified. For Lincoln had prosecuted the war—and appeared prepared to press the peace—on the theory that civil war did not dissolve the Union. Indeed, the Union could not (constitutionally) be dissolved. And Northern military victory was confirmation not only of that principle but also of the Constitution *as it was*. On Lincoln's account, the Civil War neither provoked nor signified a radical alteration of the constitutional fabric. On the contrary, it had mended that fabric. Hence reconstruction was ap-

[11] See the Democratic Party's argument that the Thirteenth Amendment not only suffered from procedural irregularities but also altered substantively the form of government in the United States (and in the states themselves) and destroyed vested constitutional rights in property. "The So-Called Constitutional Amendment," in *The Democratic Almanac for 1866* (1866), at 27–30. But see Murphy, supra note 2.

propriate and reconstitution unnecessary. Any repair of the Union could be accomplished within the logic and institutions of the existing order. (One exception to this seamless picture was emancipation, which, on Lincoln's account, did require constitutional justification ex post facto.)

After Lincoln's death and the ascension of Congress as the principal institution responsible for imposing and enforcing the terms of the peace, the radical nature of Congressional Reconstruction subverted the theoretical foundation for pursuing reunion from within the existing order. But powerful forces, both pragmatic and psychological, impelled Congress to continue to embrace the strategy of reconstruction and to disavow the need for reconstitution.

First, because the Civil War had been fought by both sides as a constitutional war—indeed, as a war to preserve the Constitution—the forces of Union would have found it unbearably uncomfortable to abandon their Constitution on the heels of military victory. To reconstitute at such a time would have lent too much credence to the Southern position precisely when devotion to the old Constitution was politically imperative.

Second, achieving a genuine reconstitution would have required, in some fashion, the acquiescence of the vanquished South. Having recently attempted to withdraw from the antebellum regime, however, most white Southerners would have been hard pressed to assent to a new marriage after the war or even to reaffirm original vows. (In fact, like many Northern states, every Southern state except Tennessee initially rejected the Fourteenth Amendment.) Acquiescence would have been impossible to achieve without a form of duress that may have been much harder to justify than was the compulsion exerted to obtain ratification of the postwar amendments. At the very least, generating conditions that would have both ratified a Radical constitution and satisfied Hamilton's criteria of reflection and choice would have been difficult indeed. Under the circumstances, to permit a level of reflection and choice consistent with reconstitution would have risked ultimate failure, which would have allowed Southerners to accomplish through the back door what they could not achieve through secession at the front. In the Congress—though much less so among Reconstruction governments in the Southern states—revenge and punishment became important motivators and militated against giving ex-Confederates anything resembling victory.

Third, within human beings there may innately reside a kind of inertia, a native conservatism, that inclines them to resist most forms of change, especially radical change. As Locke noted, people will suffer massive indignity and oppression before rousing themselves to resistance. This inertia manifests itself in other ways as well. For example, people sometimes dress up change in the most unassuming garb possible and promote it as though it were simply a means for preserving the status quo. Promoting Radical Reconstruction through constitutional amendment may have been an attempt to appeal to such passive forces, but it did so at the cost of disguising how genuinely fundamental, at least on its face, was the proposed alteration of the regime.

Even were we to put aside the substantive newness of the institutions and values of the Radicals' program and thus ignore the need to enact the program by a procedure akin to those in Article VII, the procedure by which the amendments were enacted was nonetheless deficient, for, as Ackerman notes, it did not even comport with Article V. The point is not that we should be slaves to process but that the failure to adhere to basic processes of constitutional change can undermine the very conditions necessary for underwriting constitutional authority. As was discussed in chapter 1, the notion of constitutional authority generates a set of expectations in those who are to be constituted. Among those expectations are that a constitutional regime will follow its own procedures and that those procedures will reflect a degree of reflection and choice.

The expectations are not naive assumptions about how the best of all constitutional worlds ought to operate; rather, they represent realistic appraisals of the conditions that attach to the constitutional enterprise. Those conditions are not ideal abstractions. They are precepts that form part of the very logic of a constitutional order's authority, part of what is required for the order to present itself to the world as authoritative.

But the manner in which the Radicals ratified their program violated those expectations among a substantial segment of the citizenry. We see this violation in the claims of postwar Democrats that the Reconstruction Amendments were unconstitutional because they were ratified under invalid procedures and under coercion.[12] Coercion took two forms, both direct and indirect. First, Reconstruction was conducted under military occupation. Second, Congress rejected Southern refusal to ratify the postwar amendments and made ratification a condition for "readmission" of the Southern states into the Union and for attaining both local self-government and representation in Congress.

We should not permit the repugnance of Southern Democrats' aims to blind us to their perceptions on this point. For in the process of securing ratification, the Radicals inhibited the capacity of their program to command the respect and attachment of those citizens who most threatened the program's success. Such was the Radicals' dilemma;

[12] See "The So-Called Constitutional Amendment," supra note 11, at 27; "The So-Called Fifteenth Amendment," in *The Democratic Almanac for 1870* (1870), at 41.

they could not gain approval of their program without the acquiescence of the South. But evading that inability in turn undermined the authority of the program and of the new regime itself.

With respect to reconstitution, the Radicals' solution denied the possibility of constructing foundational myths, plausible to both North and South, that might have supplied (or obviated the need for) metaphysical props for the new order. There was no tenable myth, like James Bradley Thayer's, of the people descending from the heavens to remake the polity. There was certainly no myth that God had done so. With respect to reconstruction, the Radicals' approach precluded a credible claim that their revision was consistent with the minimal requirements of Article V.

V

But perhaps there was another way to establish the constitutional authority of the new regime after the war. In fact there may have been two. On one account, the institutions and values of the Reconstruction Amendments reflected the true values that existed in the original Constitution all along. In short, Lysander Spooner got the Constitution right, and some portion of the polity presumably recognized that and instantiated it textually in the postwar amendments.[13]

One optimistic conclusion about the authority of the amendments that might follow from this view is this: If there were procedural flaws in the amendments' instantiation, the flaws were not fatal, perhaps because process is always subordinate to substance or, in any event, because no procedural change was required to reveal what was always the best account of the Constitution's meaning. If the standards of truth and rectitude and goodness that inform this position are basically transcendental, deriving from outside the Constitution, polity, or constitutional enterprise, then for reasons discussed in chapters 6 and 7, they may be constitutionally suspect. But even if they derive from "within," they face other difficulties, both textual and experiential. For example, many of Spooner's claims—including his contention that "the Constitution" includes or incorporates human dignity[14]—are fundamentally in-

[13] This account resembles that of Murphy, supra note 2. It also resembles Sotirios A. Barber's (different) aspirational view of constitutional meaning in *On What the Constitution Means* (1984).

[14] Spooner's constitutionalist invocation of human dignity has twentieth-century adherents. See Murphy, supra note 2; William J. Brennan, Jr., "The Constitution of the United States: Contemporary Ratification," (Speech of October 12, 1985), reprinted at 27 *S. Tex. L. J.* 433 (1986).

consistent with what I take to be undeniable attributes of the original document. It matters not which antebellum myth—federalist or antifederalist—one invokes, for each was inconsistent in its own way with the institutions and values of the Reconstruction Amendments. Thus if Spooner's accounts are to survive and thrive, they require an alternative mythic foundation; more on that shortly.

A second way we might think of the Radicals' program as a kind of reclamation relates back to the original constitutional founding. This claim draws directly on principles that go to the heart of the constitutional enterprise. In chapter 1 I claimed that a fundamental deficiency of the original Constitution was its failure to establish conditions under which slaves—maybe also free blacks—could constitute themselves politically by reference to the Constitution. It might make sense, then, to think of the Reconstruction Amendments as attempts to cure that defect and to reform the institutions and values of the Constitution along lines more compatible with basic principles of constitutionalism. One difficulty with that approach, however, is that the change in institutions and values which such a reformation implied was so substantially at odds with those of the antebellum polity that it still begged for some new myth to authorize it.

But perhaps some such myth was available. For the postwar regime had crawled out of catastrophe, its roots nourished by blood and suffering on all sides, North and South, black and white. Perhaps the very catastrophic character of slavery and civil war supplied the basis for a new mythos for the new republic. Perhaps a great civil war to end slavery was an event of such cataclysmic horror and glory that it might mythically be said to have created a new political order along fundamentally new lines or reclaimed one submerged in the existing order.

Of course this notion contradicts my earlier claim that war is insufficient to ground *constitutional* authority. But let us put that objection aside for now and assume *arguendo* that war might underwrite authority. Even so, the history of the war and the nation's postwar experience belied the claim that such a myth might make. If the Civil War for the South was a war for slavery (and that was not entirely so), the war for the North was not intrinsically a war against slavery (especially not at its inception). Lincoln certainly did not initially prosecute the war as an indictment of slavery. Even the Emancipation Proclamation, which in retrospect has been promoted as embodying the meaning of the war, was almost exclusively an instrument for weakening the Southern military effort and hence for promoting nationalism, which was the ultimate value for Lincoln and for most Northerners who supported the war. Perhaps most tellingly, the Proclamation exempted slaves outside the Confederacy from emancipation. The Gettysburg Address contained nary a word about slavery. During the war, moreover, Lincoln tried unsuccessfully to persuade black leaders to agree to emigration to Central America.[15]

After the war Lincoln emphatically repudiated racial equality as a postwar value. He disavowed even the most rudimentary of political rights for blacks and did not take remotely seriously the idea of social equality. Notwithstanding a brief period of commitment to racial equality among Radicals and other white Northerners during Reconstruction, the commitment was appealing primarily for its value in punishing the South. After a few years, white Northerners proved weak friends of racial equality.[16]

In short, the Civil War did not stand unambiguously for either the abolition of slavery or an alteration of the basic values of the old order, at least with regard to slavery and race. Instead, it clearly stood for a myth of the indestructibility of Union—which, as I argued in chapter 7, was an *anti-constitutionalist* myth.

VI

But maybe it is misguided to be preoccupied with the theory and psychology of constitutional legitimation, with the power of myth and the weakness of war as modes of establishing constitutional authority. More to the point, perhaps the postwar amendments signified a sufficient break with the past that they effectively remade the old Constitution without the standard foundational props. Thus whatever the Constitution might have meant before Reconstruction, it meant something radically different afterward. The addition of the postwar amendments, the argument might go, made it possible to see new things—new forms and values—in the text of the Constitution that augured new ways of being in the political world of the United States.

Such a transformation through amendment might be akin to a serial novel in which the story of a single "work" is created by many authors over time.[17] Each author takes as part of his or her task to be true to the aim or theme of the work. In our context, the matter is complicated

[15] David Herbert Donald, *Lincoln* (1995), at 367–368. Lincoln's commitment to colonization was persistent and longstanding. See id., at 165–167, 343–345, 355.

[16] See Kenneth M. Stampp, *The Era of Reconstruction: 1865–1877* (1965), at 24 et seq.

[17] This notion is a variation on a theme suggested by Ronald Dworkin and Stanley Fish, who argue—in different ways and to varying conclusions—that constitutional *interpretation* is akin to a serial novel. Ronald Dworkin, "Law as Interpretation," 60 *Texas L. Rev.* 527 (1982); Stanley Fish, "Working on the Chain Gang: Interpretation in Law and Literature," 60 *Texas L. Rev.* 551 (1982).

since the story proceeds along two dimensions—one a text, one a polity—whose congruence is not always perfect. But as the story proceeds, clarifying moments may arise that permit one to see text and polity in a significantly different light than before. Imagine the Constitution, through gradual alterations of text and experience, stepping from one paradigm to another and, in one unassuming step, becoming something fundamentally different from what it was.

From this perspective, we need not worry so much about the Constitution's presenting in one fell swoop a completely new thing under the sun. We need only be concerned with the Constitution as a "made" thing, though the making occurs slowly, across generations. Such a view supplies a happy ending to the problem of Reconstruction, for in avoiding the need for a refounding, we are able to hold onto our vision of the new world toward which Reconstruction seems to point.

Or perhaps we simply reconceive the character of founding in this context, seeing it as part of a tradition or history that stretches far back like a river, a history whose course can be altered by the slightest erosion or accretion. Because it is a history that carries with it the hearts and minds of the people, the change it makes requires only slight textual recognition, if any, and can be accomplished through a relatively "ordinary" process of revision. This seems to be the happy implication of Ackerman's thesis.

Thus even if the Reconstruction Amendments could not claim authority by riding atop antebellum myths of the original founding, even if the Civil War was inadequate to establish a new foundational myth, the amendments might gain authority from their consistency with a newfound ethos in the country. In this light, the Civil War seared the conscience of the people (with some help from Congress) and thus transformed the ethos of the polity. The Thirteenth, Fourteenth, and Fifteenth Amendments were merely the textual emblems of this moral transformation.

What a wonderful people they would be. Having endured generations of slavery and caste based largely on race, having habituated themselves to a politics of aristocracy and exclusion (whatever its democratic characteristics and pretensions), having experienced the divisiveness and obstructionism and national political debility of regional factionalism, they could throw off the shackles of such patterns and embrace new forms of freedom and equality and national self-confidence. They would not require the intrusion of divine forces. Nor would they require the precipitation of the mythic constitution-making people who had retired into the sky. For the people in the world could find their way to accomplish this reciprocal change in their Constitution and in themselves.

This is a happy story indeed, but it is not our story. In our story, by

1877 the Radical forces that drove Reconstruction were severely depleted. Anticipating exhaustion, Republican leaders (who still controlled the national political apparatus) perceived the need to strike a bargain. But with whom? They could deal with (or continue to support the position of) newly enfranchised African-Americans. Or they could deal with recalcitrant and alienated Southern whites. For reasons both pragmatic and perverse, Republicans chose the latter.

Thus in the South, slavery was replaced by sharecropping and other forms of economic organization that tied free blacks in servitude to the soil and to a new aristocracy that eerily resembled the old. And a system of social segregation emerged that became a public marker of inherited inequality. The process by which these changes occurred in Southern society was complex and was not completed until the late 1890s. Concerning these changes two ironies are noteworthy. First, they were carried out with the knowledge and acquiescence of Northern liberals. Second, they were perfected only after blacks left their former alliance with the populists for a new one with the Bourbons, which led the populists to try to get blacks out of politics altogether.[18]

One year before the end of the Civil War, Karl Marx drafted an "Address to Abraham Lincoln," presenting the views of the General Council of the First International on the meaning of the war. He proclaimed:

> The workingmen of Europe feel sure that as the American War of Independence initiated a new era of ascendancy for the middle class, so the American anti-slavery War will do for the working classes. They consider it an earnest of the epoch to come, that it fell to the lot of Abraham Lincoln, the single-minded son of the working class, to lead his country through the matchless struggle for the rescue of an enchained race and the reconstruction of a social world.[19]

Even in the North after the war, however, events belied Marx's teleology. For there free labor became the prisoner of triumphant capital, which was the genuine winner of the Civil War. And Northern blacks suffered de facto a fate similar to the fate of blacks under law in the South.

Everywhere the old racial disabilities were replaced by the systematic exclusion of former slaves and their descendants from the most basic of political rights (such as voting)[20] and civil rights (such as access to pub-

[18] See C. Vann Woodward, *The Strange Career of Jim Crow* (1974), especially at 67–109.

[19] "Address of the International Workingmen's Association to Abraham Lincoln," in Karl Marx and Frederick Engels, *Letters to Americans, 1848–1895* (1953), at 65–66.

[20] In the case of voting, restriction was enforced through terrorism, intimidation, and legal barriers to the exercise of the right.

lic accommodations and benefits).[21] Moreover, states were resurgent, free to regulate their new domestic institutions except where such regulation impinged on relations of capital and labor.

The postwar regime wrought a brave new world. But perhaps its form should not surprise us. For a polity that lacked the will or the means to reconstitute itself along fundamentally new lines—or even properly to amend its way into a new regime—could not have been expected to remake itself in the image of the new forms and values of the postwar amendments. If those amendments were to be a device for making a new form of politics, a new thing under the sun, they were, as Edmund Burke might have predicted, stillborn.[22] If, on the other hand, they were designed to be consistent with the logic of the old order, then that order arose, reborn and strangely invigorated, from the ashes of civil war.

[21] See *The Civil Rights Cases*, 109 U.S. 3 (1883), and *Plessy v. Ferguson*, 163 U.S. 537 (1897).

[22] Compare Justice Swayne's dissent in *Slaughter-House*, proclaiming the postwar amendments to be "a new Magna Charta" and bemoaning the Court's evisceration of the amendments. *Slaughter-House Cases*, supra note 2, at 125.

Epilogue

I

Despite the curious similarities the postwar order was not in all respects identical to the old. For example, notwithstanding the persistence of regional differences and the romantic refinement of Southern stories of the "Lost Cause," North and South were surprisingly united by the end of the nineteenth century. As I have already suggested, however, this unity came at a price. The price was the emergence of a new constitutive division in the constitutional order: that between whites and blacks.

The division was not entirely new, of course. Its roots were long. One could not have explained, for example, the peculiar institution or the perverse distinctions among citizenships in the antebellum polity without a strong sense of the fundamentality of race. But from a constitutional standpoint, at least until *Dred Scott*, the racial presuppositions of institutional structure and political culture were ironically hidden precisely because so many basic assumptions of whites about racial superiority seemed so natural, so apparent. In short, they could go without saying.

After the war many of those racial assumptions persisted, but the inherited institutional and normative forms could not reliably sustain racial superiority, especially if the Fourteenth Amendment were to be interpreted expansively. Some such worry undoubtedly underlay the refusal of every Southern legislature except Tennessee's to ratify the Fourteenth Amendment and animated opposition to the Amendment in the North. In fact worries over the radical implications of the Amendment, including its racial egalitarianism, led the legislatures of Ohio and New Jersey to rescind their ratifications. Congress ignored the rescisions and certified adoption, but even after Congress had certified the Amendment, Oregon's legislature also rescinded ratification.[1]

There emerged, in the North, South, and West, a kind of "we/they" (or, in Carl Schmitt's terms, *friend/enemy*) frame of mind.[2] It split the

[1] John Hope Franklin, *Reconstruction: After the Civil War* (1961), at 67–68; Horace Edgar Flack, *The Adoption of the Fourteenth Amendment* (1908), at 161–209; Joseph B. James, *The Ratification of the Fourteenth Amendment* (1984); *Coleman v. Miller*, 307 U.S. 433 (1939), at 448–449.

[2] Carl Schmitt, *The Concept of the Political* (Schwab, trans., 1976). Schmitt claims that the identification of domestic friends and enemies is inevitable, especially in what Schmitt

polity because it divided "the People" on which the Constitution ostensibly relied for its authority. From the perspective of many whites, blacks were *in* the polity but not *of* it. And the democratic cast of political power meant that whites had the means to attach disabilities to "them." Thus in most places, by means informal and formal, the disabilities appeared as naturally as the sun rose. As Myrdal later would intimate and the Kerner Commission explicitly affirm, there were two Americas, one black and one white.[3]

Again, one of the most visible markers of disability was segregation. Segregation had to be de jure in the South, for the races there were neither physically nor culturally separate to the extent they were in the North. But whether de jure or de facto, the policy of segregation reinforced the divided polity. Contrary to the implication of *Brown v. Board of Education*,[4] the injury of segregation was not that the development of blacks would be retarded if they could not associate with whites. Although there were deep and abiding inequalities in the segregations practiced in the United States, they had nothing inherently to do with the extent to which blacks could learn or develop or flourish in a black world. In fact despite the constitutional language we now use to talk about our racial legacy, the inherent constitutional problem of segregation was not merely a matter of equality, but that whites and blacks were denied the space to meet and talk to one another about the world(s) they inhabited. This injury was inflicted on both blacks and whites,[5] though the political and material consequences of separation were obviously and inordinately suffered by blacks.

Compare this condition with that of the North and South before the Civil War. As alienated as Southerners were in the polity, never was there a time when they could not discuss or negotiate the terms of their constitutional world. After the Civil War, however, segregation not only forced blacks and whites into separate worlds but denied them the means to traverse the territory between them.

---

calls a "constitutional state," particularly in the absence of foreign war. The claim of inevitability seems overstated. But it would be a mistake to disregard the special power of the impulse, even in constitutional orders, to create domestic friends and enemies as markers of political boundaries and political identity. Id., at 45–53.

[3] Gunnar Myrdal, *An American Dilemma: The Negro Problem and Modern Democracy* (1944). Of course this dichotomy is overly simple, as race was not the only cleavage in the polity, and, even where race was concerned, "black and white" captured only part of the picture.

[4] *Brown v. Board of Education*, 347 U.S. 483 (1954).

[5] In recognizing the mutuality of harm, Harlan's dissent in *Plessy v. Ferguson*, 163 U.S. 537 (1896), at 552, 563–564, was much more perceptive than the Court's opinion in *Brown*, supra note 4.

II

It is a wonder that events did not entirely undermine the attachment of blacks—now one could plausibly begin to use "African-Americans"—to the Constitution. That this did not occur was owing partly to the capacity of African-Americans to generate their own accounts of what the postbellum Constitution meant. In ways that Frederick Douglass foreshadowed but Abraham Lincoln could not, African-Americans after the war and into the twentieth century readily distinguished nation from Constitution. They distinguished, that is, the facts of political institutions and practices from the meaning of the Constitution. As late as the mid-1960s Martin Luther King could press a radical critique of the political *order* while proclaiming fidelity to the *Constitution*. Thus, as disparate as they sometimes were, the separate worlds of blacks and whites continued to be *constitutional* worlds. And there even seemed a time when events might engender their reconciliation.

But events did not rest. Of course the civil rights acts of the 1960s declared many forms of racial segregation and discrimination illegal. Saying so did not necessarily make it so, but many prominent forms of segregation and discrimination were in fact ended, though some were not and the vestiges of others remained. More important for our purposes, racial divisions persisted and ironically may have deepened after the 1960s. I am neither a sociologist nor an expert on racial relations and thus am not competent to explain the reasons for these trends, but I might be able to offer an impressionistic account of their contours and a preliminary sense of their constitutional significance.

With respect to African-Americans two rough forms of constitutionally significant division have emerged in the United States—an interior division (one *within* "the Constitution") and an exterior division (a separation *from* the Constitution).

The interior division is an inheritance of Martin Luther King's constitutionalism. Although King's attachment to the constitutional order was ambivalent, his devotion to the Constitution seems not to have been. One can see evidence of both in his "Letter from a Birmingham Jail." Although the Letter paid primary homage to what he called "the most sacred values in our Judeo-Christian heritage," it also invoked democracy, the Constitution, and the Declaration of Independence without apology or irony.[6] King's fidelity to Constitution was most clearly visible in his speech to those assembled for the March on Washington in 1963. There he explicitly cited the Constitution and Declaration as contracts,

[6] Martin Luther King, "Letter from a Birmingham Jail" (1963), in *I Have a Dream: Writings and Speeches That Changed the World* (Washington, ed., 1992), at 83–100.

specifically as promissory notes whose promises he insisted the nation was obliged to honor.

There were two distinct elements to King's characterization of the promises. The first consisted of a straightforward claim to equality, dignity, and decency of treatment for African-Americans. It was, in his terms, a claim to "justice" that implicated the basic quality of life of blacks in the polity. The second element was that of integration. As King put it in his speech in Washington, "I have a dream" that even in Alabama "little black boys and black girls will be able to join hands with little white boys and white girls as sisters and brothers."[7]

Rarely was it clear whether King intended the latter element as instrumental to the former (or vice versa) or saw them as standing on an equal plane as ends in themselves. It is apparent, though, that there was little tension between the two in King's thinking. For in tandem they represented a constitutional vision not merely of toleration but of belonging. That vision has resonated profoundly among a great many African-Americans and has appealed to other Americans as well. In fact many of the African-American adherents to King's constitutionalism have been as intensely committed to (their vision of) the Constitution as anyone in the country. One thinks of the words of Barbara Jordan in another context: "My faith in the Constitution is whole. It is complete. It is total. I am not going to sit here and be an idle spectator to the diminution, the subversion, the destruction of the Constitution."[8]

In its simultaneous ambivalence toward the constitutional order and devotion to the Constitution, King's constitutionalism and the place of African-Americans in the polity are structurally similar to the relationship of Southerners to their Constitution in the nineteenth century. The concerns that animate Lani Guinier's response to racial majoritarianism, for example, bear a familiar resemblance to the worries that drove John C. Calhoun's concurrent majorities, though white Southerners are usually oblivious to the similarity.[9]

Of course there are differences. One is that the dominant constitutional position of nineteenth-century Southerners aimed not at making a world that did not exist, as did King's, but at keeping a world that was slipping away. Another difference is that the myth that supports King's constitutionalism—including the convergence of the Constitution and the Declaration and the invocation of Lincoln as emancipator and patriarch—is plainly inconsistent with the myth that supported the domi-

[7] Martin Luther King, "I Have a Dream" (1963), in id., at 101, 105.

[8] Barbara Jordan and Shelby Hearon, *Barbara Jordan: A Self Portrait* (1979), at 187.

[9] Lani Guinier, *The Tyranny of the Majority: Fundamental Fairness in Representative Democracy* (1994).

nant nineteenth-century Southern Constitution, before or after the Civil War. (With respect to mythology, a more apt comparison is between King's constitutionalism and the antislavery constitutionalism of Frederick Douglass.)

Present-day African-American adherents to King's constitutionalism are themselves divided. In part their differences have grown out of frustration over the scope, pace, and practicability of racial change in the country. But the division has also grown out of disagreement over the relative primacy of the two elements of King's constitutionalism: (1) basic rights and equality for black Americans, or (2) universalism and integration. Different assumptions about and commitments to these values have led African-Americans in different directions at the level of policy, and in fact have led many of them, if not most, away from unequivocally integrationist aims.[10] For all their dissimilarities, however, most African-American adherents to King's constitutionalism continue to share space under the Constitution.[11]

III

One cannot easily make the same claim about the second, *exterior* division among African-Americans. Its main significance is less that it is a division among African-Americans, although undoubtedly it is, than that it represents a split between African-Americans and the rest of the polity. The causes of this division are complex and its sources and manifestations numerous.

One example is that of young blacks, especially young men in enclaves of the country's largest cities, who now stand a greater chance of going to prison than to college. The alienation from the political order that many young blacks feel today is profound, but it seems to derive less from a reflective response to the Constitution or constitutional mat-

[10] For an account of the breakdown of the aim of integration, among both blacks and liberal whites, see Gary Orfield, "Race and the Liberal Agenda: The Loss of the Integrationist Dream, 1965–1974," in *The Politics of Social Policy in the United States* (Weir et al., eds., 1988), at 313–355. See also Jennifer Hochschild, *The New American Dilemma: Liberal Democracy and School Desegregation* (1984); Judith L. Failer, Anna Harvey, and Jennifer Hochschild, "Only One Oar in the Water: The Political Failure of School Desegregation in Yonkers, New York," in *Beyond Desegregation: The Politics of Quality in African American Schooling* (Shujaa, ed., 1994), at 53 et seq.

[11] Compare, for example, Derrick Bell, *And We Are Not Saved: The Elusive Quest for Racial Justice* (1989); Glenn C. Loury, "'Matters of Color'—Blacks and the Constitutional Order," in *Slavery and Its Consequences: The Constitution, Equality, and Race* (Goldwin and Kaufman, eds., 1988), at 150–164; and Shelby Steele, *The Content of Our Character* (1990).

ters per se than from frustration and despair over the possibility of finding a place for themselves in America.[12] Although these sentiments are not explicitly constitutional, they might imply much about the material and social preconditions for constitutional attachment.

Alienated youth aside, however, other African-Americans have expressed a similar sense of estrangement in explicitly constitutional terms. Like nineteenth-century Southerners and Garrisonians, they have sought physical separation as a solution to what they perceive as intractable problems: racism, subordination, and oppression which are reinforced by the numerical majority that whites enjoy in the national political order. Whatever else one might think of them, the black proponents of racial separation have been neither naive nor ill-informed. Marcus Garvey and Malcolm X were thoughtful, articulate, and frequently eloquent in their condemnation of the polity and their defense of a policy of a black homeland.[13]

In our own time Louis Farrakhan of the Nation of Islam is the most prominent proponent of the policy. He is certainly not the only proponent whom we might name, but his prominence makes him a useful exemplar. Even if he does not speak for most African-Americans, I suspect that his critique of the American polity resonates among many, even among those who do not embrace him.

The difficulty of discussing Farrakhan, aside from people's often visceral reactions to the man and his ideas, is that he is a moving target. In fact, on many matters he is simply inconsistent. I make no attempt to read him systematically or comprehensively here but merely sketch the contours of his thinking as it touches on the Constitution and the American constitutional order.

For our purposes Farrakhan presents three faces to the world, each implying a distinct rationale for and version of racial separation. The first is an argument from a kind of natural law, which yields in his hands a biologically determined racialism. Each race, he says, has its own nature, which is part of the physical and moral makeup of the races.[14] But what are the natures of the respective races? One gets a hint of his answer from his "Speech on the Black Woman": "[W]hen the

[12] For a fine account of conditions that underwrite the alienation of black men, see Mitchell Duneier, *Slim's Table: Race, Respectability, and Masculinity* (1992), especially at 25–26.

[13] Gary Peller offers an excellent account of the contours and implications of black nationalist thought. Gary Peller, "Race-Consciousness," in *Critical Race Theory: The Key Writings That Formed the Movement* (Crenshaw, Gotanda, Peller, and Thomas, eds., 1995), at 127 et seq.

[14] Louis Farrakhan, "Black Solidarity Day Address," in his 7 *Speeches* (1974), at 118 et seq.

white man put his blood in us he did not help us. When he put his blood in us, . . . he was . . . making us to lean naturally in his wicked way instead of leaning toward the natural way of our own original Black self which is toward righteousness." Farrakhan metaphorically associates the white man with the beast of Revelation and condemns lying down with the beast.[15] This condemnation aims at keeping the black race biologically distinct and separate from others. For this reason, what Farrakhan's newspaper calls "the Muslim Program" seeks to prohibit "intermarriage or race mixing."[16] But biological purity is not politically sufficient. Ultimately, he says, blacks will rule others, "not as another slave master but as a better ruler, teacher and guide of the people,"[17] for African-Americans are "the people of God's choice."[18]

Resting on this incarnation of natural law, Farrakhan's first face is not recognizably "constitutional" (in the sense of supplying an account or critique of the Constitution) or "constitutionalist" (in the sense of speaking to the general norms or institutions that the use of written constitutions implies or presupposes). Consequently I shall not dwell on it here. His second face, however, is more suggestive for our purposes, for it resembles the Garrisonian critique of the nineteenth-century Constitution. Farrakhan's version of this critique rests partly on an intentionalist reading of the original Constitution. In a speech in Philadelphia on July 4, 1996, he said, "The Declaration of Independence and Constitution had none of us (Blacks) in mind. . . . What you are celebrating is somebody else's independence."[19] So framed, the gist of this position is that because the Declaration and the Constitution were framed by and for the white race, the texts do not now include blacks.

Any number of policies might follow from this constitutional claim. One, which Farrakhan presses, is territorial separation of the races. "We want our people in America whose parents or grandparents were descendants from slaves, to be allowed to establish a separate state or territory of their own—either on this continent or elsewhere. We believe

[15] Louis Farrakhan, "On the Black Woman," in id., at 31–32. See also Farrakhan, "Are Black People the Future World Rulers?" in *Back Where We Belong: Selected Speeches by Minister Louis Farrakhan* (Eure and Jerome, eds., 1989), at 247–249.

[16] From "The Muslim Program," *The Final Call*, August 6, 1996, at 39. This piece appears on the penultimate page of every issue of *The Final Call*, a newspaper whose publisher is Louis Farrakhan as "national Representative of The Honorable Elijah Muhammad and the Nation of Islam." Id., at 2.

[17] Louis Farrakhan, "Are Black People the Future World Rulers?" supra note 15, at 226–233; Farrakhan, "Speech at Rally for Angela Davis," in *7 Speeches*, supra note 14, at 101.

[18] "The Muslim Program," supra note 16.

[19] Quoted in "Independence Day Speech in Philadelphia," *The Final Call*, July 16, 1996, at 3.

that our former slave masters are obligated to provide such land." The statement specifies that the land should be "fertile and minerally rich" and that the "former slave masters" must "maintain and supply our needs in this separate territory for the next 20 to 25 years."[20]

In short, the policy is a special kind of secession in which the territory is neither defined nor yet occupied by those who would eventually live in it. Like Southerners' claims in the nineteenth century, Farrakhan's rests on an account of the founding. The particular reasoning is one Southerners would have recognized, even embraced, though they would not have conceded the implications that Farrakhan draws. Specifically Farrakhan's version might go as follows: Because blacks neither participated in the creation of the polity nor were members at the time of its creation, they had no way to attach to the Constitution to which the polity traced its authority. Blacks, as noncreators at the beginning, are not now bound to remain.

This argument has the ring of historical truth to it; thus if Farrakhan were fleshing out his constitutional claim, he might assert that his account of the founding is not merely mythically true, but simply true. As with many such truths, however, the historical record of the constitutional order may be more complex than this depiction of exclusion at the founding would allow. As Justice Curtis claimed in dissent in *Dred Scott v. Sandford*,

> [The] Constitution was ordained and established by the people of the United States, through the action, in each State, of those persons who were qualified by its laws to act thereon, in behalf of themselves and all other citizens of that State. In some of the States, . . . colored persons were among those qualified by law to act on this subject. These colored persons were not only included in the body of "the people of the United States," by whom the Constitution was ordained and established, but in at least five of the States they had the power to act, and doubtless did act, by their suffrages, upon the question of its adoption.[21]

Thus, on Curtis's reading, blacks were not categorically excluded from but in fact participated in the founding of the order. That there was nothing to which blacks could attach, then, would simply be inaccurate, and the justification for secession might fail as a consequence. On the other hand, even if blacks were not excluded per se, most blacks in fact were, and slaves certainly were. This observation might merely suggest that Farrakhan—were he willing to frame an argument in these

[20] "The Muslim Program," supra note 16.

[21] *Dred Scott v. Sandford*, 60 U.S. (19 How.) 393 (1857), Curtis dissenting, at 576.

terms—revise his claim to account for foundational ambiguity and so perhaps salvage one constitutional ground for his policy of secession.

Whatever the historical plausibility of this account, however, it is now almost impossible to cite it as a possible device for determining the Constitution's current meaning. To make the claim stick would require a rigidly intentionalist approach to interpretation that even today's most ardent advocates of intentionalism would refuse to embrace. Farrakhan himself may suspect as much, which could explain his third face. It begins—but does not end—with arguments that echo Martin Luther King's constitutionalism: "The Kingdom of God is an egalitarian kingdom structured on truth, where each of us will be treated with fairness and justice. America could become the basis for the Kingdom of God. She has within her borders every nation, kindred and tongue. If they could be made peaceful, productive and mutually respecting, you would have the basis for the Kingdom of God right here on earth."[22] Thus in his more expansive moments, Farrakhan rejects the Garrisonian critique of the Constitution, repudiates what he calls the inherently racist vision of the founders, and embraces the view of Declaration and Constitution as "inspired" and "moral." But "it would take moral and spiritual men to make such documents flesh," he says. And the problem has been that such people have not come forth—or at least not in sufficient numbers—to make real the values of freedom, justice, and equality.[23]

At this point Farrakhan might easily be taken as a successor to King, but Farrakhan's solution to the problems of American constitutional experience—the problems, that is, of "white supremacy" and of "government that has failed in its responsibilities"—departs dramatically from King's. "Integration," says Farrakhan, "is not working to bring true freedom, justice, and equality to America's former slaves." What is called for, then, is "the separation of the so-called Negroes and the so-called white Americans." The form of separation is identical to that presented in Farrakhan's second face, but its justification is no longer tied to a story of the founding. Instead it rests on what one might read as a pragmatic claim about current social realities: "Since we cannot get along with them in peace and equality, after giving them 400 years of our sweat and blood and receiving in return some of the worst treatment human beings have ever experienced, we believe our contributions to this land and the suffering forced upon us by white America, justifies [*sic*] our demand for complete separation in a state or territory of our

[22] Louis Farrakhan, *A Torchlight for America* (1993), at 159.

[23] Id., at 151–154; "Independence Day Speech," supra note 19, at 3.

own." This policy, he says, is "the best and only answer to the problem between the two people."[24]

Although the conclusion of this third argument is identical to that of the second, the structure of this one is quite different. Here, the thinking goes, the Declaration of Independence and Constitution both embody foundational values to which all might attach. Thus the failure, from Farrakhan's perspective, has not been one of the Constitution but of the political order, for the polity has persistently failed to realize the values that the Constitution enshrines, in fact is systemically incapable of realizing those values. So framed, the argument may push beyond simple pragmatism to a claim that rests on the ostensible character of the Constitution itself. Borrowing from King's metaphor, the Constitution is a kind of contract, but the polity has broken the agreement and seems unwilling ever to redeem its promises. Although I have imputed a fuller constitutional argument than Farrakhan himself supplies, if the implication is fair, then Farrakhan's position is strikingly similar to that which Southerners adopted in 1861.

IV

If Louis Farrakhan were the only separatist on the political stage, one might dismiss him as an extremist demagogue. But he is not the only African-American harboring such sentiments and resentments. Nor are African-Americans the only group whose members are pressing for autonomy.

The treatment of Native Americans throughout the continent and their peculiar legal status as separate, conquered peoples have produced an array of attachments decidedly ambivalent. Further, their reservations are permitted to a limited extent to operate as entities separate from the United States, though doubtless they lack the autonomy, material resources, and territory that Farrakhan imagines for his African-American homeland.

For reasons that might well be constitutionally comprehensible, a number of Hispanics in the American Southwest continue to regard as illegitimate the nation's conquest of that region in the Mexican War. For these individuals the war failed to engender conditions that would allow them to attach to the new regime, even to this day.

The military conquest of Hawaii, which led to settlement by whites and the admission of Hawaii as the fiftieth state, did not promote a

[24] Farrakhan, *Torchlight*, supra note 22, at 151–154; "Independence Day Speech," supra note 19, at 17; "The Muslim Program," supra note 16.

sense of attachment among Native Hawaiians. In fact many of them still consider themselves "an occupied people" and deny the authority of the government of the State of Hawaii. Some insist that certain native lands be returned and that the State of Hawaii acknowledge the sovereignty of natives over those lands. Others claim that the vote for statehood should be rescinded.[25]

Various groups of Asian-Americans have pressed for rights to maintain culturally autonomous groups. Disaffected whites, invoking a genetically altered antifederalism, have formed klans and militias and neo-Nazi groups that challenge the nation's constitutional authority. And whites of all classes have abandoned many of the nation's cities, in part because of an unwillingness to live with "others."[26]

Arthur M. Schlesinger, Jr., worries that "multiculturalism" is exacerbating these tendencies, contributing to what he calls "the disuniting of America."[27] His worries about multiculturalism may be overblown, in fact may simply be wrong. But there is little doubt that centrifugal tendencies, based importantly on race and ethnicity, are neither isolated nor insignificant. We cannot easily know whether or how the Constitution or the constitutional order can withstand these tendencies. Much may depend on people's capacity to engage in serious conversation—in which the outcome is genuinely open—to reflect on, perhaps also to choose, the conditions under which they can create or sustain a political life that is capable of securing authority under a common constitution.

The cost of resisting such a conversation may not be anarchy, revolution, or civil war, but rather a slow disintegration, reflecting forms of constitutional failure all the more powerful for their subtlety.

[25] Mindy Pennybacker, "Should the Aloha State Say Goodbye? Natives Wonder," *The Nation* (August 12–19, 1996), at 21.

[26] For an account of "white flight," see Derrick A. Bell, Jr., "*Brown v. Board of Education* and the Interest Convergence Dilemma," in *Critical Race Theory*, supra note 13, at 20 et seq.

[27] Arthur M. Schlesinger, Jr., *The Disuniting of America: Reflections on a Multicultural Society* (1992).

Bibliography

Ackerman, Bruce A. "The Storrs Lectures: Discovering the Constitution," 93 *Yale L. J.* 1013 (1984).

———. *We the People: Foundations* (1991).

Altman, Andrew. "Legal Realism, Critical Legal Studies, and Dworkin," 15 *Phil. & Pub. Aff.* 205 (1986).

Amar, Akhil. "Of Sovereignty and Federalism," 96 *Yale L. J.* 1425 (1987).

———. "Some New World Lessons for the Old World," 58 *U. Chi. L. Rev.* 483 (1991).

Ames, Herman V. *The Proposed Amendments to the Constitution of the United States during the First Century of Its History* (1896; repr. 1970).

Aquinas, Thomas. *Summa Theologica*, in *The Political Ideas of St. Thomas Aquinas* (Dino Bigongiari, ed., 1953).

Bailyn, Bernard, ed. *Pamphlets of the American Revolution: 1750–1776* (1965).

Bancroft, Frederic. *Calhoun and the South Carolina Nullification Movement* (1928).

Barber, Sotirios A. *On What the Constitution Means* (1984).

———. *The Constitution of Judicial Power* (1993).

Beard, Charles A. *An Economic Interpretation of the Constitution of the United States* (1935).

Bell, Derrick. *And We Are Not Saved: The Elusive Quest for Racial Justice* (1989).

———. "*Brown v. Board of Education* and the Interest Convergence Dilemma," in *Critical Race Theory: The Key Writings That Formed the Movement* (Kimberlé Crenshaw, Neil Golanda, Gary Peller, and Kendall Thomas, eds., 1995).

Bendix, Reinhard. "The Mandate to Rule: An Introduction," 55 *Social Forces* 247 (1976).

———. *Kings or People: Power and the Mandate to Rule* (1978).

Berlin, Isaiah. *The Crooked Timber of Humanity: Chapters in the History of Ideas* (Henry Hardy, ed., 1991).

Berns, Walter. "The Constitution and the Migration of Slaves," 78 *Yale L. J.* 198 (1968).

Bestor, Arthur. "State Sovereignty and Slavery: A Reinterpretation of Proslavery Constitutional Doctrine, 1846–1860," 54 *J. Ill. St. Hist. Soc.* 117 (1961).

Beveridge, Albert J. *The Life of John Marshall*, 4 vols. (1916–1919).

Bork, Robert H. *The Tempting of America: The Political Seduction of the Law* (1990).

Bowen, Catherine Drinker *Miracle at Philadelphia: The Story of the Constitutional Convention, May to September 1787* (1966).

Braden, George D. "The Search for Objectivity in Constitutional Law," 57 *Yale L. J.* 571 (1948).

Bradford, M. E., *Remembering Who We Are: Observations of a Southern Conservative* (1985).

Brandon, Mark E. "The 'Original' Thirteenth Amendment and the Limits to Formal Constitutional Change," in *Responding to Imperfection: The Theory and Practice of Constitutional Amendment* (Sanford Levinson, ed., 1995).

Brennan, William J., Jr. "The Constitution of the United States: Contemporary Ratification" (Speech of October 12, 1985), repr. at 27 *S. Tex. L. J.* 433 (1986).

Brest, Paul. "Interpretation and Interest," 34 *Stanford L. Rev.* 739 (1982).

Brubaker, Stanley. "Taking Dworkin Seriously, 47 *Rev. of Pol.* 45 (1985).

Buchanan, Allen. *Secession: The Morality of Political Divorce from Fort Sumter to Lithuania and Quebec* (1991).

Buchanan, James. *The Works of James Buchanan* (John Bassett Moore, ed., 1910).

Buchanan, James M. "Europe's Constitutional Opportunity," in *Europe's Constitutional Future* (Graham Mather, ed., 1990).

Buchanan, James M., and Roger L. Faith. "Secession and the Limits of Taxation: Toward a Theory of Internal Exit," 77 *Am. Econ. Rev.* 1023 (1987).

Burger, Warren E. "Lawyers and the Constitutional Convention," 34 *Fed. Bar News & J.* 106 (1987).

———. "Tell the Story of Freedom," 72 *ABA J.* 54 (May 1986).

———. "We the People," 37 *Case W. Res. L. Rev.* 385 (1987).

Burke, Edmund. *Burke's Speech on Conciliation with America* (Hammond Lamont, ed., 1897).

Calhoun, John C. *The Works of John C. Calhoun*, 6 vols. (Richard K. Cralle, ed., 1855, 1856).

———. *Disquisition on Government* (Richard K. Cralle, ed., 1883).

———. "Address in the Senate of the United States, on the Subject of Slavery" (March 4, 1850) (Princeton University Microfiche Collection).

———. "Speech on the Reception of Abolition Petitions" (February 6, 1837), in *Slavery Defended: Views of the Old South* (Eric L. McKitrick, ed., 1963).

Carpenter, Jesse T. *The South as a Conscious Minority, 1789–1861* (1930).

Christy, David. "Cotton Is King; or Slavery in the Light of Political Economy" (1860), in *Cotton Is King, and Pro-Slavery Arguments* (E. N. Elliott, ed., 1860).

Clausewitz, Carl von, *On War* (Michael Howard and Peter Parat, eds., 1984).

Cohen, I. Bernard. *Science and the Founding Fathers: Science in the Political Thought of Thomas Jefferson, Benjamin Franklin, John Adams, and James Madison* (1995).

Commager, Henry Steele, and Milton Cantor, eds. *Documents of American History*, vol. 1 (1988).

Corwin, Edward S. "The 'Higher Law' Background of American Constitutional Law" (1928, 1929), in *Corwin on the Constitution*, vol. 1 (Richard Loss, ed., 1981).

———. *Liberty Against Government* (1948).

Cover, Robert M. "Foreword: *Nomos* and Narrative," 97 *Harv. L. Rev.* 4 (1983).

———. *Justice Accused: Antislavery and the Judicial Process* (1975).

Croly, Herbert D. *The Promise of American Life* (1909).

Current, Richard N. "God and the Strongest Battalions," in *Why the North Won the Civil War* (David Donald, ed., 1960).

Dahl, Robert. "Decision-Making in a Democracy: The Supreme Court as a National Policy-Maker" (1957), in *The Borzoi Reader in American Politics* (Edward Keynes and David Adamany, eds., 1971).

———. *A Preface to Democratic Theory* (1956).

———. *Who Governs? Democracy and Power in an American City* (1961).

Davis, David Brion. *The Problem of Slavery in the Age of Revolution: 1770–1823* (1975).

The Democratic Almanac for 1866 (1866).

The Democratic Almanac for 1870 (1870).

DeRosa, Marshall L. *The Confederate Constitution of 1861: An Inquiry into American Constitutionalism* (1991).

Diamond, Larry, and Marc F. Plattner, eds. *Nationalism, Ethnic Conflict, and Democracy* (1994).

Dillon, Merton L. *The Abolitionists: The Growth of a Dissenting Minority* (1974).

Donald, David [Herbert]. "Died of Democracy," in *Why the North Won the Civil War* 79 (David Donald, ed., 1960).

———. *Lincoln Reconsidered: Essays on the Civil War Era* (1961).

———. *Lincoln* (1995).

Douglass, Frederick. *The Life and Writings of Frederick Douglass*, 5 vols. (Philip S. Foner, ed., 1950, 1975).

———. *Narrative of the Life of Frederick Douglass, an American Slave* (1845), in *The Classic Slave Narratives* (H. L. Gates, Jr., ed., 1987).

Duneier, Mitchell. *Slim's Table: Race, Respectability, and Masculinity* (1992).

Dworkin, Ronald. *Taking Rights Seriously* (1977, 1978).

———. "No Right Answer?" in *Law, Morality, and Society* (P.M.S. Hacker and Joseph Raz, eds., 1977).

———. "Law as Interpretation," 60 *Texas L. Rev.* 527 (1982).

———. *Law's Empire* (1986).

Eisgruber, Christopher L. "Justice Story, Slavery, and the Natural Law Foundations of American Constitutionalism," 55 *U. Chi. L. Rev.* 273 (1988).

———. "Justice and the Text: Rethinking the Constitutional Relation Between Prudence and Principle," 43 *Duke L. J.* 1 (1993).

Elazar, Daniel J. "The Biblical Theory of Covenant: Biblical Origins and Modern Developments," in *Covenant, Polity, and Constitutionalism* (Daniel J. Elazar and John Kincaid, eds., 1980).

Elazar, Daniel J., and John Kincaid, eds. *Covenant, Polity, and Constitutionalism* (1980).

Elkin, Stephen L. "Constitutionalism: Old and New," in *A New Constitutionalism: Designing Political Institutions for a Good Society* (Stephen L. Elkin and Karoł Soltan, eds., 1993).

Ely, John Hart. *Democracy and Distrust: A Theory of Judicial Review* (1980).

Erskine-Hill, Howard, and Graham Storey, eds. *Revolutionary Prose of the English Civil War* (1983).

Ewald, William. "Comparative Jurisprudence (I): What Was It Like to Try a Rat?" 143 *U. Pa. L. Rev.* 1889 (1995).

Failer, Judith L., Anna Harvey, and Jennifer Hochschild. "Only One Oar in the Water: The Political Failure of School Desegregation in Yonkers, New York," in *Beyond Desegregation: The Politics of Quality in African American Schooling* (Mwalimu J. Shujaa, ed., 1994).

Farrakhan, Louis. *7 Speeches* (1974).

———. *Back Where We Belong: Selected Speeches by Minister Louis Farrakhan* (Joseph D. Eure and Richard M. Jerome, eds., 1989).

———. *A Torchlight for America* (1993).

Fehrenbacher, Don E. *The Dred Scott Case: Its Significance in American Law and Politics* (1978).

———. "Slavery, the Framers, and the Living Constitution," in *Slavery and Its Consequences: The Constitution, Equality, and Race* (Robert A. Goldwin and Art Kaufman, eds., 1988).

Filler, Louis. *The Crusade against Slavery, 1830–1860* (1960).

Finkelman, Paul. *An Imperfect Union: Slavery, Federalism, and Comity* (1981).

———. "Slavery and Bondage in the 'Empire of Liberty,'" in *The Northwest Ordinance: Essays on Its Formulation, Provisions, and Legacy* (Frederick D. Williams, ed., 1989).

———. "Story Telling in the Supreme Court: Prigg v. Pennsylvania and Justice Joseph Story's Judicial Nationalism," 1994 *Sup. Ct. Rev.* 247 (1994).

Finn, John. *Constitutions in Crisis: Political Violence and the Rule of Law* (1991).

Finnis, John. *Natural Law and Natural Rights* (1980).

Fish, Stanley. *Is There a Text in This Class? The Authority of Interpretive Communities* (1980).

———. "Working on the Chain Gang: Interpretation in Law and Literature," 60 *Texas L. Rev.* 551 (1982).

Fisher, Herbert W. *Considerations on the Origin of the American War* (1865).

Fiss, Owen. "Objectivity and Interpretation," 34 *Stanford L. Rev.* 739 (1982).

Fitzhugh, George. *Sociology for the South, or the Failure of Free Society* (1854), in *Slavery Defended: Views of the Old South* (Eric L. McKitrick, ed., 1963), and in *Ante-Bellum* (Harvey Wish, ed., 1960).

———. "Southern Thought—Its New and Important Manifestations," 23 *De Bow's Review* 337 (October 1857).

Flack, Horace Edgar. *The Adoption of the Fourteenth Amendment* (1908).

Flanz, Gisbert H., ed. *Constitutions of the Countries of the World*, Release 96-5 (August 1996).

Fleming, James E. "Constructing the Substantive Constitution," 72 *Texas L. Rev.* 211 (1993).

———. "We the Exceptional American People," 11 *Constitutional Commentary* 355 (1994).

Foley, Michael. *The Silence of Constitutions: An Essay in Constitutional Interpretation* (1989).

Foner, Eric. *Reconstruction: America's Unfinished Revolution, 1863–1877* (1988).

Frank, Jerome. *Law and the Modern Mind* (1930) (Peter Smith ed., 1970)

Franklin, John Hope. *Reconstruction: After the Civil War* (1961).
Freehling, William W. "The Founding Fathers and Slavery," 77 *Am. Hist. Rev.* 81 (1972).
———. *The Road to Disunion: Secessionists at Bay, 1776–1854* (1990).
Friedman, Lawrence M. *A History of American Law* (2d ed., 1985).
Geertz, Clifford. *The Interpretation of Cultures* (1973).
Genovese, Eugene D. *Roll, Jordan, Roll: The World the Slaves Made* (1972, 1974).
George, Robert, P. *Making Men Moral: Civil Liberties and Public Morality* (1993).
Goodman, Nelson. *Ways of Worldmaking* (1985).
Gordon, Robert W. "New Developments in Legal Theory," in *The Politics of Law* (David Kairys, ed., 1982).
Graebner, Norman A. "Abraham Lincoln: Conservative Statesman," in *The Enduring Lincoln* (Norman A. Graebner, ed., 1959).
Grey, Thomas. "Do We Have an Unwritten Constitution?" 27 *Stanford L. Rev.* 703 (1975).
Guinier, Lani. *The Tyranny of the Majority: Fundamental Fairness in Representative Democracy* (1994).
Hacker, Louis M. *The Triumph of American Capitalism: The Development of Forces in American History to the End of the Nineteenth Century* (1940).
Hall, Kermit, ed. *Oxford Companion to the History of the Supreme Court of the United States* (1992).
Halperin, Morton H., and David J. Scheffer, with Patricia L. Small. *Self-Determination in the New World Order* (1992).
Hamilton, Alexander, James Madison, and John Jay. *The Federalist* (1787–1788).
Hammond, Bray. *Banks and Politics in America from the Revolution until the Civil War* (1957).
Hammond, James Henry. "Speech on the Admission of Kansas" (March 4, 1858), in *Slavery Defended: Views of the Old South* (Eric L. McKitrick, ed., 1963).
Harris, William F., II. "Bonding Word and Polity: The Logic of American Constitutionalism," 76 *Am. Pol. Sci. Rev.* 34 (1982).
———. *The Interpretable Constitution* (1993).
Hart, Albert Bushnell, and Edward Channing, eds. *American History Leaflets, Colonial and Constitutional*, nos. 12 and 35 (1912, 1906).
Hart, H.L.A. "American Jurisprudence through English Eyes: The Nightmare and the Noble Dream," 11 *Ga. L. Rev.* 969 (1977).
———. *The Concept of Law* (1961).
———. *Law, Liberty, and Morality* (1963).
Herzog, Don. *Happy Slaves: A Critique of Consent Theory* (1989).
Hobbes, Thomas. *Behemoth, or the Long Parliament* (1668, 1682); also *Behemoth: The History of the Causes of the Civil Wars of England* (1682) (William Molesworth, ed., 1840, 1969).
———. *Leviathan* (1651) (C. B. Macpherson, ed., 1968).
Hochschild, Jennifer. *The New American Dilemma: Liberal Democracy and School Desegregation* (1984).

Holmes, George Frederick. "Uncle Tom's Cabin" (1852), in *Slavery Defended: Views of the Old South* (Eric L. McKitrick, ed., 1963).

Holmes, Oliver Wendell. *The Common Law* (1881) (Mark D. Howe, ed., 1963).

———. "The Path of the Law," 10 *Harv. L. Rev.* 457 (1897).

Holt, Wythe. "Now and Then: The Uncertain State of Nineteenth-Century American Legal History," 7 *Ind. L. Rev.* 615 (1974).

Horowitz, Donald L. *Ethnic Groups in Conflict* (1985).

Horwitz, Morton J. *The Transformation of American Law, 1780–1860* (1977).

Hume, David. "Of the Original Contract," Essay 12 (1748), in *Social Contract: Essays by Locke, Hume, and Rousseau* (Ernest Barker, ed., 1948).

Hurst, Willard. *The Legitimacy of the Business Corporation in the Law of the United States, 1780–1970* (1970).

Hyman, Harold W., and William M. Wiecek. *Equal Justice under Law: Constitutional Development, 1835–1875* (1982).

Jaffa, Harry A. *Crisis of the House Divided: An Interpretation of the Issues of the Lincoln-Douglas Debates* (1959, 1982).

James, Joseph B. *The Ratification of the Fourteenth Amendment* (1984).

Jefferson, Thomas. *Thomas Jefferson: Writings* (Merrill D. Peterson, ed., 1984).

Johannsen, Robert W. *Stephen A. Douglas* (1973).

Jordan, Barbara, and Shelby Hearon. *Barbara Jordan: A Self Portrait* (1979).

Jordan, Winthrop. *White over Black: American Attitudes Toward the Negro, 1550–1812* (1968).

Kammen, Michael. *A Machine That Would Go of Itself: The Constitution in American Culture* (1986).

Kendall, Willmoore. *The Conservative Affirmation* (1963).

Kennedy, Duncan. "Form and Substance in Private Law Adjudication," 89 *Harv. L. Rev.* 1685 (1976).

Kenyon, Cecelia M. *The Antifederalists* (1985).

King, Martin Luther. *I Have a Dream: Writings and Speeches That Changed the World* (James M. Washington, ed., 1992).

King, Willard L., and Allan Nevins. "The Constitution and Declaration of Independence as Issues in the Lincoln-Douglas Debates," 52 *J. Ill. St. Hist. Soc.* 7 (1959).

Leverett, Rudy H. *Legend of the Free State of Jones* (1984).

Levinson, Sanford. "'The Constitution' in American Civil Religion" 1979 *Sup. Ct. Rev.* 123 (1979).

———. "Law as Literature," 60 *Texas L. Rev.* 373 (1982).

———. *Constitutional Faith* (1988).

Lijpart, Arend. "Comparative Politics and the Comparative Method," 65 *Am. Pol. Sci. Rev.* 682 (1971).

Lincoln, Abraham. *The Collected Works of Abraham Lincoln* (Roy P. Basler, ed., 1953).

Lincoln, Abraham, and Stephen A. Douglas. *Political Debates between Abraham Lincoln and Stephen A. Douglas* (1894).

Llewelyn, Karl. *The Bramble Bush* (7th printing, 1981).

Locke, John. *Second Treatise of Government* (1690) (C. B. Macpherson, ed., 1980).

Loury, Glenn C. "'Matters of Color'—Blacks and the Constitutional Order," in *Slavery and Its Consequences: The Constitution, Equality, and Race* (Robert A. Goldwin and Art Kaufman, eds., 1988).

Lutz, Donald S. "From Covenant to Constitution in American Political Thought," in *Covenant, Polity, and Constitutionalism* (Daniel J. Elazar and John Kincaid, eds., 1980).

Lynd, Staughton. *Class Conflict, Slavery, and the United States Constitution* (1967).

Macedo, Stephen. *Liberal Virtues: Citizenship, Virtue, and Community in Liberal Constitutionalism* (1990).

Madison, James. *Notes of Debates in the Federal Convention of 1787, Reported by James Madison* (Adrienne Koch, ed., 1987).

———. *Letters and Other Writings of James Madison*, 4 vols. (1865).

———. *The Writings of James Madison*, 9 vols. (Gaillard Hunt, ed., 1910).

———. *The Complete Madison: His Basic Writings* (Saul K. Padover, ed., 1953).

Magliola, Robert R. *Phenomenology and Literature* (1977).

Marx, Karl. "The German Ideology: Part I" (1846), in *The Marx-Engels Reader* (R. Tucker, ed., 1978).

Marx, Karl, and Frederick Engels. *Letters to Americans, 1848–1895* (1953).

McDowell, Gary L. *The Constitution and Contemporary Constitutional Theory* (1985).

McIlwain, Charles H. *Constitutionalism: Ancient and Modern* (1947).

McLemore, Richard Aubrey, ed. *A History of Mississippi*, 2 vols. (1973).

McPherson, James M. *Battle Cry of Freedom: The Civil War Era* (1988).

———. *Abraham Lincoln and the Second American Revolution* (1991).

Merrill, Walter M. *Against Wind and Tide: A Biography of William Lloyd Garrison* (1963).

Middleton, Henry. *Economical Causes of Slavery in the United States and Obstacles to Abolition* (1857).

Miller, John Chester. *The Wolf by the Ears: Thomas Jefferson and Slavery* (1977).

Moore, Michael S. "A Natural Law Theory of Interpretation," 58 *So. Cal. L. Rev.* 277 (1985).

———. "The Interpretive Turn in Modern Theory: A Turn for the Worse?" 41 *Stanford L. Rev.* 871 (1989).

Moore, Wayne D. *Constitutional Rights and Powers of the People: A Theory of Constitutional Politics* (1996).

Morris, Thomas D. *Free Men All: The Personal Liberty Laws of the North, 1780–1861* (1974).

Murphy, Walter F. "The Art of Constitutional Interpretation: A Preliminary Showing," in *Essays on the Constitution of the United States* (M. Judd Harmon, ed., 1978).

———. "Constitutional Interpretation: The Art of the Historian, Magician, or Statesman?" 87 *Yale L. J.* 1752 (1978).

———. "An Ordering of Constitutional Values," 53 *So. Cal. L. Rev.* 703 (1980).

———. "*Slaughter-House, Civil Rights*, and Limits on Constitutional Change," 32 *Am. J. Jurisprudence* 1 (1987).

———. "Staggering Toward the New Jerusalem of Constitutional Theory: A Response to Ralph F. Gaebler," 37 *Am. J. Jurisprudence* 337 (1992).

Murphy, Walter F., James E. Fleming, and Sotirios A. Barber, eds. *American Constitutional Interpretation* (2d ed., 1995).

Myrdal, Gunnar. *An American Dilemma: The Negro Problem and Modern Democracy* (1944).

Nedelsky, Jennifer. "American Constitutionalism and the Paradox of Private Property," in *Constitutionalism and Democracy* (Jon Elster and Rune Slagstad, eds., 1988).

Nelson, Truman, ed. *Documents of Upheaval: Selections from William Lloyd Garrison's "The Liberator," 1831–1865* (1966).

Norton, Anne. *Alternative Americas: A Reading of Antebellum Political Culture* (1986).

Nott, Josiah. *Indigenous Races of the Earth* (1857).

———. *Types of Mankind* (1857).

Nye, Russel B. *Fettered Freedom: Civil Liberties and Slavery Controversy, 1830–1860* (1963).

Orfield, Gary. "Race and the Liberal Agenda: The Loss of the Integrationist Dream, 1965–1974," in *The Politics of Social Policy in the United States* (Margaret Weir, Ann Shola Orloff, and Theda Skocpol, eds., 1988).

Ostrom, Vincent. "Hobbes, Covenant, and Constitution," in *Covenant, Polity, and Constitutionalism* (Daniel J. Elazar and John Kincaid, eds., 1980).

Peller, Gary. "Race-Consciousness," in *Critical Race Theory: Key Writings That Formed the Movement* (Kimberlé Crenshaw, Neil Gotanda, Gary Peller, and Kendall Thomas, eds., 1995).

Pennybacker, Mindy. "Should the Aloha State Say Goodbye? Natives Wonder," *The Nation* (August 12–19, 1996).

Phillips, Wendell. *Review of Lysander Spooner's Essay on the Unconstitutionality of Slavery* (1847).

———. *Speeches, Lectures, and Letters* (1891).

———. *Speeches, Lectures, and Letters* (1894).

Plato. *Crito*, in *Four Texts on Socrates* (Thomas G. West and Grace Starry West, eds., 1984).

Polanyi, Michael. "Genius in Science," 38 *Encounter* 43 (1972).

Posner, Richard. *The Economic Analysis of Law* (1972).

———. *The Economics of Justice* (1981).

Potter, David M. *The Impending Crisis, 1848–1861* (1976).

———. *The South and the Concurrent Majority* (1972).

Powell, H. Jefferson. "The Original Understanding of Original Intent," 98 *Harv. L. Rev.* 885 (1985).

Randall, James G. *Lincoln the President: Springfield to Gettysburg* (1945).

———. *Lincoln the Liberal Statesman* (1947).

Rawick, George P., ed. *The American Slave: A Composite Autobiography* (1941, 1972), and Supplement, series 1, vols. 1–12 (1977).

Rawls, John. *A Theory of Justice* (1971).

Raz, Joseph. "Morality as Interpretation," 101 *Ethics* 392 (1991).

Rehnquist, William. "The Notion of a Living Constitution," 54 *Texas L. Rev.* 693 (1976).

Richards, David A. J. *Foundations of American Constitutionalism* (1989).

Richardson, James D., ed. *A Compilation of the Messages and Papers of the Presidents, 1789–1897* (1896).

Robinson, Donald. *Slavery in the Structure of American Politics: 1765–1820* (1979).

Roche, John P. "The Founding Fathers: A Reform Caucus in Action," 55 *Am. Pol. Sci. Rev.* 799 (1961).

Rothman, Rozann. "The Impact of Covenant and Contract Theories on Conceptions of the U.S. Constitution," in *Covenant, Polity, and Constitutionalism* (Daniel J. Elazar and John Kincaid, eds., 1980).

Ruffin, Edmund. *The Political Economy of Slavery; or, the Institution Considered in Regard to Its Influence on Public Wealth and the General Welfare* (1857).

Rumore, Samuel A. "Building Alabama's Courthouses: Winston County," *The Alabama Lawyer* 320 (November 1989).

Sartori, Giovanni. "Comparing and Miscomparing," 3 *J. Theoretical Pol.* 243 (1991).

Scalia, Antonin. "Originalism: The Lesser Evil," 57 *U. Cin. L. Rev.* 849 (1989).

Schlesinger, Arthur M., Jr. *The Age of Jackson* (1945).

———. *The Disuniting of America: Reflections on a Multicultural Society* (1992).

Schmitt, Carl. *The Concept of the Political* (George Schwab, trans., 1976).

Schochet, Gordon J. "Introduction: Constitutionalism, Liberalism, and the Study of Politics," in *Constitutionalism: NOMOS XX* (J. Roland Pennock and John W. Chapman, eds., 1979).

Seymour, Glen Huron. *An Analysis of the Political Principles of Stephen A. Douglas* (Ph.D. diss., Department of History, University of Illinois, 1929).

Skocpol, Theda, and Margaret Somers. "The Uses of Comparative History in Macrosocial Inquiry," 22 *Comp. Stud. Soc. & Hist.* 174 (1980).

Smith, Rogers M. *Liberalism and American Constitutional Law* (1985).

Spivak, Gayatri Chakravorty. "Constitutions and Culture Studies," 2 *Yale J. of Law & the Humanities* 133 (1990).

Spooner, Lysander. *The Unconstitutionality of Slavery* (1845, 1860).

Stampp, Kenneth M. *The Peculiar Institution: Slavery in the Ante-Bellum South* (1956).

———. *The Era of Reconstruction: 1865–1877* (1965).

———. "The Concept of a Perpetual Union," 65 *J. Am. Hist.* 5 (1978).

———. *America in 1857: A Nation on the Brink* (1990).

State Papers on Nullification (1834; repr. 1970).

Steele, Shelby. *The Content of Our Character* (1990).

Stewart, Alvan. "A Constitutional Argument on the Subject of Slavery" (1837), reprinted in Jacobus tenBroek, *Equal under Law* (1965).

Storing, Herbert J. "Slavery and the Moral Foundations of the American Republic," in *Slavery and Its Consequences: The Constitution, Equality, and Race* (Robert A. Goldwin and Art Kaufman, eds., 1988).

Story, William W., ed. *Life and Letters of Joseph Story*, 2 vols. (1851).

Stowe, Harriet Beecher. *Uncle Tom's Cabin; or, Life Among the Lowly* (1852; repr. 1965).

Stringfellow, Thornton. "The Bible Argument: or, Slavery in the Light of Divine Revelation," in *Cotton Is King, and Pro-Slavery Arguments* (E. N. Elliott, ed., 1860).

———. *Slavery: Its Origin, Nature, and History, Considered in the Light of Bible Teachings, Moral Justice, and Political Wisdom* (1861).

Stuckey, Sterling. *Slave Culture: Nationalist Theory and the Foundations of Black America* (1987).

Sunstein, Cass. "Constitutionalism and Secession," 58 *U. Chi. L. Rev.* 633 (1991).

Thayer, James Bradley. "The Origin and Scope of the American Doctrine of Constitutional Law," 7 *Harv. L. Rev.* 129 (1893).

Thoreau, Henry David. *Walden and Other Writings by Henry David Thoreau* (William Howarth, ed., 1981).

Thucydides. *The Peloponnesian War* (T. E. Wick, ed., 1982).

Tocqueville, Alexis de. *Democracy in America* (J. P. Mayer, ed., 1969).

Tribe, Laurence H. "Statement," U.S. Senate, Subcommittee on Separation of Powers, *The Human Life Bill: Hearings on S. 158*, 97th Cong., 1st Sess., Vol. 1, 249–252.

Tushnet, Mark V. "Following the Rules Laid Down: A Critique of Interpretivism and Neutral Principles," 96 *Harv. L. Rev.* 781 (1983).

———. "A Marxist Analysis of American Law," 1 *Marxist Perspectives* 96 (1978).

———. *The American Law of Slavery, 1810–1860* (1981).

———. "A Note on the Revival of Textualism in Constitutional Theory," 58 *So. Cal. L. Rev.* 683 (1985).

Unger, Roberto. "The Critical Legal Studies Movement," 96 *Harv. L. Rev.* 561 (1983).

Warren, Charles. *The Supreme Court in United States History* (rev. ed., 1947).

Weber, Max. "Politics as a Vocation" (1919), in *From Max Weber: Essays in Sociology* (H. H. Gerth and C. Wright Mills, eds., 1946).

Weld, Theodore Dwight. "The Power of Congress over Slavery in the District of Columbia" (1838); reprinted in Jacobus tenBroek, *Equal under Law* (1965).

Wells, Damon. *Stephen Douglas: The Last Years, 1857–1861* (1971).

Whitman, Walt. "Song of Myself" (1855).

Wiecek, William M. "'The Blessings of Liberty': Slavery in the American Constitutional Order," in *Slavery and Its Consequences: The Constitution, Equality, and Race* (Robert A. Goldwin and Art Kaufman, eds., 1988).

———. *The Sources of Antislavery Constitutionalism in America, 1760–1848* (1977).

———. "Slavery and Abolition before the United States Supreme Court, 1820–1860," 65 *J. Am. Hist.* 34 (1978).

Williams, T. Harry. "Lincoln and the Radicals: An Essay in Civil War History and Historiography," in *Grant, Lee, Lincoln, and the Radicals: Essays on Civil War Leadership* (Grady McWhiney, ed., 1964).

Wills, Garry. *Inventing America: Jefferson's Declaration of Independence* (1978).
———. *Lincoln at Gettysburg: The Words That Remade America* (1992).
Wiltse, Charles M. *John C. Calhoun: Nullifier, 1829–1839* (1949).
Wood, Gordon S. *The Creation of the American Republic, 1776–1787* (1969).
Woodward, C. Vann. *The Strange Career of Jim Crow* (1974).
Wooster, Ralph A. *The Secession Conventions of the South* (1962).

Index of Cases

General Index

About the Author

MARK E. BRANDON is Assistant Professor of Political Science at the University of Michigan.